God makes lemonade

true stories that sweeten & inspire

created by don jacobson

Lemonade Books LLC

GOD MAKES LEMONADE™

Published by Lemonade Books LLC
3689 Carman Dr., Suite 300
Lake Oswego, OR 97035 USA

ISBN 978-0-578-08221-9

Cataloging-in-Publication Data is on file with the Library of Congress

Printed in the United States of America

First Edition

Book cover design by Brand Navigation
Interior Design by Brand Navigation and Katherine Lloyd, The DESK

11 12 13 14 15—10 9 8 7 6 5 4 3 2 1

God makes lemonade

God Makes Lemonade is dedicated

to single moms and their kids:

you need encouragement more than anyone,

and your faithfulness inspires us.

Thank you.

table of contents

acknowledgments

My name's on the cover of this book, but the truth is that my behind-the-scenes team made this project possible. A huge *thank you* is in order for the following folks:

> to Marty Raz, for doing everything and then some

> to David Jacobsen, for helping our team have fun and artfully lemonizing each of our stories

> to Steffany Woolsey, editor extraordinaire

> to Jason Myhre, for killer marketing and sales materials

> to Brenda, for being my partner and inspiration on this journey

And to everyone who shared a true story of hope and inspiration with the *God Makes Lemonade* community...this is your book as well, and your honesty and encouragement are changing people's lives.

Don

introduction

God Makes Lemonade is more than a series of books—it's a community where true stories of real hope and encouragement are shared.

Stories have always been the way people help each other hold on to hope. The stories in this book are about everyday folks who are surprised by unexpected sweetness in the midst of sour circumstances. In these difficult times, most of us don't need to be told to work harder—we're already working as hard as we can! What we need is encouragement...to keep hoping even when things seem hopeless.

If you're struggling beneath the weight of unemployment, depression, broken relationships, an unexpected death, or any of life's other difficulties, God Makes Lemonade might be exactly the refreshment you need.

Don't give up—you're not alone! The stories in this book are written by all sorts of people about almost every imaginable circumstance. Some are funny, others are thoughtful, and more than a few will have you running for a box of tissues. But one thing they all have in common is a sense of hopeful honesty. Yes, life gives us lemons—truly sour experiences. But when it does turn into lemonade, it's as refreshing as a cold drink on a hot August day. We hope you'll find that kind of refreshment in the stories you're about to read.

We all know "stuff" happens in life—but so does lemonade!

courting
through
cancer

A nurse had given my husband a dry erase board to use after his surgery. Unable to speak because of his tracheotomy, David constructed his first question letter by letter, his hand shaking with the effort.

Inwardly wincing at the pain he was in, I guessed his question before he finished: "How are the kids?"

He stopped writing and nodded.

I took his hand. "They're doing fine," I said gently. "They're actually having fun with the babysitters. But they miss you." I paused. "And I miss you, too."

David smiled and reached for the pen again. I couldn't wait to read his next thought.

♂ ♂ ♂

You might think of a dry erase board as a difficult way for a married couple to communicate. But only one month before, when my husband could still speak, we were communicating far less. I'd even wondered if our family would be better off without him around. On the way home from the doctor's office—the day David was diagnosed with a cancerous tumor on the base of his tongue—I knew I would faithfully care for my husband, but as I looked at him across the front seat of the car I wondered where our relationship was headed. More than a quarter-century earlier, we were two starry-eyed lovers who'd begun our marriage as best friends and allies. Where had it all gone wrong?

If asked, I would have said it was all David's fault. Early in our marriage I discovered that my husband had a hair-trigger temper, and he volleyed angry words at me and our children with little provocation. His temper seemed to be exacerbated by our young ones. Whenever one of the kids cranked up the decibel level, whether from fun or strife, David was liable to yell or storm out of the room. In an effort to "protect" David from his own children, I learned to absorb all of the children's energy myself—to the extent of taking my infants along with me to my college classes even when David was at home.

Through the years the kids and I never knew what would trigger David's anger, so we lived with a constant level of stress. Something as innocuous as a spilled glass at dinner or a screen door allowed to slam could set him off. I knew it wasn't fair for our children to be growing up with the uncertainly of that unpredictable rage, but it was years before I insisted David seek professional help. By then our family dynamics—including our marriage—was, at best, damaged. At worst, it was dysfunctional.

But that wasn't the whole story, of course. I wasn't the saint to my husband's sinner. Even after David started seeing a counselor, and he began to make progress, I doggedly continued to absorb all the family stress. Playing the martyr came so readily that I refused to share normal family stress with David, such as budget dilemmas or disciplinary issues. He was becoming a different father and husband, but I continued to wrap myself in the cloak of resentment. I berated David in front of the kids, teaching them it was okay not to respect their father. I rationalized that he didn't deserve any respect because of all the years he'd held us under the thumb of his anger.

We would need a lifetime of words to work through all the issues that plagued us.

♂ ♂ ♂

My husband's surgery successfully removed the cancer, but he was unable to speak or take care of himself for months. As I sat at the bedside of my mute husband, away from our children and the everyday busyness of life at our house, I was forced to confront two things for the first time: our marriage was truly on the rocks, and the man in front of me was not the man I had married.

But as I simply sat with him in silence—no longer bogged down by bills and babies—I gradually stopped seeing him in terms of adjectives: angry, selfish, unsupportive.

Instead, in his voiceless pain he became a man again. And not just any man, but the man I'd married so many years before. David. My love. In the silence created by cancer, I no longer heard his cruel and angry words—and he no longer heard mine. A tiny seed of hope began to grow in the space between us: perhaps things didn't have to keep getting worse.

One morning I readied myself to go to the hospital and see David. It would be just the two of us again, and we'd spend more time in companionable silence than we would in speech. I knew he would gaze at me, and in the absence of words I would notice his attention acutely. I chose a flattering outfit and sprayed on David's favorite perfume. As I looked in my full-length mirror, I almost laughed aloud as the realization hit me: I was courting my husband! As I sat beside his hospital bed, day after day, we were rekindling the flame of our first love, saying things with our eyes and clasped hands that we hadn't heard for years in our tense, noisy house.

Our courtship continued when David returned home from the hospital. I became his daily caregiver through the long months of chemotherapy and radiation. I changed his blood-soaked dressings, cleaned his wounds, and made sure his feeding tube was in place to deliver his medicine. At first I worried that our children would once again trigger David's anger, and that the quiet respite we'd enjoyed in the hospital would prove fleeting. Instead, he observed us from the couch, contentedly and silently, as if he were seeing his family for the first time. When he became fatigued, our youngest—three-year-old Abby—would follow him into his bedroom. Somehow her intuition sensed what he did and didn't need, and she would sit at the foot of his bed for hours, quietly turning the pages of storybooks and watching her father.

As the days and weeks of David's convalescence turned into months, he responded to my tender care with gratitude, and I responded to his gratitude with more tender care. I rubbed his feet and he sighed blissfully; I recorded his favorite shows so he could watch them when he had the energy. For perhaps the first time in his life, David felt cherished—and I felt free of the bile of bitterness I had swallowed for so many years.

We were forming a real partnership, and I knew this one would never succumb to the same stresses that nearly broke us before. Now we understood how bad things could get—but more importantly, we had been given a fresh glimpse of how good things could become.

David's surgery was five years ago. Looking back, we can both say with certainty that his cancer saved our marriage. At home David and I support each other now, both in our individual pursuits and in our parenting. We enjoy regular dates—even if they sometimes include a trip to the oncologist!

Recently I looked deeply into David's eyes and told him that the thought of spending the rest of my life with him filled me with awe and gratefulness. He took my hand for a moment, and then—without saying a word—he leaned toward me and kissed my lips. He tasted as sweet as he had the day we were married. How many people are given a second chance at love, by cancer?

That magic moment quickly ended as our watching kids pelted us with a chorus of groans and complaints. David and I understood: children don't like to see their middle-aged parents smooching in the middle of a crowded restaurant! But that didn't stop my husband from playing footsie with me beneath the table while the server took our orders.

Mary Potter Kenyon

the
perfect fit

I had the perfect job. I ran the front desk at a posh country club—so posh it cost more than $100,000 a year to join! It provided me with a great paycheck and medical benefits, both of which my family needed. My husband was a pastor with a modest salary, and my three kids can eat through a paycheck's worth of groceries in no time flat. But thanks to my job, we were beginning to pay down some debt and even put a little money toward retirement.

But the job was about more than the financial benefits. I loved the work, too. During a typical week, I might design dinner menus, plan events, assist the decorators, create name cards, and organize elaborate wine tastings. My executive chef–prepared lunches were on the house, and if things slowed down in the afternoons I could froth myself a hazelnut cappuccino to savor back at my post. Mondays I could golf for free on a course designed by Jack Nicklaus. Even visiting the restroom was a high-class experience: the toilet paper was folded into a neat triangle and stamped with the club's stylish logo.

I assumed I would be there for years, working my way up with exceptional and friendly service. Except that one Thursday afternoon, when I joined the general manager for our weekly meeting, I found a woman from human resources sitting in the office as well. As the door closed behind me, my heart began to race.

"Kimberly," said my manager, "you're just not a good fit for our company."

My mouth instantly felt like it was lined with dry cotton, and my already racing heart went into overdrive. "What do you mean? I don't understand!" My stammered protests sounded shrill and desperate even to me, but what else could I say? I was being blindsided, my years of exemplary work dismissed like they'd never happened.

"Today is your last day," my manager said, cutting me off. "The decision has been made. I'll escort you out."

I cried all the way home and didn't sleep a single minute that night. How were we going to make ends meet? Questions ran through my mind ceaselessly.

The next day I updated my résumé and began e-mailing and calling about every job opportunity I could find. Then, hoping to stretch my final paycheck as far as it could go, I hit the local food pantry and resale shop in town, looking for the absolute cheapest things that we needed.

At the resale shop, the woman working the counter could tell I was distraught, and she offered to pray with me. I was so desperate that I agreed right away, and she took my hands in hers and began to speak. She asked God to help me find the right job, and to lead me to the right place where I could make a real difference. After the prayer, I left with a strange sense of peace.

Two days later, I got a call from the director of the nonprofit that ran that resale shop. She told me that she had two job openings, and asked me to meet with her. Her directions took me out into the countryside. As I drove by green pastures and quiet ponds dotting farmland, I felt the same sense of peace return.

The nonprofit director's office was at a women's rehabilitation center set on nearly one hundred acres. It had a dormitory, kitchen, classrooms, and everything needed to help shelter, heal, and educate down-and-out women. The two job openings were both at the rehab center: one in the office, the other as a teacher.

I had experience teaching, and that second job seemed like the perfect fit. "You would be teaching women who are here instead of in jail or prison, who have been abused, addicted, rejected, and even lost their children," the manager told me, and my heart leaped. I felt compelled to be their teacher.

I drove home with tears in my eyes, but this time they were tears of grateful hope.

I have been teaching at that rehabilitation center for more than a year now. My salary is a lot less than I was making at the fancy club, and my position doesn't come with medical benefits—or hazelnut cappuccinos! However, my family has never once lacked the things we need each week.

Being fired wasn't easy, but I'm grateful that I ended up somewhere I was greatly needed, and somewhere I needed to be. I didn't know it at the time, but my life was missing something important. I needed to learn some lessons, and God had to make me a teacher to get my attention. Working with the dear women at the rehab center, I learn every day about practicing forgiveness, avoiding temptation, and seeking what really matters.

Most importantly, I learned that life isn't about planning bigger and better parties or feeling appreciated by the rich and famous. Instead, it's about helping each other discover that a life filled with faith and family is the richest life of all, and the only life worth living.

Kimberly Sutton

expect
a feast

*H*ave you ever signed up for a weekend getaway, like a conference or a retreat, and returned home even more tired than before?

I attended a weekend gathering with friends that was filled with great ideas and inspired teaching. The problem wasn't the conference itself, but *my* self: I returned home to the same stresses I'd left behind. I was in the same place as before, and I couldn't figure out how to change things. The weekend away helped me realize how much time I spent thinking about myself: *Am I keeping everyone happy? Does everyone like me?* Same old questions, but still no answers in sight.

Monday morning found me drained and weary. I was tired of feeling like I had failed—just the *thought* of all my responsibilities threatened to overwhelm me. But I couldn't sit around processing. I had a family and kids to take care of.

By Tuesday I'd gathered a bit of energy and felt a bit more capable. As I prayed and thought about life that morning, I decided that I just needed to be more intentional about caring for others. Certain people came to mind: my brother, my cousins, and my friend Maria, who was struggling through a difficult pregnancy. I found myself strategizing ways to squeeze more into my already busy schedule. I would make more detailed lists, be more organized, and give my loved ones the care and attention they deserved. That would make everyone happy. Right?

As I was thinking and praying, this thought came into my mind: trying harder to love people by making more lists is like inviting people over to dinner and setting empty plates and cups in front of them. It was like I heard God whispering, "Let *me* prepare the feast. Fill up at *my* table and then invite others to join you."

The words pierced my heart. What if it's less about *doing* extra tasks and more about *being* the kind of person so filled with love that it can't help but overflow?

All day long I savored that thought like a warm cup of tea. To be sure, Tuesday was no less hectic than Monday. I was still on my feet nonstop, attending to the thousand details that make a household run. Five o'clock snuck up on me, and with the kids racing helter-skelter I headed to the kitchen to throw some dinner together.

In the kitchen I found a disaster. My daughter Emma had been experimenting with her latest smoothie recipes while simultaneously making homemade salsa. The countertop was littered with dishes, the floor was a mess, and diced tomatoes and green peppers dotted every surface like so much confetti.

As I surveyed the scene, planning how I might fix dinner and help my daughter clean up at the same time, I happened to glance out the window.

Maria—my almost-ready-to-give-birth friend Maria—was making her way slowly up the front walkway, her husband and toddler patiently keeping the pace she set. Maria was radiant, and I was—as always—happy to see her. But she was most definitely not on my Tuesday evening to-do list.

Could my friend have chosen a more convenient time to visit? Yes. Was I embarrassed by the state of my house? Definitely. But as I opened the door to greet her, I realized something important: nothing I could *do* would make her feel as welcome as simply *being* her friend.

Soon we were all sitting around the table, enjoying food and savoring each other's company. We talked about life; we passed second helpings. And never once did smoothie stains or salsa leftovers make their way into the conversation. Okay, I'll admit I thought about my messy floor a time or two—but always I was called back to the present by the laughter of my friends.

It wasn't until I was watching that precious family make their slow, expectant way back down our driveway that it came to me: this night wasn't about me or my dinner or my clean house. It wasn't about making better lists or loving people more efficiently.

It was about the willingness to simply be: to be thankful, to be open, to be present for the feast.

marked by love

hortly after our youngest daughter was born, my husband learned that he had a rare genetic kidney disorder. We were supposed to be celebrating the birth of our little girl, and instead we found ourselves caught up in a swirl of medical diagnoses. We learned that a transplant could be postponed for a time, but Quinn nevertheless had to change his eating habits, adjust to frequent hospital visits for tests and consultations, and take a seemingly endless number of pills to manage his blood pressure.

Over all of this hung the dark cloud of uncertainty: when exactly would Quinn need a transplant? And when the time came, would a match be available?

During that period, Quinn's brother discovered that he suffered from the same disease. He found out the hard way—when he suffered kidney failure and was hospitalized—and we almost lost him. A third brother was able to provide a matched kidney at the last moment, and we prayed that when the time came for Quinn's surgery the right donor could be found.

After six years, we were no longer able to manage Quinn's disease from home. He would need a transplant in the next few months. We met with the transplant team at the hospital and were informed that we had been placed on a cadaver donor list. The doctors asked whether one of Quinn's family members might be able to donate instead, thus speeding up the process.

I blurted out, "I want to be tested as a donor."

The doctors looked at me in amazement, but I continued to insist that I wanted to be tested. Their reaction quickly turned to concern. Clearly I hadn't been paying attention when they told us how slim a spouse's chances were of being a successful donor. Still, they agreed to perform the basic blood test, probably in order to shut me up while they considered more realistic options.

What the doctors didn't know was that I had a feeling I was supposed to help my husband beat this disease. In the time since he had been diagnosed, Quinn and I had both started going to church, and one thing I'd learned was that long odds don't bother God in the least.

Three days later I listened to someone from the hospital tell me over the phone, "Not only are you a match—you're an almost perfect match!" I would be able to give a kidney to Quinn, and we would come out the other side of this tunnel together.

Despite our excitement about the match, we had to defend our decision constantly. Friends and family asked us to reconsider, since we had children and both my husband and I would be undergoing major surgery at the same time. Yet none of their objections loosened the sense of peace we felt holding us tightly.

Two weeks before the surgery, I was called in to meet with a hospital psychologist to talk about what to expect. He asked me if I knew that many live donors go through a difficult time after the surgery. I could end up resenting my husband for causing the scar—we might never be able to look at each other in quite the same way again. He told me that it wasn't too late to change my mind, and encouraged us to wait for a kidney from a cadaver.

I told the psychologist that my mind was already made up, but that night I did feel fear begin to creep in. I'd seen the scar Quinn's brother had received—it looked like he'd been in a bar brawl with a shark.

Up to then I'd pushed aside all thoughts relating to *my* part of the surgery, but as I soaked in the bathtub, I began to cry. Was I really meant to go through with this when there were other options? Would the ugly scar change the way Quinn looked at me? Would I still be beautiful to him? I heard my tears dripping into the water as I prayed. *I'll do this, but I need strength. Take away my vanity. Please help me.*

♂ ♂ ♂

The morning of the surgery, Quinn and I were wheeled into pre-op on separate stretchers. I wish I could say that we gazed meaningfully into each other's eyes, like a scene in a romantic movie; but the truth is that we were too doped up to do much more than offer each other lopsided smiles and a final hand squeeze. As we were rolled away from each other, everything turned black.

♂ ♂ ♂

Two weeks later, still heavily bandaged, I went to my post-op appointment to have the dressing removed from my back. I would finally see the extent of the damage to my skin, which I had only been imagining since the surgery. Quinn was healing perfectly, and the transplant had been a success, but fear for myself was still lurking.

As the doctor removed my bandage, he chirped, "That looks beautiful!"

I responded to what I assumed was sarcasm with a quip of my own: "Oh, is it healing well? How ugly is it, doctor?"

Looking at me strangely he asked, "Don't you know?"

When I said that I didn't, a small smile played on his lips. "We were able to have a visiting plastic surgeon come in to finish your operation," he explained. "Your scar will hardly be noticeable in a year or so."

Still processing his words, I stood and walked to the mirror, gently twisting so I could see my back. The scar was a vertical line no wider than a pencil, and it stretched from my hipbone to the bottom of my bra strap. Just two weeks since my surgery, and already the angry red was fading—as if a gentle hand had traced a smooth line across my skin.

It was beautiful.

♂ ♂ ♂

Fourteen years after the transplant, my husband remains perfectly healthy. I don't think about my scar every day anymore, but when I do I take a moment to touch it with my fingertips. It is now a thin, pale line. In my scar I don't see pain or sacrifice. Instead I see a mark traced on my body by love, connecting Quinn and me and inviting us to trust that there will be even more goodness and grace in the years to come.

Sharie Robbins

sophie

his latest blow felt like one too many—as though it might knock us down for good. Our oldest daughter had been in and out of rehab for alcohol and drug addictions before she turned twenty. Now we learned she was pregnant at twenty-one, the father was nowhere to be found, and she was being counseled to give up the baby for adoption.

Our first instinct was to offer to raise the child ourselves, or at least care for him or her until our daughter was sober and ready to be a mother. But my wife and I were counseled not to; due to our daughter's instability and uncertain future, the baby could be caught in the middle, or even taken by our daughter during one of her binges. All we could do, it seemed, was watch as she prepared to give away our grandchild—and that felt like we were doing nothing at all.

Sophie was born on August 28, 1987, and we were at the hospital with our daughter when she gave birth.

The moment a grandparent first holds a grandchild is sacred, the culmination of long years of parenting and praying. I also wanted it to be the start of something—the moment I began to pour love and wisdom into my granddaughter's life.

Instead, it was the end. Alone with Sophie for less than an hour, I took her in my arms, shocked by how light she felt. She was the pinkest, tiniest, most gorgeous baby I'd ever seen. I watched her sleep. I noticed the way her translucent eyelids flickered while she dreamed, the way her short breaths counted down the remaining time we had together. When she woke, I was the first thing she saw, and a bright burst of love sparked between my heart and hers.

What happened next felt like a violation. A nurse entered the room to take Sophie. Sophie's adoptive parents would be arriving soon to meet her and bring her to her new home. All of my being cried out *No! No! You can't take her! She belongs to this family. I am her grandfather. I want to watch her grow!*

Even as these thoughts raced through me, I stood up and handed Sophie to the nurse. When she took Sophie from me and left the room, something inside me was torn apart. Broken.

I staggered through the door and into the arms of my wife, who had held Sophie the hour before me. No words passed between us. We wept tears that were heavy with bitterness and grief.

Our only grandchild had been taken from us—by people we didn't know to a home we'd never visit. It was a closed adoption, so we knew we'd said good-bye to Sophie for good.

♂ ♂ ♂

We mourned, but we never forgot our Sophie. I carried a picture of Sophie that was taken at the hospital the day she was born. In it, she is cradled in the arms of a giant stuffed rabbit. She looks impossibly small nestled in its soft fur. That picture held a place of honor in my wallet, and I took it out often to study it and think about my granddaughter.

As the years passed, two other granddaughters were born into our family. We treasured them, yet often there fell across our joy the shadow of Sophie's absence. Watching our granddaughters grow up made us wonder: where is Sophie living, and is she happy? Every significant life event, from holidays to birthdays to graduations, reminded us that Sophie was living somewhere without us.

Through an intermediary, our daughter received a picture of Sophie every few years. Whenever a new picture arrived, we studied it like forensic detectives, desperate for any clues with which we might stitch together the story of her life. Yet I continued to carry only the picture of newborn Sophie in my wallet, a memento of the moment our eyes first met and I knew I would love her forever.

Friends sometimes wondered why I was so attached to Sophie. I still had the rest of my family, including other grandchildren, and it wasn't as if I'd ever really known Sophie. It was hard to explain, but in my heart the connection to Sophie felt unbreakable. I'd always known she was meant to be part of our family, and time had done nothing to weaken that conviction.

For twenty-three years I carried that picture of baby Sophie in my wallet. She was living with another family, but she never left my heart.

ó ó ó

On March 11, 2011, five of us stood at the top of the ramp at the Portland airport: myself, my wife, our daughter, and our two grand-daughters, now teenagers. More than once we shouted, "There she is!"—only to be disappointed. As the flow of departing passengers slowed to a trickle and finally stopped, we wondered if it had been a mistake to arrange to meet our long-lost Sophie. What if she had changed her mind and didn't want to reconnect with us? What if we didn't recognize her because she was a stranger?

Then we saw her, and everything froze.

Later, Sophie would tell us how she'd found us. When Sophie turned eighteen, she started to search for her birth parents. Her adoptive mother gave her the name of her birth mother, and after several years Sophie managed to contact her through Facebook. Sophie was torn between her desire to meet her birth mother— and us, her grandparents—and her fear of being hurt. In the end, family ties pulled her more strongly than her fear and she traveled to Portland for a week. She told her two half-sisters—my other granddaughters—she was coming and wanted to meet us.

Which is why the five of us were all at the airport, craning our necks and straining our eyes. Then: Sophie! She began to run, her wheeled suitcase bouncing along behind her. She ran up the ramp and into the waiting arms of her birth mother. In that moment, two decades of absence were erased. Soon all of us were hugging, laughing, bawling, and hugging again. Our daughter would later say that it felt like a hole in her heart had just begun to heal.

Sophie stayed with us, at our home, that week. One night after dinner, I opened my wallet and took out her baby picture. It was fading and creased, but I could still see clearly my tiny day-old Sophie nestled in the embrace of the stuffed bunny. I held it at arm's length, looking back and forth between the baby and the grown woman before me. When I held my first granddaughter that day in the hospital, I didn't think I'd ever see anyone more beautiful; yet there she sat across from me, an impossibly beautiful adult.

I began to cry, but these tears were pure joy. In them was all the love, all the affection, of the twenty-three years we'd been apart. There was something else in my tears, too; it was hope.

The picture of Sophie that I carried in my wallet for twenty-three years is now in storage in our garage. I don't need it anymore. Whenever I want, I can look at a picture of her taken recently, and if I need to hear her voice I can call her. Or she can call me, like she did this Father's Day when she made plans to come visit again this summer.

I've always been her grandfather…and now I can watch her grow.

Lemon Drop

Wouldn't you like to have a friend like Paul—
someone who will never give up on you or stop
dreaming about you? I'm privileged to call Paul my friend,
and seeing his story in print encourages me to keep
more "snapshots" in my own heart of people I love.
Twenty-three years is a long time to wait,
but some things are worth it. —Don

more than bread alone

The sunny summer morning my husband lost his job, I repeated a single prayer: *God, whatever happens, don't let my kids go hungry.*

This wasn't a particularly passionate prayer. It was more like the kind I pray when I think I already have everything figured out. A safety-net prayer. After all, we would have good severance pay, and there were quite a few promising job opportunities in the pipeline. I was so used to things working out for us that I figured this temporary unemployment would free my husband to find a more fulfilling job—and one that paid more, too!

My perspective began to shift that evening when our neighbor's father stopped by to ask if we would like some frozen bread. He just happened to have a trunk full of it that he needed to get rid of. And so I started our time of unemployment with a freezer stocked with bread—and a sneaking suspicion that we might actually need it.

As the weeks and months trickled through the hourglass, so did our severance pay. Our credit cards were maxed out, and my husband heard "You were a good candidate, but..." more times than he could count. The day we needed milk and I found myself searching through drawers for change was the day the truth sunk in. We were flat broke.

My grocery list became my prayer list. I'd never asked God for things like diapers before, but it seemed that every time I did, the next day a neighbor or someone from church would hand me a bag of diapers their child had outgrown.

During this difficult time, my children were an inspiration. Their basic needs were always met, and their hearts were full of joy. Carolina, my two-year-old, loved my "special" pizza: tomato paste, a few scraps of lunch meat, and a thin layer of cheese on a slice of white bread. And Daniel, my three-year-old, could happily play outside in the dirt for hours, without a toy in sight. They knew we would be okay, even if I was still learning that lesson.

We tried not to burden people with our circumstances. Yet time after time, even as my husband was receiving yet another rejection notice, people lifted the weight from our shoulders. A friend gave us enough money to eat turkey and open presents on Christmas morning. A neighbor set a bag of groceries on our porch. Someone at church planted flowers in our garden. Having our basic needs provided by others hurt—until our hearts began to heal, and grow.

But then we discovered that we were pregnant with our third child. We wanted more children, but this felt like the wrong time. Leaving our caring community was the last thing we wanted to do, but it seemed like we had no choice.

One year after being laid off, my husband found a job several hours away. It required us to relocate, leaving behind the friends who had carried us through that exhausting year. We'd learned that life is sometimes about receiving help, and leaving our community of gracious givers would be difficult—especially now that we were expecting another baby. While we had a steady income at last, there were still questions. Would we make it in our new home? Would we find new neighbors and church friends to come alongside us? And would we continue to trust in God's provision?

One day my pregnancy craving for ice cream reduced me to tears; I knew even the few dollars that a cone would cost was a luxury beyond our means. My husband was volunteering at a local fishing derby that day. When he returned home that evening, he was carrying a bag full of brightly colored leaflets.

I looked closer: they were coupons for free ice cream. More than we could use. More than we could save. More even than we could give away.

But that didn't stop us from trying! And as I watched my small children eating ice cream, their lips and chins coated with sticky goodness, I realized that sometimes the little things are what help us get through the big things. As we slowly put down roots in our new community, we discovered that provision isn't about a particular place; it's about being willing to receive—and when you're filled up, about being ready to give.

Emily Vazquez

a match made in mud

Personal Ad:
Divorced, overweight grandma with minimal baggage
seeks educated, charming man with no vices,
no small children, and plenty of money.

Okay, I never actually placed that ad, but I thought about it. When my marriage of twenty-four years ended, my self-esteem took a wallop. I'd enjoyed being married, and I was open to it again, but I was going to approach it with eyes wide open.

I was the executive director of a health agency, after all, so I had a certain image to maintain. In the time since my divorce, I'd developed a few rules for dating: never date someone from work; never meet men in bars; and never, *never* expect to find a single man at church—all the good ones were already taken.

That's why, with encouragement from a friend, I joined a dating service—my one stipulation being that it not use photos or videos. Soon I was introduced to Doug, and we dated on and off for several months. Doug warned me that he was slow to warm up to people: no handholding, no arm around my shoulder, and certainly no kissing.

He wasn't just *slow* to warm up, I told a friend; he was freezing cold!

Since my self-esteem was still recovering, I assumed his line about being slow to warm up was just a cover for an inconvenient truth:

Doug didn't find me attractive. Maybe it was time to ask the dating service for another introduction.

Meanwhile, my agency was gearing up for its annual fundraiser. It wasn't a silent auction, as you might expect, or a family fair. No, it was a mud volleyball tournament. I'd inherited the event from the previous director, and axing it was out of the question. I warned Doug that if he wanted to see me, he'd have to drive out to the fairgrounds—and if he came, a large iced tea, heavy on the ice, would be his entry ticket.

The day of the fundraiser, the temperatures rose as the mud thickened. The gelatinous goo sucked the shoes right off players' feet and coated their diving bodies from head to toe. Everyone seemed to be having a good time, but I felt sure they were just putting on good faces. Or was I the only one who found the whole production both demeaning and disgusting?

I tried to project a responsible, administrative aura, and any errand that took me away from the mud immediately became my first priority.

At lunchtime, my clothing and skin remained blessedly mud-free. However, while I unloaded some fresh bags of ice at the concession stand, someone grabbed me from behind. One of my volunteers had me locked in a full embrace—one of my covered-in-mud-from-head-to-toe volunteers, fresh out of a volleyball match in the pits. I froze, but the hug got worse as the volunteer rotated my body until every side of me was covered.

I must have looked like a giant chocolate Easter bunny with her ears nibbled off. This was *not* projecting the executive image I wanted! I needed to get clean right away. Unfortunately, the nearest solution was an inflatable pool and a garden hose, from which flowed only a trickle of water—and it had a long line, to boot. Unless I wanted to shove aside waiting children—even worse for my executive image—my only choice was the fire hose.

At the edge of the parking lot, I stepped up onto the wooden pallet and nodded my readiness. The waiting firefighters seemed just a little too anxious to blast me, but who could blame them? When the water smashed into my body, it nearly swept me off my perch. Fighting to keep my balance, I knew I'd never be able to turn my back on that jet of water. I'd have to be satisfied with a clean—if soaking—front, and take care of my filthy back later.

As I stepped unsteadily to the ground, I saw Doug walking toward me. Of course. At least he was carrying a large iced tea. I *needed* that iced tea, but I didn't need to see Mr. Slow Warmer, not looking like I did. Should I feign some pressing administrative business and flee in the opposite direction?

My iced-tea craving won. I knew Doug would probably never want to see me again, but the drink was so delicious. Maybe it was for the best, I thought. I showed him around, sheepishly introducing him to my volunteers and secretly hoping one of the muddier ones would wrap him up in a bear hug. For most of the tour, Doug lagged a step or two behind me, with a perfect view of my muddy derriere.

That night, when I was finally clean and settled in my favorite chair at home, I listened to some voicemails. There were messages from my son and several telemarketers. Then the last message.

Beep. *Hey Karen, this is Doug. When you get home, give me a call. I have a couple of questions for you.*

I was way too tired to run that relational race, but on the other hand, if Doug wanted to end things, it would be nice to just get it over with. The day wasn't *quite* over yet, so surely there was room for a final traumatic event!

I called the number I'd memorized after our first date. When Doug answered on the second ring, my voice sounded shrill and irritated, even to me, when I asked him what he wanted.

His first question was, "Do people really pay money to do that?"

"Don't ask me why, but they do," I responded. Then, with more impatience than necessary, I asked, "And your second question?" I already knew what it would be: a gentle question designed to let me down without hurting my feelings. Which is why his *actual* question practically knocked my socks off.

"Do you know how *good* you looked today?"

Now I was warming up, and not slowly. Doug's question was the perfect end to a horrible day, the unexpected beginning to a lifetime together.

Karen Hessen

crash landing

om and Dad married on December 26, 1953, between the Korean and Vietnam Wars. Dad was a naval aviator, and in the course of his service flew missions in the China Sea.

Mom was proud of her husband, but his flying scared her. Over time, her mild fear became a full-blown phobia of flying. After all, she knew an airplane might be responsible for her husband's death, and she always felt safer when she knew he was on terra firma.

When his tour ended and he returned to the States, Dad often found work piloting small planes. He loved to fly and the money was good. Occasionally he worked for the Bureau of Land Management, doing aerial surveys. More often, he carried papers for the *Wall Street Journal* as a glorified paperboy.

During those years, while Mom was happy to have her husband home from the war, she continued to worry whenever he took to the skies. She knew the odds of a pilot's eventually crashing a small plane. Every minute Dad was home, she secretly hoped that somehow he wouldn't return to the air.

In January of 1995, the day Mom dreaded finally came. Dad was flying a twin-engine Beechcraft 18 across the Rocky Mountains in western Montana. The wings became covered in ice, and the aging engines couldn't lift the plane high enough. He died instantly upon impact. Mom's worst fear had come true.

Several years later found Mom remarried and living with her new husband on a remote ranch across the state. She was often alone at their house while her husband was out mending fences or taking care of the cattle.

One day as she did her housework, old habit had her listening to the rhythmic drone of a nearby crop duster. When the noise of its engine suddenly stopped, she froze, senses tingling. Racing to the window, her heart nearly stopped: a plume of black smoke rose from a nearby wheat field. Mom dialed 911, but soon realized the phone line was dead. If the pilot was still alive, she was his only hope.

Fear whispered in her ear as she drove down the gravel road, but she paid it no attention. She knew the crash site could hold no terror like what she had confronted years before. As she got closer to the crash site, Mom saw flames surrounding the tangled fuselage. She raced from her car toward the wreckage, only to spot the pilot lying beside the crumbled cockpit. Was she too late?

Then the pilot spoke. He was still alive! His desperate plight spurred her into action. Knowing she could do nothing for him directly, she leaped back into her car and raced the several miles to a nearby dam. There she found others to help, and a working phone. A MedEvac flight was called, and within an hour the pilot, still fighting to stay alive, was on his way to the nearest hospital.

That pilot lived to fly again, thanks to Mom. While she didn't approve of his continuing to fly after he recovered, she didn't have any say about that!

In life, sometimes our worst fears come true despite every prayer to the contrary. But when this happens, we find—like Mom did—that fear's power over us is no longer absolute. Living—and loving—means taking risks, and accepting the outcome…whether you're in the cockpit or on the ground.

Ann Bardell

come on over

obin, I'll ask Ma after school today," Linda promised. "Now blow your nose before the bus gets here. Holy moly—you look like something the cat dragged in!"

Maybe this doesn't sound like an endearing way to speak to a weeping teenager, but let me tell you: when my friend Linda spoke those words to me, my future was transformed.

I was a wreck at sixteen. Besides juggling a full load of college prep classes in school, I worked a job every day after school. That might have been bearable if my situation were better at home, but my mother had died when I was twelve, and my alcoholic father often forgot to buy groceries or pay the heating bill.

The reason I was a weeping mess at the bus stop that morning— the reason my best friend, Linda, decided to ask her mother if I could come live with them—was that the previous night my father had stumbled home sometime after midnight and decided to shoot our cats. Inside the house.

Linda and I had been best friends since the first day of kindergarten, when Miss Fisher assigned us to the same table. So it stood to reason that when Linda told her mother—who everyone called "Ma"—what my father had done, the matter was quickly settled. I would move in with them immediately.

That same day I packed up my shabby clothes and meager belongings and moved into Ma's house. As a mother of eight, with half her children already grown and gone, Ma insisted there was more than enough room for me, and she was right: there *was* enough room. Extra space wasn't what I needed, and we both knew it. My real need was for family—people I could count on to love me through thick and thin. The first night I slept at their house, I felt like I was coming home.

It's been nearly forty years since that tearful morning at the bus stop. Ma has become my mother in so many ways, and Linda has been my best friend for every single day of those four decades. She is my rock when my world threatens to collapse and my cheerleader when I'm chasing my dreams. Through every conceivable up-and-down, Linda's earthy, honest love has been the soundtrack of my life:

"Quit crying so hard, I can't understand you. What? You're getting a divorce? Oh, Robin…after all these years. Tell you what. We're gonna go get a beer and a burger and figure things out."

"Oh, Lordy, what happened? I can't believe it! Are you gonna be okay? I'll be there as soon as I can. Hang in there, kiddo. We'll figure out a way to get through this."

"Michael did what? Who's the girl? Are they getting married? Cowabunga, you're gonna be a granny! Quit crying and come on over. Brucie finally learned how to make chicken soup without screwing it up, and Ma's making noodles right now."

In life, I've found that friends enjoy gathering for celebrations, but things change when you're down in the muck. Those who were quick to raise a glass in cheer suddenly get too busy to answer your calls. Not so with Linda. She has walked beside me through thick and thin—love, birth, jobs, the loss of a child, failure, success, and aging. Most amazingly of all, she didn't do this at a distance, but by inviting me into her own home.

Friendship, I've discovered through it all, isn't a sprint. It's a lifelong walk, and the friends who have walked beside me have saved my life and become my family.

Robin Hewitt

almost home

Only five years shy of a century, Oscar Bailey felt old. He was bone-tired. Surprisingly, that wasn't natural for this ninety-five year old man. Old age and Oscar had never really been on speaking terms with each other. From cleaning his chimney to helping a neighbor pull out a stump, and from mowing the lawn to cultivating a verdant, weedless garden, Oscar simply didn't have time for weariness.

That all changed a few years earlier when his beloved wife, Mildred, fell ill. On a freezing day in January, Oscar and Mildred stopped at the market for a jug of milk. Without warning, Mildred collapsed in the parking lot. Oscar was powerless to save her; he could only watch helplessly as the ambulance roared away with his wife inside.

Mildred spent six weeks in the hospital, but she never fully recovered. To make matters worse, she began to manifest the first symptoms of Alzheimer's disease: difficulty making plans, speech deficits, and—hardest of all for Oscar—flashes of memory loss during which she didn't recognize her husband.

Oscar and Mildred had been happily married for seventy years. The children of European immigrants, they rose early, worked hard, ate well, and slept soundly. Oscar had been a forester, and he knew the name of every plant and tree that greened the woods around their home. In the fall, he would harvest blackberries, blueberries, and grapes for making his own wine. Mildred had cooked every meal from scratch, decade after decade, with fruits and vegetables grown in their garden. The house was always spotless, and often the buttery-sweet smell of a homemade cake wafted through the polished hallways.

Two years after Mildred's accident, Oscar knew those days were gone for good. Mildred now spent most of her time in bed, the covers stretched across her frail body and tucked beneath her chin. Even when the sun shone outside, the curtains were pulled closed. She slept, and mumbled, and slept again, usually waking only when Oscar came to spoon soup into her mouth.

Oscar was now responsible for anything and everything that needed doing, inside and outside. At ninety-five, doing everything takes a toll—even on a man as hale as Oscar Bailey. The seemingly endless list of chores was difficult enough: laundry, cooking, cleaning, gardening, paying the bills. But the hardest part was going into Mildred's bedroom, perhaps to give her pills or feed her some lunch. She'd take the pills, eat the food, and not once would her eyes light with recognition. It was like caring for a stranger.

Retiring and moving to an assisted-care facility where they could get more help wasn't an option for a man like Oscar. "We've been in this house for years," he would proudly proclaim, "and we'll die in this house, not some *home*." He pronounced the last word as if it were a curse.

He meant every word, but that didn't remove his exhaustion—or the pain of caring for the woman he dearly loved, but who was no longer the same woman he married. Oscar's body was starting to break down. His back got the worst of it, and each vertebra throbbed with irritation and fatigue. How could he possibly go on?

He couldn't. One day Oscar collapsed on the ancient sofa in the living room. Night was lowering across the woods, the yard, the house—and Oscar felt the darkness in his heart, too. He tried to sit up and rub his own back, but the effort was too much, and it only caused fresh jolts of pain to shake him. The man who could do everything himself was suddenly helpless. Oscar began to cry, and in his soul a desperate prayer for help rose up. *I can't do this, but I can't abandon the only woman I've ever loved.*

With his hands on the small of his back, Oscar felt them clasped by another pair of hands.

"Mildred, what on earth are you doing out of bed?"

Oscar turned and squinted. The room was dim, but he could still see fine with his glasses on. And he was the only person in the room. Shocked, he turned back around, bringing his hands into his lap.

Still he felt the warm, strong grip of another pair of hands enfolding his own. Then the unseen hands began to massage Oscar's, gently but firmly rubbing his palms, his bony wrists, the aching joints in every finger. Oscar stared ahead, seeing nothing but feeling every detail.

Through Oscar's hands spread waves of warmth and comfort, waves that washed into every corner of his cold and weary body. His fingers, touched by a mysterious visitor, became the epicenter of encouragement, and soon a feeling of peace and relief settled over his entire being. Long after the massage ended, Oscar sat on the couch, savoring the blessing, and certain he had been visited by God.

That night Oscar experienced the gifts night is meant to bring: rest, calm, and the hope of a new day.

In the morning, Oscar's aches and pains returned. When he brought Mildred her breakfast, she didn't recognize him. After breakfast, he did a load of wash and swept the porch, feeling the familiar burning in his lower back. That night, his body was as tired as ever, and the next morning he woke up and did it all again.

The mysterious touch that massaged Oscar's hands wasn't meant to solve all his problems or do all his work for him. Oscar was ninety-five years old. He didn't need a bottomless well of strength with which to live a whole new life. What he needed was simply a cup of cold water so he could run the final lap. After that encounter, he could almost hear the cheers as he rounded the final turn—*Well done, good and faithful friend*—carrying his wife of seventy years to the finish line in love, in peace, in the house that had been their home for all those sweet and tender years.

no longer a nuisance

The moment my husband told me the mutt's name was "Natty," I privately nicknamed him Natty the Nuisance—I could tell he was going to be nothing but trouble. When Ken picked him up from the local hardware and feed store where folks give puppies away, he was told that Natty was a Great Pyrenees mix. To me, however, his lineage looked more like Heinz 57.

At least everyone *else* in the house was happy about the new puppy. "Look, isn't he a lively one?" gushed Ken as he set the hyperactive black furball on the floor and our normally aloof Akita bounded over to nuzzle him. "I just know Natty will be a great companion for her," my husband continued. "She's been lonely."

All I saw was another creature to pick up after—and a shaggy one at that. Nothing but a nuisance.

I liked animals. In *theory*. In practice, cleaning up after our three cats and a dog—now two dogs—was a lot of work. Ken's health had been slowly deteriorating over the last few years, so caring for the animals was increasingly my responsibility. I fed, walked, picked up after, bathed, and groomed—and when Natty came to live with us I experienced anew the joy of potty training a dog that would grow to weigh almost as much as me.

Natty's animal intuition alerted him to the fact that I was not his biggest fan, and he spent most of his time curled at Ken's feet. Whenever I walked through the living room, I'd see Ken and Natty occupied with their favorite pastimes: my husband watching reruns of *Gunsmoke* and *Cheyenne*, and Natty resting his massive head on Ken's knees and drooling contentedly.

The only time Natty ever seemed to want me was when I groomed our Akita or held one of our cats in my lap. Then he'd lope over and nose my hand away from the other pet—and if I ignored him, he'd whine and whimper and use his powerful frame to push my hand away again. "I've never seen an animal that demands so much attention," I'd complain to Ken.

"He's just a puppy—he'll outgrow it," my husband would always tell me. But Natty didn't. A total nuisance.

♂ ♂ ♂

Last spring, my husband passed away after a long decline. In the weeks that followed, Natty's neediness increased exponentially. The big dog shadowed me as I walked from room to room, and anytime I sat down at my desk or on the couch, he'd nudge my arm until I consented to pet him.

Even in my grief, I felt sorry for Natty. I'd known for years that I would probably lose my husband, but Natty had no such awareness. To him, it seemed as if his best friend had simply vanished, and the pain of that loss was obvious on his canine face.

Nevertheless, I didn't appreciate the way he interrupted my life. I was grieving, too, and caring for Natty felt like an additional burden that I'd prefer not to carry. I wondered if I should find another home for him, one where he could receive all the attention that he obviously craved. I needed to deal with my own grief, not his.

♂ ♂ ♂

As Natty approached his sixth birthday, he should have been enjoying his dog-years middle age. Instead, he seemed to be sliding into early senescence. He spent most of his time in the backyard, lazing on the grass, watching the birds, and barking at the occasional truck that passed the house. When Ken was alive, Natty used to race back and forth between the patio and our apple tree, but now he'd plod lethargically across the lawn.

Kind of like me, I thought to myself. Since my husband passed away, I'd become a bit sedentary myself. *But I have arthritis,* I rationalized, *and Natty is too young for that.*

Our vet agreed. "Natty's pretty healthy," he told me, "but he's overweight. He needs to lose around twenty-five pounds. I know it's hard, but see if you can find a way to walk him more."

On the way home from the vet, I sighed. Natty wasn't the only one who needed to lose twenty-five pounds and be more active. During Ken's decline and subsequent passing, I'd comforted myself with creamy casseroles and carrot cake. And though I lived on a rural loop frequented by joggers and walkers, I always found an excuse to stay inside: too hot, too cold…too old.

The next morning I somehow willed myself to find Natty's leash and slip on sensible shoes. The moment I snapped the leash onto Natty's collar, his tail began wagging. And much to my surprise, as soon as we stepped out the door Natty took the lead, keeping a steady pace and tugging me in his wake.

As we walked, a series of small insights surprised me. I enjoyed breathing in the scent of the lilac bushes that we passed. The feeling of my heart beating filled me with a sense of life. And— shockingly—when I ran my fingers through Natty's coarse fur while we waited at an intersection, I felt a thrill of attachment. Maybe walking Natty wasn't so bad; maybe *he* wasn't so bad.

The next day Natty and I went for another walk. And the day after that. Soon we settled into a routine, and in time a day without walking Natty became almost unimaginable.

Now, when I get too engrossed sending e-mails or reading a book, Natty will pad up to me and gently—but firmly—nuzzle my arm.

When I become distracted by chores around the house, he'll station himself at the front door and rumble until I remember our date. Scruffy Natty is no longer a nuisance. Instead, he's my personal therapy dog. Together we're striding into shape, my dog and me, and walking toward whatever's next in life. Both of us still miss Ken, but I'm grateful for the companionship of my unexpected friend.

Terri Elders

blooming lilacs

*E*very child has a special place—be it a fort, a tree house, or that cozy space under a parent's desk—where the world fades away and everything is safe. When I was a little girl, my refuge was the most magical spot imaginable: the wide, fragrant hollow under the arching branches of three lilac bushes in my yard. I crawled beneath those bushes whenever I needed time alone; it was there, in the speckled sunlight, that I solved the pressing problems of childhood. How would I save enough money for a new set of jacks? Could I win back my lucky aggie marble at school the next day?

One day I got home from school and came face-to-face with a horrible sight: my father was pulling up my lilac bushes! He had decided our yard didn't need them anymore—never mind that *I* needed them! He looped a rope around their branches at root level and heaved, pulling them straight out of the ground. As I cried my eyes out, the lilac bushes were heaped together in a pile where they would be left to dry.

And when they were dry enough, they would be torched.

♂ ♂ ♂

Life moved on, of course. I began to care about things other than jacks and marbles, and my problems could no longer be solved beneath the branches of a lilac bush. I grew up, moved out, married, had six children, and—in the blink of an eye, it seemed—Verne and

I were ready to retire. In 1998, we moved to a home where we would spend our golden years.

In the yard of this home was a single stunted lilac bush. It was so far gone that Verne wanted to pull it up as soon as we moved in, but I stopped him. For some reason—perhaps as an homage to my lavender childhood getaway—I wanted to keep it. As the years passed, and the lilac bush failed to produce blossoms or even green up, I gave up any hope that it would ever bloom. Nevertheless, it seemed right to allow it to stay, and eventually Verne quit trying to persuade me otherwise.

Ten years after Verne and I retired in that house, he passed away. We had enjoyed fifty-six years of marriage, and he was truly my best friend and the love of my life. It was a difficult time, and things got even worse when I was in a car accident that resulted in a bruised and battered body and significant hearing loss. I became depressed, and every day I moped about the house and felt sorry for myself.

Then, on a bleak day in November, something changed. I was staring lifelessly out the window at the same unvaried palette of browns that I saw every day. Except it wasn't entirely brown. In the middle of the yard was my lilac bush, and it was blooming.

In cold, damp November, a month when every outdoor plant is dormant, my never-bloomed-before lilac held out its branching purple flowers in defiance of winter's approach. I threw on my coat and hurried outside, still not believing.

But it was true. The flowers were small but unbelievably bright. And suddenly I wondered if Verne was trying to get my attention. He knew I needed to keep living, and he understood my faith in the power of a blooming lilac.

Year after year the lilac had done nothing other than prove it was lifeless. But that November day, standing in my chilly yard and staring in awe at the purple flames warming my heart, I knew I could bloom again, too.

ර ර ර

I spent a wonderful Christmas with my children in Iowa. Over the course of my visit, we concluded that I should sell the house Verne and I had lived in and move closer to my kids and grandkids. So after Christmas we drove through the streets near their homes, and—despite the deep drifts of snow—found a perfect little house for me. The sale closed at the end of February, and we decided I would move in May.

In May, the little house looked even better without four feet of snow surrounding it, and I couldn't wait to move in! As I walked into the backyard for the first time, I nearly fell over in shock: three huge lilac bushes were growing there, healthy and green and glad in the sunlight. I'd returned to my special place.

After Verne died, depression almost robbed me of the ability to appreciate countless memories of my wonderful husband. The miracle of a lilac bush blooming in November gave me strength to emerge from the winter of my discontent. As I put down new roots, my flourishing lilac bushes reminded me that I, too, could keep blooming and once again grow in a place of safety and beauty.

Mary Griffith Chalupsky

lost and found

The day I learned my parents were divorcing, it felt like every light in our house suddenly got turned off.

I was five, and their divorce woke me up to the reality that life can change even when you don't want it to. People can change too, even people who say they never will.

Worse than the divorce, however, was what happened afterward. My father deserted our family, running away from my mom and my younger brother and me. It was like he wanted to run far enough away to forget I'd ever been his daughter.

Perhaps he was able to create a new life for himself. Perhaps he went for days, or even weeks, without thinking of me. But I wasn't so lucky. My world had a daddy-shaped hole in it. Every day that I woke up to a quiet house or played by myself in the yard, I was reminded of being a small girl without a father.

♂ ♂ ♂

When I was seven, my mother introduced me to Mike. I didn't know how serious my mom was about Mike, but for *me* it was love at first sight. Mike was as kind as he was tall, and his warmth and love seemed to light up our home. During their engagement, I called him "Daddy Mike," my own affectionate take on *Little Orphan Annie.* As soon as he and Mom said "I do," I dropped the "Mike" and kept only that single, sweet word I'd been longing to use since I was five: Dad.

Not everyone who loses a father gets the chance to find another; even at my young age, I knew my stepdad's loving presence was a special gift. I treasured it.

Sadly, time took its toll on their marriage. By the time I was fifteen, Mom and my brother and I had moved out and divorce papers were drawn up. I worried about what would happen next: would he run away from me, just as my biological father had, and try to forget me? I knew I would never forget him, or the pain of his departure.

Mike did live in another house, but he never ran away: his love for my mother changed, yet his love for me remained sure and steady. Despite the divorce, despite the move, despite the fact that I was in the throes of my teenage years, Mike's love for me was a rock that never moved. It turned out that even though he wasn't my mother's husband, he was still my dad.

I'd made a lot of mistakes already by the time I was fifteen, but I've never been so glad to be so wrong about something.

And being wrong has never been so important. Mike loved me through my teenage years and into adulthood, and I loved him right back. Then last year, Mike's only biological daughter died, suddenly, at the age of twenty-seven. The shock knocked us down, and the flood of grief that followed was so fast and deep that we felt like we would never swim to the surface.

In the midst of that heartrending time, a realization came to me. Mike's life and mine were like mirror images. So many years before, when I was an abandoned child who longed to be held by a new father, Mike was the one who walked through my door and took hold of my heart, never to let it go. Now, what seemed like a lifetime later, Mike had lost a daughter and was looking for a port in his storm of grief. He found rest in me, the hurting girl he'd loved like his own—the stepdaughter who was now his only daughter.

In some ways it was easy for me to love Mike through those awful months and years. After all, I already knew in my bones that love holds tight through every storm. That was a lesson I'd learned from Mike—from the man I'll always call Dad.

I can never compensate for the daughter Mike lost, and Mike wouldn't want me to. But I am able to be the daughter he needs, just as long ago he became the father I needed. A lost child can never be replaced, but broken hearts always have a chance to heal.

Billie Criswell

...but now i see

Was I imagining things, or was that boy in the third row of the art class I was teaching actually *asleep* on top of his charcoal drawing?

I always knew that I'd be an artist; I'd been drawing and painting since before I could remember. Yet here I was, teaching bored middle schoolers the same old lesson about shading and perspective.

Somewhere along the way, my lifelong dream of *being* an artist had blurred, as if someone had wiped a rag across one of my pencil drawings. Instead of creating art, I was teaching people *about* art—and as the sleeping boy made clear, that wasn't making a real difference.

I'd lost track of my dream.

♂ ♂ ♂

Several days later, I was tucking my son into bed when he saw our dog in the hallway and impulsively threw a hard plastic toy to her. Unfortunately, he let go of the toy a fraction too late—and instead of soaring across the room to the dog, it hit my right eye.

It was so unexpected, so close—his hand was only inches from my head—that I didn't even have time to blink. An explosion of pain seared my eye, and I doubled over on his bed. With my eye clenched tight, I could see multicolored sparks firing against a black background.

I was trying not to scare my son, but inside I was panicking. *What's happening to my eye?* I screamed silently. My eye felt like it was dying, and I wanted to vomit.

Nothing could be done that Friday night, but I found a specialist who could see me first thing Saturday morning. My father-in-law, an optometrist, had practical advice: "Don't bend over—you're losing your retina."

The next day, I listened to the specialist explain that the curative rate for retinal damage is unpredictable. "It might heal totally, or not at all," he said flatly. Not the most compassionate way to lay out what might happen to a patient, but I understood what he meant. This was totally out of my control, and all I could do was wait.

So for the next few days I let go and waited. I quit my teaching job, I stayed home and rested, and I prayed. I spoke calmly to my son and didn't mention my eye, hoping he wouldn't worry that he'd hurt me. Waiting was the only thing over which I had a small measure of control. I could wait anxiously, or I could wait in peace. And every time I found myself beginning to freak out—*What good is an artist with only one eye?*—I tried to choose peace.

I started to do something else: draw. In that season of half-darkness, I saw more clearly than ever before that God had given me a love and talent for art. Talent is never abstract: it can be seen and appreciated only when it is used, and it is meant to be used in the moment, not hoarded for the future. As my pencil moved across the blank page—now in long, looping arcs, now in short bursts of tight shading—I discovered again the joy of creation, even as I saw it through only a single eye.

 delta delta delta

Progress was slow, but both my eye and my art slowly improved. As I saw more clearly with my damaged eye, I experienced a clearer sense that I was again *being* the artist—making art, thinking creatively—that I was called to be. Working with limited vision meant that I had to move slowly and carefully, and in the process my skills became sharper than ever before.

Over the next few years, I witnessed my art career stretching outward and bearing sweet fruit: I illustrated an original curriculum for a church's summer children's program; I returned to teaching with a fresh passion that stemmed from making my own artistic discoveries; I partnered with a master painter to create a massive mural celebrating creation; and I launched an online resource center for churches and parents who need illustrated children's materials.

As I write this story, I close my good eye and look at the screen through my injured eye. Years after the accident, my right eye still has a blind spot the size of a pencil eraser, directly in the center of my vision. When I look at what I'm typing, I can't see the exact word I'm trying to focus on—but I *can* see all the surrounding words with my peripheral vision. And when I paint and illustrate and draw, I take a second and a third look, and in the act of looking again I see more clearly than I ever did before. I've come to see my blind spot as a blessing because it reminds me both of what I still have and of what I almost lost. I don't know what my future as an artist will look like, but I do know that I'll see every step along the way clearly.

Gina Graham

Lemon Drop

A successful visual artist with trouble seeing? Only in *God Makes Lemonade*! I spoke with Gina recently, and her eye is doing better than ever, though she'll always notice a tiny spot there. She's currently working on an ambitious series of six Easter paintings for her own home—and without the injury she never would have taken the time for it. Her less-than-perfect vision will always remind her of what she almost lost…and what she still has. —Don

{ in his own words }

n Maryland in 1968, a fourteen-year-old girl became pregnant by a nineteen-year-old boy.

The girl's father was livid. She was his first daughter, his namesake, and they had always shared a special bond. Yet when she told her father that she wanted to keep the baby, he exploded. He screamed at her, warned her that she would never amount to anything, and—as things escalated out of control—punched his own daughter in the face.

The girl's mother took her to another state for a few months, hoping things would calm down back at home. They did, but the family was damaged irreparably. They eventually returned to Maryland, but the girl's father was never again welcome in their home.

As Christmas approached, the girl wasn't expecting a whirl of presents and lit trees and special meals like all of her friends. Instead, she was adjusting to life without her father, and preparing to give birth to a daughter. Finally, as night fell across the city, I entered the world.

Because my mother was so young—still a girl, really—her mother took care of me. Nana was a beautician, and since her shop was in the back of our house, she was able to look after me and work at the same time. My mother went back to high school, eventually earning her degree by the time I was three.

My mother hadn't had a lot of contact with my father as she was finishing school, but when she graduated, both families pressured my parents to marry. My father found a job in New Jersey, and after the wedding the three of us moved there. As we settled into our new life together, things were rocky. My father was enrolled in a crash course on becoming a hands-on dad and present husband, while my mother was—for the first time—raising her child without the immediate support of her extended family.

Life changed again one year later with the birth of my younger brother, Kevin. My parents' already fragile relationship was cracking, and Kevin's arrival added additional pressure. They were too young and too unprepared; they had been thrust together by their families. Ultimately, Mom and Dad decided to separate.

Not long afterward, my father was found dead in his apartment. A brain aneurysm killed him at the age of twenty-three. I was left, at the age of four, without a father, and only vague memories of happy times together.

As I grew into a young woman, I always felt as if I had a father-shaped hole in my heart. I often wondered how different my life would have been had he lived. The tragedy could have cast a shadow over my whole life but for one source of light that continued to inspire me: family photographs.

My parents took many pictures during their brief period of happiness before they separated. As I thumbed through photo albums, I spotted my father in scene after scene: holding me in front of the lion cage at the zoo, pushing me in a swing at the park, and laughing with family at a backyard barbecue. The more I studied these pictures, the better I remembered some of the happy times I was able to share with my father before he died.

Still, despite the pictures, I was wounded. Having lost my father at such a tender age, there were countless questions about our relationship that would forever go unanswered. Or so I thought.

One day, many years later when I was a grown woman with children of my own, my Nana discovered a letter that my father had written to me when I was a baby. I opened it with trembling hands, unfolding the aging paper and carefully smoothing it. There in front of me was his beautiful handwriting—loops and curves that my proud young father had set down in ink before I could even pronounce his name.

It wasn't just any letter, either—it was a love letter. As waves of sadness and joy simultaneously broke across my heart, I understood for the first time the depth of joy my father had felt upon meeting me and holding me in his arms. He was blessed beyond measure, he told me in the letter, to be my father. He loved me deeply, and that love would last forever.

When I set the letter down, I was a new woman. Decades after his death, I was finally able to come to a place of peace. The love I feel for my own children suddenly came into sharper focus, and I determined to make every day my own living love letter to them. And although my father left this world far too soon, he was able to speak to me the words I needed to hear from beyond the grave. I will never lose that most precious of all gifts, his letter to me—yet even if it were lost, its words are written forever on my heart.

Krista Matthews

ending
and
beginning

*I*t wasn't until I was a mother myself that I asked *my* mother to tell me about the night she came home from work to find our house on Orchard Way empty and her children gone. She sat across from me and I watched her familiar face shift, soften, as she traveled into the past. Mum pushed her glasses back on her forehead and began to speak.

You know I worked the three-to-eleven shift, and how it was more than a mile from there to catch the streetcar home. By the time I walked to the streetcar stop, waited for it, and walked home from Monongahela Street, it was well past midnight.

She shrugged her slim shoulders, as if to shake off the weight of a heavier time that had taken a toll from her.

I was a single mom before anyone heard the term. It broke my heart to leave you kids alone, but I knew you would be okay, and I knew I could depend on you even though you were only eleven.

Mum looked at me, her eldest daughter. Twelve was a lot different back then—twelve going on twenty. But the years following the Great Depression changed a lot of things. She continued her story.

Back then, everyone in the neighborhood kept an eye out for you kids. They knew I had to work to keep a roof over our heads and food on the table. The hours weren't good, but the job was. It was the best way to take care of the four of you.

I smiled at my mother, sitting gracefully on a couch that her younger self would have found unimaginably luxurious. "Nowadays," I said, "leaving four young children alone from after school until midnight might be considered child abuse."

Back then it was called surviving. Your dad died in 1934, before Social Security. There was no pension or insurance. We couldn't feed you children and pay insurance premiums. Besides, your dad was thirty years old, strong and healthy. We had to make a choice, so we chose food on the table. Who would guess a year later he would be gone?

I twisted in my chair, trying to picture my widowed twenty-seven-year-old mother with four children under the age of six and no steady income. I watched her shake her head, as if she was answering her own question before continuing her story.

When I got home that night, I turned the lock and reached for the light switch. There was no electricity. The company had turned it off again. I hadn't been at my job long enough to get caught up on old bills. When I made a payment, we had electricity for a while, but when I got too far behind, off it went. You know, I did the same job as the men on that production line—I put out as many pieces per day—but my hourly wage was less because I was a woman. It was hard.

Hard doesn't begin to describe what she did for us. I flashed her an admiring smile. "You got us kids ready for school, cleaned, did the laundry, shopped, and had a hot meal waiting for us when we came home for lunch. After all that, you went to work, stood on your feet for eight hours helping to make wartime gas masks, then came home and started all over again. I don't know how you did it. When I was a child I didn't think about it, but now I see what you did."

She seemed embarrassed by my words, and quickly returned to the story I'd asked her to tell. She got to her feet and walked, arms and hands extended, pantomiming that night long ago.

I felt my way around the walls of the living room to make sure I didn't bump into that big cast-iron potbelly stove in the middle. Then I went up the steps to my bedroom. The streetlight outside was shining in the window and I saw the room was completely empty. No furniture. Nothing. I knew what I would find in the room the four of you shared.

She sat down again and took a long breath before continuing.

I went down the stairs, made sure I didn't walk into the stove, locked the door to that deserted house, and dragged myself to Nana's house. I didn't want to cry, but I couldn't help it. I knew Nana would be making decisions for you every day, now that she'd taken you to her house. As I walked the two miles to her place, the only people I saw were drunks hanging around the taverns on Monongahela Street. That was the longest walk of my life.

Silence hung in the air between us. I watched her body settle slightly, as if that walk had once again drained her energy. I broke the quiet. "Well, obviously we all survived." She kept talking as if we'd never paused, as if I hadn't spoken.

Nana had been after me for a long time to move back home. She was always reminding me that only your Uncle Packy was still at home, and there were two empty rooms on the third floor. You remember how our house on Orchard Way had only two small bedrooms. We could've used the space, no doubt about it. Moving made sense.

Mum sighed, and then named the heart of the matter.

Making sense didn't take away the pain of knowing that if we moved to Nana's, I'd be your mother in name only. But when the electricity went out that last time, the decision was made for me. But who knows what would have happened to you kids if we'd kept living on our own. Maybe it was for the best.

"It was, Mum," I said. "I hated that old house. I was just too young to understand that we didn't have any other options. We had to go down to the basement to use the toilet, and that dirt floor..." I shuddered before continuing. "There was no bathtub or sink. You had to bring that galvanized tub up out of the basement and fill it by hand so we could take turns taking a bath, one at a time, in the same water. I *despised* that," I added, my nose wrinkling at the memory.

Yes, and then I had to empty the darn tub the same way and haul it back into the cellar when we were finished. Nana's house had a bathroom with a sink and real tub. It had a refrigerator, too, and that meant no more boxes nailed to the windowsill to keep food cold in winter. Remember when we'd open the window to get something to eat and cold air would rush into the house?

Mum's arms automatically wrapped around her middle, and a chill shook her body—whether from the memory of icy winter nights or from reentering a time of such hardship, I couldn't tell.

And there was the other side of the coin, too.

Now I shivered. "Grandpap and the Triangle Grill. I remember." I looked at the floor as I continued. "Saturday nights he'd get drunk and all hell broke loose when he got home. I could never figure that out. Monday through Friday he was even-tempered, never missed a day at work, and was always kind and loving to us. But come Saturday…"

Both of us were silent. There are some things darker, more tragic, than electricity being turned off. After a time, I gently asked my mother for a few more details about the day Nana took us to her house.

You know your grandmother—she had an army of volunteers. That afternoon, the quickest and easiest thing to do was take everything on the second floor and pitch it out the bedroom windows, bending it if it didn't fit. Bed frames, mattresses, chests of drawers, clothes, linens: everything landed on the cobblestones out back. Her helpers below tossed everything into that rusty old Ford pickup that belonged to Mr. Epps and then drove it to the dump. The only thing they saved while I was at work that night was my cedar chest—but every last thing inside it was sent to the dump.

I watched Mum fold her hands in her lap, and then the first three fingers of her right hand closed around her left ring finger and twisted back and forth.

Every last thing, including the diamond engagement ring your dad gave me. The diamond had fallen out of it, and I was storing the ring and the diamond away until I could afford to get it fixed. Nana never saw it.

A memory came into my mind, a question I had lived with for many years. "Our neighborhood was called Bedbug Row! Was *that* why Nana threw out all our stuff?"

That, and the fact that everything we owned belonged in the dump. My cedar chest and the few pieces of clothing Nana saved sat on her back porch until they'd been hand-inspected for creepy crawlies, washed in boiling water, and dried in the sun. My cedar chest got an extra week outside, and a bath in Lysol. Only then could I take it inside to my bedroom.

Mum paused again. Then she let herself recline against the soft back of the couch, and I knew the next thing she said would bring her storytelling to an end until the next time I asked her to tell me one.

Life was different after that night I came home to a dark, empty house. But that's what it was still—life—and I'll always be grateful that Nana came for you that night. Life wasn't easy after that, but it was easier. We were all together…and no more trips to the basement to use the bathroom!

We smiled at each other.

They say all's well that ends well, but as my mother's story took me back to my childhood, I realized that it wasn't just the ending—living in a nicer home with Nana—that was well. So was the beginning, when Dad was still alive. So was the middle, living on Orchard Way without him, when the force of Mum's love held us together like gravity. And as I sat across from my mother, many years later, I knew the story we were still writing would be well, too. We'd see to that, together.

Mary Lou Wilson

lunches with mike

The birth of a baby is meant to be a joyous event. The adoption of a baby—especially when a baby is adopted by a couple unable to have children of their own—is supposed to be joyous as well. Profound gratitude and happiness should accompany the arrival of any baby to a family, with a great swell of love and appreciation to carry the baby's parents through the difficult early months.

Unfortunately, my adoptive parents must have missed that memo. The night they brought me home, they wrote a different script. My midnight cries for milk produced a reaction in my father as unexpected as it was violent: he yelled at my mother to "shut that kid up!" and kicked her out of their bed. Literally.

That early hostility set the stage for years of abuse. Both of my adoptive parents battled alcoholism throughout their adult lives, and those nearly nightly episodes of rage became all too familiar. My mother wanted a baby, and my father grudgingly agreed, but my presence only made their problems worse.

Daytime and nighttime became like separate compartments during my childhood. While the sun was shining, my family seemed completely normal. We went on picnics and swam at the beach. Then, as night fell, rage stormed into our house, and with it came terror. Many nights I would retreat to my closet and close the door; my refuge was three feet square and lit only by the faintest crack of light. Some nights my parents found me there, hiding, and the madness escalated into abuse.

At sixteen I tried to run away. When that plan was thwarted, I made a half-hearted attempt to kill myself. That didn't work either, so I decided to keep living in spite of my parents. Maybe since I'd survived this far, I could keep surviving. Maybe all that I'd endured could one day help *me* help someone else.

◌ ◌ ◌

Many years later, when my daughter was in eighth grade, she called me at lunchtime to ask if I would drive her and a group of friends off campus for lunch. I was happy to oblige, and our one-time excursion turned into a standing date, and then a ritual. The faces changed from week to week, according to the shifting teenage friendships, but besides my daughter there was one constant: Mike.

Mike's childhood reminded me of my own, but his was even worse. His father was in prison, his mother was doing and selling drugs in another state, and his stepmom—who had custody of him—was an unstable alcoholic. Mike demanded that any adult in his life pass a test of commitment. He'd been betrayed too many times to naively trust any random authority figure. If someone tried to insert themselves into his life, he'd push them away—not because he didn't want to be loved, but because he didn't want to be hurt again.

Not many adults were patient enough to try to care for Mike. They called him a troublemaker and said he was "acting out." I just figured he was smart. I recognized what Mike was doing because I'd done it myself—what wounded child wants to be hurt again? I understood him, and maybe that's why Mike slowly started to trust me. It probably didn't hurt that I was chauffeuring him to lunch every week.

◌ ◌ ◌

Mike had two selves, just like all of us do: his public self, and the self he was in private. Most people in Mike's life made the mistake of thinking his public persona was his real and only self: the tough, independent eighth grader who was so screwed up that he willfully screwed up other people's lives, too.

Mike's other self, the one he hid from nearly everyone, reminded me of myself when I was his age: wounded, desperate to discover trust and love, and unsure if he ever would.

After several weeks of listening to Mike, he started to trust me. One day he came to our house. I opened the door to find him on the verge of tears, scarcely able to get the words out about what was happening at his home. I knew he was desperate to be listened to, and I promised I'd stay faithful him.

I'll be there whenever you need someone to listen, I told him. I'll stand up for you.

The next day, as usual, I picked the kids up at school for lunch. Mike happened to be the only boy in the group that day, and at our beachside picnic, he and I found a place to sit apart from the girls. Our patch of sand was out of earshot, and I decided to share some of the missing pieces of my own childhood that I'd been keeping back. As I described how abuse and fear had dominated my childhood, I threw Mike a lifeline: What if the pain we experience provides us a choice? I asked him. What if we can either let ourselves be destroyed or be transformed into something better?

As we talked, I could see the effect my story was having on Mike. He was quiet, but in the sharp focus of his eyes and his clenched fists I could tell he was internalizing every word. I wondered if he was glimpsing any hope in his seemingly hopeless future. I knew I'd probably never know for sure, but I prayed that when he left my sphere of influence, he'd be on a better path than when he started.

On the ride back to school, the girls continued talking a mile a minute, while Mike remained quiet. He and I had a lot more to think about than the girls did. I glanced at him in the mirror: he was staring out the window, seemingly absorbed in thought. What was going through his mind? What would he do the next day, and the day after that?

Partway through the drive, I happened to glance in the rearview mirror again. This time, Mike was waiting for me. He met my eyes with his own, and silently mouthed two words in the noisy car that only passed between the two of us.

Thank you.

♂ ♂ ♂

Mike's life didn't instantly turn around that day. Taking him out for a burger and listening to him talk didn't produce a miracle. And it didn't need to—I'm living proof of that. Most of the time our screwed-up lives don't change in the blink of an eye. Instead, we allow ourselves to accumulate hope year after year, until one day we awake to find that we've made it. We've done more than survive: we're thriving. And on that day, we start to look for others straggling behind us on the path toward wholeness.

Mike's whole life is in front of him still, and he knows he can make it. The pain of his past doesn't have to determine his future. That's why I expect I'll see Mike again one day. I'll be a grandma, with gray hair and a cane, and I'll run into Mike at a fast-food restaurant. He'll be the middle-aged man in the corner, sitting on a bench with a troubled teen, talking him into his future.

Carol Statton

beyond the bay

On the forty-five-minute bus ride from Waikiki, Oahu, to Hanauma Bay, I wondered if I had made a mistake. What was I doing trekking all over this tropical island, when back home in Alabama I had a mountain of problems that threatened to overwhelm me?

The stunningly beautiful beach was crowded. Vacationing teenagers dared each other to leap into bigger waves. Snorkelers finned back and forth across the bay, the tropical fish they were hunting invisible to everyone else. On the white sand, sunbathers stretched out full-length, hoping to return home enough shades darker to arouse the envy of their coworkers.

As I looked across the idyllic scene, I felt as if something was missing. I was restless, and I knew that trying to relax on the jam-packed beach—however much it resembled a postcard from paradise—wouldn't bring me peace. I hadn't left my problems behind in Alabama; I'd carried them to Hawaii in my heart, and even here they seemed to darken the view. I felt like I could never go home because of the family issues there, yet I knew I couldn't stay away forever.

Unable to sit still, I began to explore my surroundings. At the far end of the beach a mountain rose from the water—a jagged, boulder-strewn pyramid stippled with lavender flowers. I thought I could see a trail snaking its way along the side of the mountain. I looked down at my feet, which were protected by only a flimsy pair of beach shoes. I looked at the beach, which was clogged with tourists and snack vendors. I looked at the mountain, and I took off hiking.

The trail meandered along the base of the mountain, away from the beach and beside the Pacific. Hanauma Bay quickly disappeared from sight behind me, and soon after, the sound of frolicking tourists was replaced by sounds that had been here long before there were ears to hear them: breakers crashing into the mountain's rocky base; water sucking and draining through honeycombed caves; the wind whistling through the stems and leaves of the hardy plants that called this place home.

Finally my beach shoes carried me to a place that I now believe I was meant to see. I clambered past some rough boulders that had been deposited at the base of a narrow, volcanic headland. On the other side was a sight far removed from beach blankets and snorkels.

The mountain rose straight out of the sea, and its bare sides below the trail bore the full brunt of the ocean's pounding waves. No purple flowers or green shrubs colored the dark, sloping rock. Every time a swell rolled in, the resulting crash flung bright droplets into the sky, painting a misty vortex of color. I extended my hand beyond the edge, hoping to catch some of the mist, but a steady breeze blew the disintegrating palette past my reach and up over my head, wetting the slopes behind me. Transfixed by the polychromatic explosions of seawater, I became part of another world. I felt my problems shrink before the eternal grandeur around me.

This new creation of which I was a part seemed to be an image of that particular time in my life. I sensed that my life was full of slippery, jagged rocks, but that if I was patient—if I could bear the fury of the waves—I would witness something beautiful and worthwhile rising above it all.

I don't know how long I stood there, but it was long enough for the wisdom of the message to soak into my soul, long enough to instill in me a sense of confident peace.

Returning home to my problems wasn't about inventing the perfect solutions. I didn't need to prevent difficult things from happening with my own willpower. Rather, I needed to keep walking forward—even if the trail of my life was bumpy and I was wearing flip-flops! Around a bend I *would* find the view I was meant to see, as long as I kept my eyes open.

Hope, like sea mist rising on the wind, may seem fleeting. But when fully realized, hope is also beautiful. And if we watch for it, the same wind that carries it past us will return it to us again.

Sara DuBose

waiting to ripen

*J*ust deal with it."

My husband's brusque words of advice weren't what I wanted to hear. His German stoicism meant that he dealt with our son's running away the same way he dealt with anything in life: by putting his head down and getting back to work.

My Scottish passion, however, required a very different approach. Our son had just run away, after all—how could I *not* talk about it? I needed to do some processing. Why had he run away? How should we react? Was I to blame? These questions, along with a thousand others, raced through my head. I *was* going to "just deal with it," but that didn't mean the same thing for me as it did my husband. If I couldn't talk to him about what had happened, I needed to find another outlet.

So I started writing—a decision that would shape the latter half of my life. My thoughts flowed onto the page as a series of rhymes. For verse after verse after verse, I complained and dreamed and processed and questioned. I wrote about myself, my family, God, and life as I knew it. And the more I wrote, the more I wanted to write. I penned a stack of pages that grew to monumental proportions. I shed tears along the way, but my rhymes never led me to despair. The verses always ended on a sweet note of hope, even when I was unable to see that hope at the stanza's beginning.

Over the years, I came to see my writing like a tree: rooted in the bitter experiences of my life, but in season bearing the sweet fruit of understanding and perspective. I'd always loved the *idea* of writing and being onstage before an audience, but as I approached my eightieth birthday, I discovered that I'd spent the last several decades actually *writing.*

♂ ♂ ♂

Have you ever noticed that parent/child roles begin to reverse over time? After I turned eighty, my daughter fixed me with a probing look and said, "How many more poems and lessons are you going to write before you publish? Gather your writing together and I'll make it into a book." So I did, and then she did!

Can you imagine the thrill of becoming a first-time author at the age of eighty-one? At my age, the biggest thrill I expect most days is to have someone carry my groceries to my car for me. Once I had a published book, even *that* experience became sweeter: knowing I had a captive audience for as long as it took to reach my car, I'd try to encourage my grocery-store helpers by reminding them that *all* things are possible. If they expressed skepticism, I had the perfect opening for telling my life story, including the sweet ending of becoming an author.

Those boys' surprised smiles told me clearly that my words had an effect—maybe they *could* keep chasing their dreams! The journey from fear to faith may not be direct, but it is worth it.

♂ ♂ ♂

Recently I took my book to the county fair, hoping that tales of inspiration would appeal, even next to the homemade pies and preserves. A woman walking past my table stopped and picked up the book. She seemed intrigued by it, but behind her polite smile lingered something painful. She told me she was glad I'd found my sweet spot in life, but she had such a big problem in her life that she couldn't imagine being so positive.

I looked at her and boldly proclaimed, "I can top that!"

So began a brief game of one-upmanship about the difficulties we'd suffered in life, shared with the honesty and candor that fellow sufferers reserve for each other. This brief story isn't the place to recount all of the traumatic and painful events I've experienced, but suffice it to say that my son's running away from home wasn't the worst. Or even the hundredth worst.

After we talked, the woman looked surprised that I could still be so positive when at times I'd had it so rough. As our conversation concluded, the woman told me she wanted my book, and she wished she had enough money to buy it. I think what she really wanted, however, wasn't the book itself; she wanted the hope that the book points toward. We hugged each other tightly, crying, and I wished her well.

♂ ♂ ♂

One month later, I answered the phone and heard the familiar voice of the woman from the county fair. She wanted to know if she could come to my house and buy a copy of my book. When I opened the door a short while later, I knew she'd driven to my house for more than the book. The words began to spill out: her company was downsizing, and if she wanted to keep her job she would need to move to another city. She had only twenty-four hours to decide, and leaving her beloved city was the last thing she wanted to do. It seemed like one of those lose-lose situations that we're confronted with so often in life.

As at the county fair, we cried, prayed, talked, and comforted one another. We laughed together through our tears. Then she wrote me a check for the book and we said our good-byes. I watched her walk to her car, carrying my book, as well as something even more important: the belief that things might actually turn out okay, that on the other side of fear might be faith, hope, and love. I don't know how she resolved her employment dilemma—I don't even know her name—but our time together was what both of us needed.

I never cashed her check; it's in a frame on my wall, and I see it every day.

When I was a girl, my Scottish father worked as a stagehand in Scotland, before we emigrated. I used to sit on his knee, spellbound, as he told stories about famous actors, behind-the-scenes mischief, and world-renowned performances. After we arrived in the States, he assumed that my older sister, a stunning beauty, would make a name for our family in Hollywood. He never considered that I, freckle-faced, bucktoothed, and hanging on his every theatrical word, might inherit his dreams.

I finally realized my childhood dream of "being onstage"—no matter that it took until I was eighty-one! Now I'm old enough to see that some dreams take decades to ripen to their proper sweetness. Since we don't know where life will take us, let's push on and chase our dreams, even if we can't yet see how they will turn out. Often it's the dream accomplished in old age, after a lifetime of waiting, that is the sweetest.

Eleanor Steele Porath

God's punch

The acting bug hadn't just *bitten* me—it had chomped down and wouldn't let go.

I moved to New York City in 1988, and by chance landed the lead in *Toxic Avenger 2* and *Toxic Avenger 3*. While those movies aren't considered cinematic masterpieces—okay, they're downright campy!—they were a lot of fun to make, and they naturally got me thinking: maybe I can make a living doing this.

After filming wrapped, I took a job as a bouncer at a popular nightclub to leave my days free for auditions and plenty of time lifting weights at the gym. I was six foot four, 250, and handling security and crowd control was perfect for me. The nightclub was called Stringfellows, and I loved the feeling of being close to all the famous actors, athletes, and musicians who partied there.

But I was still living paycheck to paycheck. Breakfast, lunch, and dinner were one of two things: mac and cheese, or PB&J. I checked the trade papers every day, hoping to land my next acting gig, and I spent a fortune mailing out glossy head shots to every producer and casting director I could think of. It didn't help my budget that part of the expectation for a struggling actor was to always *dress* like you made money. Whenever my mom called to ask what I was doing with my life, I told her not to worry. I was fine. Despite the long odds, low pay, and constant uncertainty, I loved what I was doing.

I probably would have kept it up, too, if not for what happened one night at Stringfellows. It was an ordinary weekday night at the club, but for some reason a group of fellows got a bit too wild.

When we asked them to leave, a glass bottle was thrown and a fight erupted. This group of guys had been drinking quite a bit, and our security team was top-notch, but just as we were getting things under control, someone punched me in the face.

That got my blood boiling! I saw who punched me, and I hit him back with a right jab to the mouth. He went down, and I continued to clean up and get the rest of those troublemakers out of the club. A few minutes later, the guy I'd dropped managed to stand up, wobble his way to a phone, and call the police. Meanwhile, a coworker told me to check my hand, and I discovered my index finger was bleeding. With a borrowed tweezers, I pulled a piece of tooth out of the cut, at the same time noticing that a tendon had been cut and was now sticking out of the wound. It wasn't bleeding badly, and I still had adrenaline pumping through my veins, so I simply wrapped my hand in a cocktail napkin.

The police had arrived by then, in response to the drunk guy's complaint. As soon as they smelled the reek of alcohol on his breath, they let me go, and I headed over to the emergency room at Cabrini Hospital on East 19th Street.

After a short wait, the doctor cleaned out the cut on my finger, but refused to stitch it up. He explained that a human "bite" wound can easily get infected, and sewing it closed would simply trap the germs inside. Instead, he sent me home with pain meds, antibiotics, and a date with a surgeon to reattach the severed tendon.

Two days later, I woke to the sight of red streaks on my hand and arm. I was quickly admitted to the hospital, and it was determined that I would need intravenous antibiotics until the infection disappeared. By God's grace, I was able to get the nightclub to pay for my weeklong hospital stay.

And by the second day of lying in bed with nothing to keep me busy, I started to do some serious thinking. I had a college degree, yet here I was earning rent by punching dumb drunk guys! There had to be something better to do with my life. If acting wasn't it, then what was?

Each day a surgical team came to visit me and evaluate my progress. It was made up of doctors and nurses, along with a new kind of specialist I'd never even heard of: physician assistants, or PAs. With nothing else to do, I struck up conversations with some of my PAs, as well as some PA students. I learned that PAs function as an extension of the doctors, specialize in different fields, and even assist in surgeries—but don't incur the massive cost and time commitment it takes to become a medical doctor.

I'm sure all the people I spoke to thought I was just another numbskull off the street. But I started asking myself, "Could I be a PA?" Shortly after I was discharged, I found a PA program at Bayley Seton Hospital in Staten Island, filled out my application, and mailed it off. This was different from sending out just another head shot for some random movie role. I was taking a big step into the unknown.

Two months later I was visiting my parents when I received a phone call from the director of the PA program, asking me to come in for an interview. For me that interview was a hundred times more nerve-racking than any casting call I'd ever answered, but the results changed my life: I was accepted into the program, and two years later I graduated with honors.

Today I have a wonderful wife, three beautiful daughters, and every day I enjoy my work as a physician assistant. Looking back on my years as a wannabe actor and bouncer in the Big Apple, I'm amazed by how suddenly my life changed. Some people refer to fate as "the hand of God," and in my case that hand took the form of a punch— a punch that knocked me into a better life.

Ron Fazio Jr.

Lemon Drop

I've never seen *Toxic Avenger 2*, but I might have to Netflix it now that I know Ron's story! When he was acting it wasn't for the money—it was for the love of what he did. Ron told me that's what's great about being a PA now: he has the privilege of doing what he loves and loving what he does. He even helped the husband of his daughter's first-grade teacher become a PA after a midlife career change— and nobody had to get punched! —Don

{ mother's day }

I spent the morning of this most recent Mother's Day scrubbing pee stains off the bathroom floor.

It hadn't always been this way. Two years ago, my husband and I celebrated a joy-filled Mother's Day with our then two-year-old. One year later, I spent Mother's Day at *my* mother's home, just a week after discovering I was pregnant with my second child—and just days after my husband informed me that he was leaving us. When I told my mom what had happened, she immediately drove the eight hours from New York to Virginia to help me pack up and move into base housing, since I was still in the Marine Corps.

That's what made this Mother's Day a far cry from the kind of day I'd dreamed about when I first got married and started a family. After all, raising two children on your own isn't exactly a recipe for relaxation or pampering. Mother's Day was now just another day—one that included potty training and cleaning up Cheerios from the kitchen floor. Except now it was even more difficult, due to my added sense of loss and sadness. I knew other moms around the base were getting bouquets and breakfast in bed. I'll admit that I started to feel a bit sorry for myself.

At least I could tell *my* mom how much I loved her. After finishing my chores and washing up, I called and wished her a happy Mother's Day. My mom has always been there for me, and I wanted her to know how much I loved her. After hanging up the phone, I went outside to bring in the mail, which I hadn't picked up the day before. Amid the usual pile of bills, notices, and junk advertisements, a sky-blue envelope attracted my attention. It had no return address, and I didn't recognize the handwriting.

Puzzled, I opened the envelope right there at the mailbox. Inside I found a Hallmark Mother's Day card, signed with my boys' names and nothing else—which was odd, since neither of them could write! Who had sent me an anonymous card?

Still trying to tease out the mystery of my card, I walked back into the house. I found my newborn contentedly asleep in his playpen, holding his favorite blanket close to his cheek. In the kitchen, my three-year-old was pushing his truck across the floor, happily lost in his make-believe world.

Suddenly my heart tightened in my chest. This day—Mother's Day—might not look like the day I'd dreamed about, but it *was* about celebrating motherhood. Suddenly I was overwhelmed by emotion. I loved my boys so much; I wanted to give them the world. I knew my love would stop at nothing to protect and provide for them.

I began to cry quietly. *I will never love anyone the way I love my kids.*

As I started to leave the kitchen, intending to place the anonymous card on the mantel, a new thought hit me: *My mom loves me that same way!* This thought literally took my breath away. Gasping for air, and choking back sobs, I raced to the phone and dialed my mom's number. The second I heard her pick up, I poured out my love for her like I never had before.

I'd always loved my mom and known that she loved me. But on that lonely Mother's Day, even as I felt discarded by divorce and unappreciated, an anonymous card changed my life. I never found out who sent it, but it caused me to reflect on just how deeply I love my own kids—and how much my own mom loves me.

That day I understood for the first time in my life the full extent of a mother's love. It is bottomless, this love. No matter what happens in life, I am held by arms of love that are as tender as they are strong, and they will never let me go.

Bryana Jordan

mulligan

*I*n the late 1970s, an eager teenager named Curt got a job selling nails at a building supply store. Thirty years later, he was the director of construction in Florida for one of the largest homebuilders in the country. Each day, my husband oversaw a staff of more than forty people and coordinated multimillion-dollar projects.

He was doing what he loved, and he was good at it.

The day they fired him, I was out of town attending the birth of our first grandchild. His voice came across the line as a whisper: "I'm gone."

After that, Curt would get a few independent building contracts, but soon jobs would dry up for good. No builders were hiring.

One warm Florida evening, Curt and I sat across from each other on our patio. The lawn was immaculate, the house was in perfect repair, and the deck was spotless. Neither of us had a clue what to do next. He flicked an imaginary speck of dirt from the arm of his chair.

We hadn't wanted to move here—away from our friends, our dream house, and the community we loved. We had done it for a job that was the next obvious step in Curt's career. And now that career was over.

Pretty soon Curt started to spend more time in his favorite chair inside. His résumé was on the desk of every possible builder, contractor, and consultant in the county. He'd stare at the wall, waiting for the phone to ring. As the days passed, his mood darkened.

Finally I suggested he get a hobby, which was something he'd never had time for before. I vetoed getting his pilot's license, but when he showed interest in a set of golf clubs that was on sale at the mall, I surreptitiously encouraged the salesman to share a few war stories.

Thirty minutes later, Curt was loading his new clubs into the car. The next day he signed up for lessons. One week after that, he heard about a volunteer job at the local golf club. And later that day he walked in the door smiling: "I'm the new afternoon pro-shop guy."

He got up early the next morning to work on his swing.

♂ ♂ ♂

For the next year, Curt continued to apply for construction jobs, work at the pro shop, and play free rounds of golf in his remaining hours. His scores kept getting better—and at least he wasn't staring at the wall or searching for nonexistent weeds in the lawn.

But despite the welcome distraction of a hobby, something crystalized in us that we'd both been avoiding for months: Curt wasn't going to get another job in his industry. Ever. He was only fifty-four, and certainly not done working. A career change was in order—but to what?

Browsing the Internet the next day, I discovered a golf academy that offered an associate's degree in less than two years; the cost was within our means. Curt was skeptical, however. He didn't think he played well enough to be an instructor—an objection I was able to counter by asking what he thought golf school was for. Then he said he didn't want to hang out with a bunch of jocks. He might've had a point there—no one would mistake my husband for a jock at this point in his life. But I requested that he at least *consider* the golf academy. "One visit can't hurt," I said.

Two months later, Curt donned a navy blazer, kissed me good-bye, and drove off to his first day as a freshman at golf school. He was a bit overweight, depressed, and sure the whole golf experiment would never pan out. As I watched him leave, I leaned against the door, holding back my tears. Had I made a mistake by pushing him toward this new venture?

The answer was clear when, one semester later, Curt was selected president of the class golf tournament. And at home, it was clear that his enthusiasm for life was returning. He even began a daily exercise routine that included long runs—this from a man who used to drive from one store to the other at the mall!

By the end of his eighteen-month degree, he'd lost thirty pounds and gained a newfound sense of hope. He wasn't going to join the senior PGA anytime soon, but his golf game was improving. Still, the question remained for us: where exactly was all this leading?

One week before graduation, Curt's golf mentor called him into his office. "They're looking for someone to do some outside work at a private club. It might lead to something," he told my husband.

I drove Curt to his interview at the private club. "How are you feeling?" I asked, remembering the compulsive tie-straightening and hand-fidgeting that had accompanied past job interviews. After years of unemployment, he'd become convinced that no one wanted to hire a fifty-something has-been.

As the flat, Florida landscape flashed past the windows, Curt turned to me and smiled, and the hard-earned lines in his face melted away. "I'm okay," he said. "Besides, if I don't get *this* job, I still have you."

Half an hour later, the job was his.

A week later, on his first day of work at the golf club, I wondered if Curt wasn't quite done in construction. After all, he was building a fresh start for both of us.

Terri Tiffany

{ one saturday morning }

open my eyes. From my bed I see my brother, Tony, and sister, Paula, sleeping soundly in the twin bed they share. Morning sunlight shines through the window. Mama's got the coffee on, and I hear the *bloop-bloop* of the Maxwell House filling the pot, just like the commercial on television. Dad loves his coffee, especially on Saturday mornings when he comes back to the kitchen after working outside. Mama's humming along with a song on the radio, but it's on so quiet that all I can hear is her sweet voice. The smell of bacon frying makes my mouth start to water, and I want to stay in bed for a bit and enjoy it.

But I can't. Everything's wet: my sheet, my pajamas, my pillow. I've done it once again. I wish to God there were some other way to start most of my days. Five years old is way too old to be wetting my bed still. Why can't I wake up in time and make it to the bathroom? I don't drink anything after six and I go pee three or four times before I fall asleep. And I still wet my bed. That's why Tony shares Paula's bed and why relatives don't like to visit. It's why Mama gets sick and tired of washing and hanging my bedding to dry almost every day. Cold, cloudy days are the worst. My sheet doesn't have time to dry, and Mama has to give me a towel to lie on top of.

I know Mama still loves me, and she tries to understand. But none of us really understand why I still do this.

Dad's going to be mad this morning. When he's at work he doesn't always know when I've wet the bed. Today he'll come in for breakfast and see Mama washing my sheet, and he'll probably give me a spanking with Mr. Big, his leather belt. I'd never tell Dad, but I wish he wouldn't use Mr. Big. I don't think it helps me stop. Neither does embarrassing me by pinning a cloth diaper on me in front of my aunts and uncles. It's not like I *try* to do this. There's got to be something out there to help a kid like me. President Kennedy is talking about flying to the moon, but they can't stop a kid from wetting his bed? Good grief!

Mom tells me every day that she loves me. She comes into my room in the middle of the night and takes me to the bathroom. She washes my stinky sheets every time I soil them. She just doesn't know how to help me.

Well, I can't lie here any longer without getting chafed. I know why mothers powder babies' bottoms when they change them. We can't afford Johnson's Baby Powder, so Mama gets me a box of cornstarch for ten cents. Besides, the smells from the kitchen are begging to be sniffed up close. I pull on a dry pair of pants and a T-shirt.

I can hear Dad outside, trying to start the lawn mower. Mama's putting the finishing touches on breakfast when I walk into the kitchen: scrambled eggs, grits, bacon, chocolate milk, and biscuits as soft as a baby's bottom—and I ought to know! The four slices of bacon are for her and Dad, but us kids will get our favorite gravy made from bacon grease. It's right Dad and Mama should get the bacon because they work so hard every day. They count the money each week at the kitchen table. Dad's so smart. He can build just about anything, change a flat tire in less than a minute, and when he tosses me into the air he catches me every time. He just can't figure why I keep making a mess of my bed.

"Good morning, Mama," I say as I shuffle into the kitchen. The smell of coffee is so rich it almost makes me dizzy.

Mama looks up from the stove. "Hey, baby. How'd you sleep?" She looks so pretty in her printed housecoat, blue slippers, and her hair up in rollers. I know what she's asking me. I know she already knows the answer, too, since I'm already out of my pajamas.

"I'm sorry, Mama. I don't know why, but I did it again. Please don't tell Dad and ruin his day, okay?"

Mama doesn't answer me. Instead she tells me to sit down. "Paula and Tony still asleep?" she asks.

"Yes ma'am, but I don't see how with all this good smelling stuff on the table!" The top of our kitchen table is smooth and colored like a lime, and I like to run my finger around the grooves in the smooth, metal edge. I wait in my chair, hoping things will keep getting better and my nighttime accident will be forgotten.

"There's my boy!" says Dad, suddenly stomping in from the back porch. "How'd you sleep?"

There's that question again. "Dad, I tried—I really did! Something just ain't right with me. I don't wet the bed on purpose, I promise." I'm starting to cry, and for some reason I look up at my parents. "I'm sorry," I say.

Mama is crying, which isn't out of the ordinary. But when I look at Dad, his eyes look wet, too. Not knowing why, I stand up from the table. I may as well get my meeting with Mr. Big out of the way before breakfast.

Dad just looks at me some more and then sits down at the table, curling his strong hands around his cup of coffee instead of taking down the belt from the wall. *Praise the Lord!* I think. I don't really know what that means, but Granny says it whenever something good happens. And not feeling the sting of Mr. Big on a sunny Saturday morning is definitely good!

As Dad talks about needing to go into town to get a spark plug for the mower, Mama sets full breakfast plates in front of us. Dad digs into his, and I get ready to follow suit. Then, to my amazement, Dad takes a piece of crispy bacon from his plate and sets it on the edge of mine. Mama watches him, and then she sits down beside me and gives me a piece of bacon from *her* plate, too! Now I've got two pieces instead of none, and I can't wait to start eating. There's nothing I like better than a breakfast cooked by my mama, Magee Wages—unless it's a Magee Wages breakfast with bacon! Her real name is Mary, just like Jesus's mama, and Granny says I need to be good like he was.

Right after breakfast, me and Dad drive into Avondale and park at Western Auto. While he gets the spark plug, I go straight for the bike and wagon section. When Dad finds me there, he's carrying a big sack, probably to protect the spark plug.

We get home and go into the kitchen, which still smells like bacon and coffee. Mama asks, "Did you get the one I said to get?"

Dad grins. "Yep! It was just where you said, and on sale, too!"

Then Dad looks at me and points to my bedroom. "Go strip your bed and bring your mother the sheet and pillowcase. But bring me the pillow."

I guess the perfect day couldn't last forever. After the best breakfast and a trip to town, now we were back to my problem. Maybe I'll meet Mr. Big after all today.

I do as I'm told, pulling everything off my bed. My pillow stinks like ammonia, since I sometimes hold it to my chest while I sleep. Wetting the bed doesn't mean I'm not afraid of the dark, so I can't help but hug my pillow even though I know what might happen. I walk into the kitchen with my shameful load, ready to take my licks. Breakfast seems like a long time ago.

Dad looks at me while I hold my pillow.

"Son, I'm sorry," he says. "I've been blaming you for something you can't control. I know, because *I* did the same thing when I was a kid.

My dad used to whip me, and it's been my shame ever since. I see you trying. I see your shame. And I know it's a medical thing that whipping and shaming won't fix."

I can't believe what I'm hearing, but I can't stop to think about it because he's still talking.

"This should pass as you get older, son. I don't know how much longer that'll be, but I'll tell you what: you've seen the last of Mr. Big. This isn't life and death—it's only money. I hope you can keep from wetting your new pillow"—which he holds out for me to take—"but we'll just keep washing things until this passes. Your mother told me how bad your old pillow's gotten, and this one was on sale. We don't have enough money to buy one each week…"

Dad is starting to cry now, and I can hear that Mama is, too. I can barely see Dad's face, what with all the tears in my eyes, but I can hear him loud and clear.

"We *will* get through this, son."

All of a sudden I'm in his arms, and they're wrapping around me. They're so strong I can barely get a breath, and they feel so much better than Mr. Big. From-here-to-the-moon better. I'm going to get through this. *We're* going to get through this, my Mama and my Dad and me. We're going to be okay.

♂ ♂ ♂

It was a while before I stopped wetting the bed, but Dad never whipped me again—at least not for that reason!—and Dad and Mama never had to scrape together the money for another new pillow.

My father is in heaven now. His eighth-grade education and simple ways never marked him as much in the eyes of the world, but I still remember his homespun wisdom. One thing he told a desperate and ashamed five-year-old has carried me and my family through more hard times than I can count: *This isn't life and death—it's only money.*

That's a truth that'll get you through almost anything. Whenever I think about what really matters in life, I can still hear Dad's voice, just like it sounded in our tiny kitchen on that Saturday morning. I can still feel his strong arms, too—arms that were strong enough to put down Mr. Big and wrap up his son in love.

Rick Wages

a new home

When my friend Toni bought her first home, she quickly learned that it came with something the realtor hadn't mentioned: an alley cat.

Every neighbor in the area knew about this cat—a slight, timid kitty as sweet as cotton candy—but no one was willing to take him in. Instead, the neighbors tried to care for "Tom Kitty" with the least possible involvement: a bowl of milk every so often, a few dinner scraps left in the alley. Tom Kitty was managing to survive, but he never had a home. Until Toni moved in.

I heard the story during my first visit to Toni's new house, while her newly adopted Tom Kitty snoozed in my lap. His contented purring reverberated through my body, and my fingers gently rubbed the smooth, silky hair behind his ears.

It was hard for me not to roll my eyes when Toni shared how every neighbor seemed to think Tom's plight was some *other* neighbor's business. The cynic in me thought, *At least there are people like Toni in the world, even if most others can't be bothered to care.*

♂ ♂ ♂

Winter arrived fierce and early. Every night the temperature dipped below zero and the wind howled. Fortunately, the holidays were fast approaching, and the promise of festive get-togethers made me look ahead with hope.

At one such party, I ran into Toni. We hadn't spoken since she moved into her new house several months before. I could hear the concern in Toni's voice when she confided, "I have to find a home for Tom Kitty."

When I asked for details, she told me the whole story. Soon after she took the stray into her home, her two other cats—which had been living with Toni's sister during the move—returned. Unfortunately, the three cats didn't get along. Toni had been forced—after briefly inquiring whether someone else might take Tom Kitty—to return him to the alley. She still fed him, but he was on his own every night.

I had expected the party to be all about catching up with friends, but instead my thoughts were consumed by poor Tom Kitty's plight. I told Toni that if she found Tom Kitty, to bring him to me. It was time to get involved.

That night, back at my house, I could hardly sleep. I kept checking the thermometer. Overnight the temperature plummeted to minus nine. I couldn't stop imagining Tom Kitty curled against the freezing side of some garage, shivering and shaking.

The next morning, Toni arrived on my front porch. In her arms was a dejected, wretched-looking Tom Kitty. His winter in the alley had been hard on him. His hair was ragged and he was missing a tooth. But I was overjoyed to see him. I knew—even if he didn't just then—that he'd finally found a safe, permanent home.

Soon after, I realized what his name really was: Poncho. "Tom Kitty" was the name of an alley cat, a neighborhood stray, a cat nobody wants. But my cat was a stray no longer. He would always be wanted.

Poncho quickly regained his luster and love for life. As I sat with him on my lap, reflecting on the circumstances that had brought us together, I realized we'd both been on a journey. He'd traveled from home to alley and back again. And I'd traveled from cynicism to personal involvement. Through Poncho, I realized that the only answer to the closed hearts of others is to open my own.

Taking in a stray cat might seem like a little thing. And it is. But that doesn't mean it's unimportant. Even the smallest of creatures deserves a home, and even the littlest act of love can provide one.

Heidi Petersen

{ love song to my daughter }

One cold winter day, my third-grade daughter came home from school wearing only her T-shirt and jeans. I fixed her with a meaningful look as she walked into the kitchen. Seemingly oblivious to my insinuation, she went about fixing herself an after-school snack. Finally, I asked her directly: what had happened to her jacket?

She shrugged. "A kid in my class was out at recess with a coat that was too small for her," she told me matter-of-factly. "Her zipper wouldn't even zip. I have two coats, and she was cold and needed one, so I gave her the one I was wearing."

For a moment I said nothing. My face must have been unreadable because she asked cautiously, "Are you mad at me?"

As if I could be mad at my young daughter for performing such a kind, selfless act. Besides, by now I was used to such "rebellious behavior" from her. Despite my best efforts at spoiling my daughter rotten, she insisted on trying to save the world.

♂ ♂ ♂

Growing up, I was the oldest of seven kids; my mother was only sixteen years older than me. We lived eight miles out of town, and the simplest way to describe my formative years is to say that they were hell on earth. The first time I heard of Charles Dickens's bleak novel *A Tale of Two Cities*, I realized that my life could appropriately be called *A Tale of Two Parents*.

Two scenes capture the stark difference between my father and mother. The first is a typical dinner scene. My father is between paychecks, or he has already blown it on alcohol, and the only thing in the house for my mother and us seven children to eat is rice. We eat rice for breakfast, skip lunch, and eat rice again for dinner. My father is somewhere else—a bar, or passed out drunk, or headed into town to buy drugs—and the rest of us are eating plain rice off our plates. Except my mother. She watches us eat, an empty plate in front of her. When we are finished, she collects our plates and scrapes the leftover grains onto her plate—which she eats for her own dinner.

The second scene goes back a few years, when there were only four of us kids, but its cruelty screeches through the years to come. I am four, and my brother is three. For some reason we are with my father on a pier at night. My father grabs my brother and swings him out over the edge of the pier. My brother's terrified scream excites my father, because he spends the next several minutes torturing his own son. Holding his small boy by one arm and one leg, he dangles him over the black water, telling him over and over he is going to throw him in.

Things finally changed when I was ten. That's when my mother— helped by a friend—moved us three hours away without telling my father. We stayed in a shelter for battered women while divorce papers were drawn up. Through the help of friends and various agencies, we found a modest home and got on food stamps. We were still poor, and things were far from perfect, but we were together, and we were finally safe.

Now you know why I swore I'd never have children.

♂ ♂ ♂

My daughter is thirteen now. She has been both the biggest surprise and the greatest blessing of my life. We can't drive by a homeless person without her asking me to stop and help. If she sees a stray cat, she immediately wants to adopt it. She plans to attend Harvard—Harvard!—and become an attorney so she can help people.

The crazy thing is, I know she can do it.

Because I was so deprived—and "deprived" is the wrong word, but really, no word is strong enough for my childhood—I tried to provide my daughter with everything I never had. I'll be the first to admit I overcompensated. Most kids, if given all the things I've given my daughter, would be spoiled, plain and simple. I knew that going in, but I did it anyway. It was the only way I knew to make sure her childhood wasn't like mine.

Funny thing is, it worked. She's smart, caring, and well-adjusted—an inspiringly compassionate young woman who wants to help everyone she meets. The miracle isn't that she turned out normal, despite my overindulgence; it's that she turned out *amazing*. She reminds me of my mother.

I wish my own childhood experience had been different, but if that's what it took to produce my daughter, then I'd go through it all over again.

accidental change

I was cresting a small hill in my employer's vehicle when I glanced down for just a moment to change the radio station. The child I was nannying for screamed from the backseat, *"Look out!"* That's when the world turned white.

There was a jarring impact and a moment of shocking noise. In the aftermath, I heard sobs from the backseat. I spluttered and tried to push the deployed airbag away from my face, still unsure what had happened. When I was free of the airbag, I saw the front of my employer's car crumpled like a tin can against the wreckage of another car.

Woozy and wobbling, I pulled myself out and opened the back door. My employer's child was still crying and an angry lump was rising quickly on her forehead. A crowd began to arrive on the scene as I tried to pull the child from the car. Everything grew blurry: accident scene, ambulance, trip to the hospital.

At the hospital, the doctors eventually told us that everything was okay. But as we trundled home, I knew it wasn't.

Up to that moment I'd been living the good life as a live-in nanny for a couple with two charming children. They owned a gorgeous three-story house that was close enough to Boston that I could visit the city's museums and cultural events, but far enough away from the big-city hustle and bustle that life felt relaxed and unhurried. A garden of friends and my tiny church helped me take root and bloom, and I looked forward to the next year of employment with an equal measure of peace and gratefulness.

Now that life was over. Guilt and fear played tug-of-war in my heart. My employers had cooled toward me, and a phone call from another nanny confirmed what I'd suspected: they were trying to replace me.

All I could do was wait for the ax to fall, and soon it did. "We're sorry. We're going to have to let you go." Then they added the words that cut right to the heart of the matter: "We just can't trust you."

I realized then that part of me had *expected* to hear those words.

ở ở ở

Back in my hometown in Indiana, five months of fruitless searching for a job in a creative field left me angry and rudderless. I'd always been drawn to storytelling and writing, and I hadn't wanted nannying to become my career, but now it seemed that every door I approached was slammed in my face. It was a cruel catch-22: employers wanted someone with professional writing experience, but no employer would give me a chance to gain experience.

Filled with frustration, and carrying an empty wallet, I went to work at a daycare center. Several days after returning to work, I felt like God was trying to tell me something: *If you have a gift, but you're unqualified, then go get qualified.* Several days later, I walked into the admissions office at a local college and said, "I want to write. Sign me up."

ở ở ở

As I write this story years later, I can see the shape my life was meant to take. The time since I went back to college is something of a blur—just like the moments after the accident. But in this case, it was a delightful, expectation-smashing blur: an amazing writing education, supportive new friends, professional connections, and plentiful experience teaching and caring for children. I've published stories in national magazines and books, and I'm currently writing children's picture books.

When I crashed that car, the impact sent my life spinning in a new direction, and now I've arrived somewhere wonderful—somewhere I was meant to be all along. My former employers told me they couldn't trust me, and at the time I wondered if they were right. Now I know trust is less about avoiding accidents and more about believing good can come from them.

Jaclyn S. Miller

perfectly normal

We were living the American Dream: perfect young newlyweds awaiting the birth of our perfect first child whom we'd take home to our perfect house. The nursery was decorated, the tiny onesies and burp rags were folded in their drawers, and everything was ready.

Except my labor wasn't perfect. My blood pressure skyrocketed and the baby's heart rate dropped. Everyone assured me there was nothing to worry about, and I was being monitored closely. But something wasn't right. When our baby boy finally entered the world—an eight-pound, nine-ounce bundle with black hair—it wasn't with the lusty cry that announces most births. Instead, Seth was silent. He had spent too long in the birth canal. His skull was elongated and misshapen, his face was purpled with bruises, and he wasn't breathing. I watched helplessly as they attached an oxygen mask to his face; a nurse picked up his tiny arm and it fell like a wet noodle. We scarcely had time to look at him before the medical team whisked him off to the NICU.

A few hours later he was wheeled back into my room. The nurse said Seth had given everyone quite a scare, but now he was breathing on his own. She explained that the swelling and bruising on his face would soon fade, and his skull—squeezed into a cone shape in the birth canal—would slowly return to normal.

Those first few weeks at home, I felt like the world's best mother. Seth was so easy to care for. He never cried or fussed, but instead lay peacefully wherever I set him down. Before many months passed, however, my sense of pride morphed into fear. Something wasn't right. Seth wasn't cooing or blowing raspberries; he wasn't holding his head up or trying to roll over. I scheduled an appointment with his pediatrician, only to be told that even though Seth's head was a bit on the large side, there was nothing to worry about. "Come back in a few months," the doctor said. "Everything will probably be fine by then."

The doctor was wrong. Seth didn't hold up his head, or grab his bottle, or wave, or do any of the other things that babies his age—and younger—were doing at our church nursery. Was I doing something wrong? Had I held him too much? Would he ever be normal? I spent my days talking and singing to him, trying to encourage him to strengthen his muscles and learn to sit up and crawl.

Finally I switched pediatricians. This doctor immediately suspected something was very wrong with Seth and referred me to a neurologist. So began a four-year journey of tests and evaluations. It wasn't until Seth was five that we received a definitive diagnosis. Our son was mildly retarded, with Asperger's syndrome, sensory impairment disorder, and hypotonia. Seth's traumatic birth and lack of oxygen had severely delayed him, and we were told that he would never be able to run or read or write. He would never be normal.

We were devastated, but somehow we never despaired. We spent countless hours on our knees, praying, and countless hours working to help our darling son be normal. After Seth was born, we had three more children, and as they grew older they began to help us take care of "big brother." Our dream was that Seth wouldn't be limited by his diagnoses, but rather that he would grow into his full potential.

We were told what Seth *couldn't* do, but today we spend every day watching what he *can* do. He plays soccer in the backyard. He reads music and is learning to play the piano. And we have beautiful conversations with Seth. At school he has been given an award two years in a row that recognizes his selfless, helpful spirit. He has never called another child a hurtful name.

I went through a painful battle coming to terms with my child's diagnoses. One thing about battles is that we should never try to fight them alone. Before Seth was born, all I could see were my own dreams for the perfect life. Now my vision is so much wider, and I've been equipped to encourage other struggling parents. I try to help other parents come to grips with their children's medical issues, and I let other people shape my life and the life of my son. All of us—parents, siblings, teachers, anyone who cares—are on the same team.

Every day is still a struggle, and sometimes I still wish there was a cure. But underneath those shifting doubts and wishes is a rock-steady belief that God has dreams for Seth that are bigger than anything I could dream.

I used to want a perfect child to add to my perfect life. What Seth taught me—what he teaches me every day—is that the word *perfect* has many meanings. Sometimes it's more about others than it is about us. Sometimes it means seeing the world through a different set of eyes. And sometimes perfect means what others might call disabled, but we call our sweet Seth.

{ truth remembered }

The atmosphere inside UCLA's Pauley Pavilion was electric. I knew the arena had played home to historic events like John Wooden's run of national championships, but now I hoped it would be the site of *my* personal history: a fourth—and record-setting—NCAA National Floor Exercise title in women's gymnastics.

We UCLA gymnasts trained and competed in a smaller arena, but once a year we hosted a national invitational that drew competitors, parents, and fans from all over the country. It was 1990, and I was in the best shape of my life. My senior year was happening according to the script. I knew that if I won a fourth consecutive title, my name would go down in college history forever. After all, it was a record that could be equaled, but never broken.

Since vault had always been my weakest event, I'd been training harder than ever. The vault requires the gymnast to sprint toward a vaulting horse and at the last instant to leap onto a spring-loaded board, which launches her into the air. She then plants her hands on the vaulting horse and pushes herself even higher into the air, at which point she executes a series of twists and flips before landing on her feet on the mat.

By the time the invitational was imminent, my handspring front tuck was higher than ever. It was so high, in fact, that at times it turned my landings into controlled crashes! Instead of stretching out from my tuck to find the ground waiting, and absorbing the shock with bent knees, I would stretch out so far above the ground that my legs had time to straighten completely. Rather than absorbing the shock into my knees, my back and neck took a brutal hit. It was similar to being in a car crash, and I suffered the effects of whiplash on a daily basis. But for me it was simply part of the cost of being an elite athlete. I was ready to pay whatever it took to win my fourth national championship.

As fans began to find their seats and the arena filled with the buzz of eager conversation, our team started to warm up in Olympic order: vault, uneven bars, balance beam, and floor exercise. I felt amazing as I prepared for the vault. I knew my mom was in the stands, having flown in from Virginia to cheer me on, and I promised myself that I'd make her proud.

On my first warm-up vault, I didn't get enough altitude when I pushed off the vaulting horse. Consequently, I pulled too tightly into my tuck and opened up an instant too late, which caused me to over-rotate. My body was leaning too far forward to "stick" the landing, and I needed to take a step and catch my balance. I knew that if I took a step like that in the competition I would lose crucial points, so on my second warm-up vault I focused on getting enough height to nail the landing. Well, I stuck it, all right—my legs were fully straightened and locked by the time I hit the mat, and I thwacked into it like an arrow into a target. With nothing to cushion my landing, my neck snapped back violently, causing me to black out briefly.

I stumbled off the mat and tried to regain my composure. This was *not* going to be the end of my dream, I told myself. I'd faced pain and adversity before, and overcome it. Summoning every bit of determination and training that had already carried me to three titles, I went on to perform the vault flawlessly in competition, and I completed the uneven bars and balance beam without any issues. My scores were solid, and the only event left was my specialty: the floor exercise.

The audience was excited to see the three-time national champion's new routine, and I was excited to show them how hard I'd been working. Unlike the over-in-an-instant vault, the longer floor routine allows the gymnast to feed off the energy of the crowd. I couldn't wait to see how the fans would respond to my innovative dance moves, but before I displayed them I needed to warm up with some flips and jumps that were a part of my routine.

I performed my double backs with ease. However, when I warmed up my middle pass, something sour happened. On the takeoff for my Russian front, which is a very easy skill, I heard a pop inside my left foot. As I landed, I had to add in a cartwheel so that my arms could take the force of my momentum. I hopped off the floor as quickly as I could, not wanting to put any pressure on my foot.

I sat down on the edge of the floor mat and tried to wiggle my foot. There was no pain at all, but I was unable to move it more than a few degrees in any direction. Buoyed by the lack of pain, and anticipating that I could gut this injury out, I called our trainer over. She ruled out dislocation after feeling my foot, and then encouraged me to put pressure on it. Anticipating that everything would be fine, I stood up—and the most intense pain I had ever felt lanced through my foot. It felt as if my entire foot were burning.

The realization was instant: my championship dreams were done.

ó ó ó

That tumbling pass marked the final time I competed in Pauley Pavilion—or anywhere else. I left the arena in tears and excruciating pain, barely limping along on crutches. Days later, the doctor's report crushed any remaining hope I had: my foot was too damaged to heal anytime soon. NCAA Nationals were in less than two months.

Everything I'd been dreaming about—the whole glorious script I'd written for myself—was over. No fourth consecutive title, no All-American award, no chance to help my Bruins win a national championship. With nearly every waking moment of the last four years I'd worked tirelessly to achieve these goals. Now all that work was utterly worthless. I'd let everyone down.

And *I'd* been let down as well—by life. Maybe that's just the way life was. Pointless. I turned my back on the world of gymnastics and, savoring the bitter flavor of self-pity, sulked for a while.

◌ ◌ ◌

Actually, I sulked for more than a while. It was closer to ten years! But I had every right to, didn't I? My bitterness had remained a constant companion in the intervening years, and I often thought about how unfair it was that my foot had given out on me just before my moment of triumph.

In 2000 I got an exciting phone call: I was scheduled to be inducted in UCLA's Hall of Fame. When I heard the news, I felt a bit unworthy, since I'd never won that fourth title and my senior year had ended in disgrace and frustration. Despite that feeling, however, being singled out for such a singular honor did begin to sweeten some of the bitterness that was still lingering in my heart. Perhaps the accolades of the ceremony would become a substitute for what I'd failed to win my senior year.

At the induction ceremony, I sat at my table and read through the program, which listed everyone's accomplishments. Naturally, I scanned the list until I found my own name, and I reminisced about the various awards I'd earned in competition. When I reached the phrase "First to win three consecutive NCAA National Floor Exercise titles," all my bitterness raced back. *It should have been four,* I said under my breath. The whole ceremony suddenly seemed pointless.

What happened next is hard to explain, and even harder to believe. I had been living with the bitter taste of my injury for more than a decade, telling myself that if I hadn't hurt my foot, my life would have been far better. I would have been the champion I was meant to be, and my life since then would have been more fulfilling and fun. Suddenly, without any obvious reason, the story of my life was... rewritten. Everything I thought I knew about my own past was changed.

As if in a time warp, my mind was carried back to a conversation I had with my coach shortly after my career-ending injury.

"That foot injury is going to end your season."

"I know, I know. Believe me, I know!"

"Look—there's something else you need to know...something the MRI revealed."

"My season's over. What else could I possibly need to know?"

"The MRI found something else. Something other than your foot."

"Something else?"

"It's your neck. The whiplash from your hard landings has damaged it."

"I know it hurts, but it'll be okay."

"No. No, it won't. If you had kept snapping it on landings...you would have paralyzed yourself."

"Paralyzed? Are you serious?"

"Yes—paralyzed. Or even killed."

Immediately, even as the Hall of Fame induction ceremony continued around me, I realized that the career-ending injury that had haunted me for the last ten years had literally saved my life. I'd even blacked out the same day I hurt my foot—perhaps that had been one blackout away from paralysis or death! Because of my injured foot, I'd never competed in gymnastics again, and my neck had never suffered the brutal force of that landing.

But why hadn't I remembered that conversation? How had I gone ten years without recalling it? Because I was so fixated on my foot injury. I'd managed to live for more than a decade while telling myself a lie, even when I knew the truth! I just hadn't made the connection...until now.

The truth came to set me free during the Hall of Fame ceremony. And believe me, the truth is *so* much richer and more fulfilling. I'd been chasing another award, a place in the record books, when what really mattered was out there waiting for me.

Now, whenever I chase my children at the park, I know I'm performing for an audience more important than any that ever filled Pauley Pavilion. No award could ever mean more to my kids than to have their mother able to run and play with them. I still don't know precisely why I was able to live for so long with a false view of my past. Once I remembered the truth, however, I understood that some disappointments are really blessings in disguise.

Kim Anthony

Lemon Drop

Can you imagine the pressure you'd feel if your mom were a three-time NCAA champion? Luckily for Kim's kids, she married a former NFL player, and her kids are way too big for gymnastics...so the pressure's off! Kim didn't tell you this in her bio, but I happen to know she's got a book coming out (tentatively called *Unfavorable Odds*) that tells her life story in more detail, so look for it on shelves soon. Her story has inspired me, and I know it'll do the same for you. —Don

father vic's gift

What would Christmas be like without my mother? Just as I became a teenager, she passed away. The three of us—Dad, my older brother Jack, and me—managed to keep the house running, but things weren't the same without her. Perhaps if my other two brothers had still been at home it would have been different, but they had already moved out and married.

So we carried on with lives suddenly grown too quiet. The weight of our grief was like heavy packs: every day we made it from breakfast to bed, but no one had the strength or energy to do anything beyond the basics—and that included the holidays. Dad felt the loss of Mom so deeply that it was impossible for him to celebrate.

When Mom was alive, we all used to pick the perfect tree each year: densely needled, symmetrical, smelling of sap and wildness. Our house in Maple Heights, Ohio, was decked perfectly for the season, and all month long we anticipated the joy of another Christmas spent together.

The year after Mom died, Dad came home with a white plastic tree scarcely half his height. It stood in our living room, forlorn and scrawny as a wet cat. Christmas passed, the New Year came, and we went about the business of trying to carry our grief through another season. The pitiful plastic tree was set up in our living room every Christmas thereafter, and every Christmas it reminded us that the holiday could never be the same.

Things got better…slowly. We never forgot Mom, but we learned to live without her. Dad occasionally walked with a bit of a bounce in his step, and the sound of laughter could be heard in our house more often.

Then, when we were finally beginning to heal from Mom's death, our beloved Dad died of a heart attack.

It was January 1960, and we'd just boxed up the artificial Christmas tree and stored it in the attic. I was a junior in high school, and Jack was living at home and working. At a family conference, my two older brothers decided that Jack and I should continue to live in our house until I finished high school, since I couldn't stay there alone as a single girl. I planned to go away to college the following year, at which point we would sell the house.

My mother's sister, Aunt Theresa, was appointed my legal guardian. She lived only a few blocks away, and she devoted herself to Jack and me. The year passed by in a blur of tears and details, and almost before I knew it the trees shed their leaves and leaden clouds trapped cold air above our town. The holidays were approaching; what would Christmas be like without my mother or my father? Should Jack and I decorate? Should we haul the white plastic tree down from the attic?

Tragically, Aunt Theresa's husband died that December. Their youngest son, Victor, had recently been ordained to the priesthood, and he returned home for his dad's funeral as Father Vic. Vic and Jack had been close friends throughout their childhoods, and I thought of cousin Vic as an older brother. The first time I saw Vic after his father's death, he hugged me like his life depended on it. I wondered, as we cried in each other's arms, if the increasing weight of tragedy would succeed in crushing our two families.

As Christmas Day approached, a wish in my heart became a certainty: I wanted a real tree in our house. Jack, ever the pragmatist, told me to just put up Dad's plastic tree and be done with it. A real tree, he said, was too much bother.

He was right, of course. It *wasn't* the right time to be worrying about something like a tree. But that didn't make it any easier for me to accept. The thought of spending my last Christmas in my childhood home with no parents and a fake tree felt unbearable.

The next day, Vic came through our front door making a good deal more noise than usual. As he called out a greeting, I walked into the living room to see what he was doing. His back was toward me as he came through the door, and then I saw why: he was dragging a real pine tree into our house. I could already smell its heady scent, redolent of Christmases past. From deep within his own sadness, Vic was reaching out to a girl who had already lost too much.

That night, as I straightened the tree in its stand, I thought of my mother and my father. The activity of decorating the tree became a sort of letter to them. Each ornament I hung was a word, each piece of tinsel a phrase, each strand of lights a memory of the happy years we spent together. And when the last ornament was hung, I sat down on the couch to bask in the warm, twinkling glow and listen to Mom and Dad read my letter.

Not many years later, a series of heart attacks forced Father Vic to retire from active ministry at a young age; a final heart attack took his life at the age of fifty. My beloved cousin is frequently in my thoughts and prayers, but never more often than at Christmastime. That's when the smell of fresh pine reminds me of the year I received the best possible present: the chance, as I stood on the edge of the rest of my life, to say good-bye to my house, my childhood, and my parents.

Loretta Nemeth

forever changed

ven though scalding hot water was pouring into the bathtub, slowly covering my body, I couldn't stop shaking. I wasn't cold, but I trembled as if I were in a snowstorm. I hugged my legs close to my chest, resting my chin on my knees. I fixed my senses on the water: my eyes watched it flow from the faucet, and my skin felt its heat traveling up my legs. The bathroom was a cloud of steam and I filled my lungs full, wishing it could cleanse me. I imagined the hypnotic roar of the water as a rushing mountain stream, an icy cataract that would somehow wash away what had happened.

Then the memory returned, and my illusion of peace dissolved.

I was a naive and insecure fifteen-year-old, a girl who had never kissed a boy before, a girl desperate to be loved and accepted. When a boy I liked told me he loved me after only one date, I believed him. I trusted him to take care of me and keep me safe.

My trust made the betrayal all the more painful. When I understood what he really wanted, I told him no. The moment that followed divided my life into before and after, changing it forever. He refused to listen, and forced himself on me. I told him no again and again, even as I realized my words no longer mattered. He was determined to take from me what he wanted, and I was powerless to stop him.

What followed that tragic night were years of destructive behavior. I searched for love and self-worth in all the wrong places: promiscuous relationships, eating disorders, and the act of secretly cutting myself. Sometimes it seemed that the only feeling I could count on was pain, and any certainty—even one as gruesome as carving my own flesh—was preferable to the black whirlpool of uncertainty and doubt that swirled inside me.

I had loved being in music and drama productions as a little girl; in high school, I discovered that I had become a consummate actress. On the outside I looked presentable and popular, yet all the while I was screaming for help on the inside. Each time I left the latest boy, or cut another line in my skin, I cried out for God to make the pain go away. For four years after being raped, I spoke to no one about that night, yet the memory never left my heart and soul. It was as if I were always looking at my life through the dark and scratched lenses of that experience.

Then, my senior year of high school, everything changed. I turned around and saw a safe way out—a way that had been there all along.

It happened at a church camp in the mountains of New Mexico. All week long I felt God's presence—it was as unmistakable as the warm, soft pillowcase against my cheek at night. The love I had craved since the night I was raped was suddenly within me, as if I were drinking it in and filling up. I felt nourished, cherished. I knew beyond a shadow of a doubt that *this* love would never take advantage of me—that it would shine like the sun into every corner of my heart. What I'd been searching for was there all along, already waiting for me.

That's when I first understood the direction my life was heading. I wasn't going to spiral down the whirlpool and drown. Instead, the darkness I'd lived through would be the very thing that would allow me to help other women heal. I'd seen so much evil that the good news of a life without shame and guilt was almost unbearably good, and I knew that every day of the rest of my life would be a chapter in a beautiful adventure.

On the other side of the darkness is a light—a light so bright it can banish any hint of shadow or sadness. When we're at the bottom of a pit, we need someone who's already left it to show us the way out. Sometimes we need to go through hell before we can see heaven. And when we finally see it, we can't help but tell others about it. If love and healing can find a trembling, terrified girl and make her whole, they can find and heal you as well.

Kasey Van Norman

tout
bagay
bien

The first time I saw my daughter was on my computer screen.

I clicked on her name—*Jenny*. It was on a Haitian orphanage's website, and Jenny's picture appeared ever so slowly. This was back in 2002, and my dial-up modem took what seemed like forever to assemble the bits and bytes that described Jenny. Pixel by pixel, line by line, I was introduced to her: first her hair, gathered in a tight topknot; then her forehead, a calm expanse troubled by two wrinkled eyebrows; and finally her eyes, wide and dark and yearning.

The rest of her picture slowly resolved, but I continued to stare at her eyes. I knew without doubt Jenny was my daughter, despite the fact that she was in Haiti and I was in California. I knew it because the moment our eyes met, even on the computer screen, I fell in love.

♂ ♂ ♂

By 2002 it seemed like my husband and I might never have the second child we both wanted so desperately. Our first child, a boy, was born after three previous miscarriages and nearly half my pregnancy spent on complete bed rest. Three more miscarriages followed his birth, and it felt like our hearts were being worn down, slowly but surely, until soon little would remain. There had to be another way.

I was almost ready to give up—until a phrase came into my mind one morning: *international adoption*. Knowing virtually nothing about the process or the requirements, I began to do some research. The first thing I learned was that nearly every international adoption was prohibitively expensive.

Except for Haiti.

Minutes later I'd posted my first query to an online message board devoted to Haitian adoptions, asking what we would need to do to adopt a girl between the ages of two and four. I received a reply almost immediately from a woman named Ruth. I sat in front of our computer, clicking the "refresh" icon in my Web browser over and over.

That same day we talked on the phone, and I learned Ruth was the stateside liaison for an orphanage in Haiti. She helped find families for the children living at the orphanage, and then she helped those families navigate the complex adoption process.

"There's a three-year-old girl waiting to be adopted named Jenny," she told me, "but don't look at the website until you and your husband are sure that you want a Haitian adoption. The minute you see Jenny, you'll fall in love."

And the minute I hung up the phone, I was already pointing my browser to the website. I clicked Jenny's name the second I saw it.

♂ ♂ ♂

That began an eighteen-month process of bringing Jenny home. Finally, on October 17, 2004, I boarded a plane to Port-au-Prince, Haiti, with my husband and six-year-old son.

On the plane, an understanding woman taught me a phrase in Haitian Creole I could say to Jenny when we met her for the first time, and I repeated it over and over to myself as we raced across the water.

We had planned ahead of time to meet the orphanage director, along with Jenny, in the airport parking lot. When we emerged from the airport, we were spit into a sea of traffic—pedestrians, vendors, taxis, mini buses. The wave of heat threatened to drown us. We made our way across the baking pavement toward the parking lot, scanning the crowds for the face of our daughter.

I saw Jenny's eyes first. She was facing the sun, but she stood straight and proud, looking for us just as we were looking for her. Her hair was pulled back, as it had been in the picture, and as I drew close I could see tiny pricks of sweat stippling her forehead. Dropping my bags, I fell to my knees in front of her. I looked into her eyes for the briefest of moments, knowing our mutual longing was over, before pulling her into my arms.

As I held my new daughter, I whispered to her the words I'd learned just hours earlier. "Tout bagay bien, Jenny. Tout bagay bien."

Everything is going to be all right.

Susan Rickey

{ little
norma's
easter dress }

*D*on't worry, honey. I'll think of something!"

With her mother's sweet words of assurance ringing in her ears, seven-year-old Norma bounded upstairs to get ready for bed. But before she climbed under the covers, she danced a happy jig, her nightgown twirling around her. Soon it would be Easter morning, and Mother had promised her she'd have something beautiful to wear to church.

With Norma upstairs for the night, Mother stood by the window, looking out and hoping inspiration would strike. She wasn't well, and hadn't been for months. Anemia left her without energy, and having six children in twelve years had taken its toll on her body.

Worse than being bone weary, however, was the heartsick knowledge that her darling Norma would have nothing lovely or new to wear on Sunday. She'd stick out like a thorn among the roses; even in the middle of the Great Depression, Easter Sunday was dress-up day at their small church in upstate New York. Ladies wore spring hats and colorful dresses, and little girls sashayed down the aisle with crinoline petticoats peeking from beneath pastel skirts.

Mother walked out on the front porch and sat beneath the orange trumpet vines. Partly screened from the street by the fragrant lattice of flowers, she began to pray. Little Norma asked for so little; a new green Easter dress would make her feel beautiful and cherished. But there was no way to buy material. Using an old dress wasn't an option either, since even a nickel for a packet of green Rit Dye was too much.

The next day, Mother was hanging wet sheets on the clothesline when a neighbor popped her head over the fence. "I've brought a dress over for you," she said. "It's plain brown, but the material is excellent. Maybe one of your daughters could use it?"

Mother accepted the folded dress and thanked the neighbor warmly. After a pleasant conversation, the neighbor left, and Mother rushed into the house. Norma was at school, and Mother quickly ripped the seams out of the dress. It separated into several pieces of usable fabric, and her excitement grew. The problem hadn't vanished, but it was shrinking.

Carrying the fabric to the kitchen sink, Mother decided to bleach the dress white. Maybe, just maybe, she would be able to think of a way to get a nickel for a packet of green dye before Sunday.

She filled a large pan with water and poured the last of her bleach into it. Taking a piece of the brown fabric, she submerged it in the pan. Mother was so surprised by what she saw that she gasped: seconds after the brown material hit the solution, it slowly but surely turned the color of new spring grass. She removed the fabric, rinsed it in cold water, wrung it out, and raced to the front porch to inspect it in the sunlight.

The color was perfect. In the same place she had prayed the night before, Mother cradled the green fabric in her hands and lifted her eyes to heaven, this time whispering a prayer of thankfulness.

Mother returned to the kitchen, bleached the rest of the fabric, and hid it away before Norma got home from school. After Norma went to sleep, Mother worked by candlelight late into the night, sewing a new green dress for her daughter. Just before dawn, she hung the dress in the closet, and then bent to kiss her sleeping girl on the forehead.

The next morning at church, Norma waltzed to her seat in a gorgeous green dress with puffed sleeves, a white collar, and a full, flowing skirt. That Easter morning, no one was as thankful as Norma's mother. And no woman or girl in the sanctuary—indeed, no spring flower in the fields outside—looked as lovely and as loved as little Norma.

Mariane Holbrook

surviving suicide

*I*f you met me in 2003, you wouldn't have noticed anything remarkable. My life wasn't perfect, but it wasn't a total mess, either. I was like countless others around this country. I was divorced, and raising my young son by myself, but I had a good job as a commercial painter. We had enough money to get by, and even though every day was a struggle to balance work and motherhood, things were pretty good. I'd been at the same company for five years, and a promotion and raise were right around the corner. The future wasn't exactly *bright*, but it was slowly getting lighter.

That's when the storm clouds rolled in. A misunderstanding at work, coupled with a vindictive coworker, cost me my job. Knowing my son was relying on me to provide for him, I immediately began to search for a new job. But as the days turned into weeks and the weeks into months, I was unable to find work. The higher my bills piled up, the lower my spirits sank. I'd worked steadily since I was fifteen, but now employment evaded me no matter how hard I looked. Being unable to make ends meet caused me to feel worthless and depressed.

My life continued to erode. My car was repossessed—I now had no way to get to work even if I somehow found a job. Then one day I opened the mailbox to find an eviction notice, and the last spark of light inside my heart felt like it was snuffed out. Desperate to provide for my son, I contacted every social safety-net program in my state. Yet despite being a single, out-of-work mother on the verge of losing my house, I was told that there was no help available—not even food stamps! I honestly didn't know how I would keep a roof over our heads and food on our plates.

Stress and helplessness pressed down on me. It was as if I were being slowly but surely crushed into the dirt, and I doubted I would ever be able to lift my head. One night it all became too much. The pain, the anger, the shame—I needed to escape at any cost. The instant the thought of suicide entered my head, I could think of nothing else. It felt like the answer to my problems. I'd tried everything, and now the only way out was to end it all.

While my son watched television in the living room, I slipped into my bedroom and locked the door. In one hand I held a fifth of liquor, and in the other a bottle of sleeping pills. After spinning some of my favorite sad songs on the CD player and drinking almost half the bottle of liquor, I began to feel numb. As the pain of my life faded, I began to work up the courage I needed to escape. I tapped about twenty sleeping pills into my shaking hand and took a deep breath—a breath I knew would be one of my last.

As I lifted my hand, ready to toss the pills into my mouth and wash them down with more liquor, I heard a tiny noise. It was the rustling of a piece of paper being slipped underneath my locked door. Hand halfway to my mouth, I froze and stared at the paper—even from the bed I could read the childish, messy script of my son.

I love you mom.

Tears poured down my cheeks as I lowered the fistful of sleeping pills. I thought of my sweet, innocent son on the other side of the door. He didn't know how deep in debt we were. He didn't worry about having a big house or what kind of car we drove. He only cared about two things: Did I know he loved me? And did I love him back?

At that moment I was certain of the answers to those questions all the way to the core of my being. As I poured the sleeping pills back into the bottle, my soul cried out with love for my son. Setting aside the pills and the liquor, I grabbed a pen. Through my tears, I struggled to write a note back to my son that told him just how much I loved him. Then I got down on my knees in front of the door, the love note clutched in fingers that moments ago had been ready to toss down my final drink. I started to slide the note back under the door, and instantly it was pulled out of my fingers.

My son was still on the other side of the door, waiting to hear from his mother.

If the moment I poured sleeping pills into my hand was the darkest of my life, the moment after my son received my note was one of the happiest. I flung open the door and scooped him into my arms, and we covered each other with tender kisses. There was no way he could understand at the time, but my son saved my life that night.

My son is twelve now, and it's been a privilege watching him grow into a young man. Life doesn't look like a fairy tale—we're not were we want to be financially, and there always seems to be something to worry about—but the important thing is that I'm still living it with my son at my side. We have a roof over our heads, food to eat, and best of all we have the faith, hope, and love to keep moving forward. No matter what life throws at me, I will never again forget that the gift of my child's love is worth more than anything in the world.

Hidden away somewhere safe, I still have my son's note. I will cherish it until the day I die because it reminds me of the night I almost died for the wrong reasons—and it reminds me that love really can save a life.

Lisa Lane

next-to-last hurrah

J was so groggy that it took several seconds for the meaning of my sister's words to sink in.

"Mom has cancer—if you want to see her alive again, come home now."

☌ ☌ ☌

The next morning, my husband and I drove the five hours to my mother's house. Her health history was complicated: she'd been diagnosed with lupus several decades earlier, and recently she'd had a sarcoma removed from her arm.

Only a few months ago we'd had a scare when Mom wasn't feeling well, but the tests for cancer had come back negative.

Now the sarcoma had returned with a fury, invading her heart and lungs. Two of my sisters were already there when we arrived. When I walked into Mom's bedroom, the small, frail figure beneath the covers startled me. She'd already lost weight, and I could tell that she was failing fast. Her eighty-four-year-old body simply didn't have the defenses to keep fighting.

A hospice nurse was scheduled to visit and help with daily care; now it was only a matter of time until Mom passed. She was entering her final act, and soon the curtain would close. There was nothing we could do to prolong her time with us.

◌ ◌ ◌

Several days later, I climbed into Mom's bed and lay down beside her. I'd been thinking, and there was something I needed to ask her.

"Mom, how would you like to have a party—a party to celebrate your life?"

She smiled at me. "That sounds wonderful."

Mom had always loved parties, and hosting and cooking were her fortes. This time, however, we'd be doing everything for her, and she'd be the guest of honor.

◌ ◌ ◌

The party was planned for the next Saturday. I made a chart to track her medications, which I hung on the wall by her bed. I began sleeping beside her so that I could wake her every four hours and help her take her pills.

At 2 a.m. on Saturday morning, Mom complained of a pain in her left side, beneath her ribs. After she swallowed her pain medications, we both went back to sleep.

At 6 a.m., I tried to wake her up for her next round of pills, but she was unresponsive. I phoned her hospice nurse, who suggested Mom had suffered a heart attack while she was sleeping. She was still breathing, but her pulse was slow and erratic. As my sisters and I looked at Mom, she appeared peaceful, as if she was in a deep sleep.

The sun was rising on the day of her celebration party.

◌ ◌ ◌

Mom's minister arrived to give her Holy Communion. She lay quietly in her bed, still unresponsive, as he entered the room and began speaking. As he prayed, he asked her to open her mouth, and much to our surprise she did, even as she remained asleep. What was she aware of? What should we do with the rest of the day?

After a short discussion, we decided to continue with her celebration party as planned. Mom had been so excited about the event that canceling it seemed wrong, no matter if she could participate or not.

The whole week before, she'd helped us decide who to invite—and there had been plenty of choices! Mom had been a regular volunteer at the Veterans Memorial Hospital for more than twenty years. Two or three times a week, she would drive herself to the hospital, where she would talk with wounded soldiers and their families. She even opened her home to wives who needed a place to stay while their husbands recovered. Countless people had been blessed by Mom's care and compassion, and we expected many of them at the party.

A lovely cake was delivered, replete with a frosted picture of Mom in her happier days. Scores of balloons—purple, her favorite color— were inflated and arranged, and my sisters prepared a scrumptious ice-cream punch. Mom, still unresponsive, was bathed and dressed in new pajamas. Her hair was curled, makeup was applied, and her nails were painted a delicate shade of pink.

At 2 p.m., the guests began to arrive. We quietly told them about Mom's setback, and we asked them to sit beside her and visit as if she were alert and visiting back. Some prayed with her, some told her stories, and some made one-sided small talk. Some simply sat in companionable silence with their old friend.

By 4 p.m., the guests were gone. My sisters left to get some sandwiches , and I walked into Mom's room. I thought about how different she looked than just a few days earlier, when I'd first arrived. She didn't look like the mother I was used to seeing, but in her party outfit she was radiant. I was glad we'd carried on with the party.

Once again I climbed into bed beside her and began to stroke her hair, describing in detail all the lovely things she'd missed: the cake, the balloons bouncing along the fence near the street, the conversations in the kitchen that celebrated her life.

Suddenly, Mom sat bolt upright. Her eyes were wide open, a smile flashed across her face, and she raised both arms toward heaven. Then she took her last breath and fell back against her pillows. One moment she had been sleeping, silent yet regal as a queen; the next, she was transfigured into a vision of ecstatic delight. And then she was gone.

A week before, I'd rushed to her side, hoping to see her alive one final time. At the instant of her death, I got to see her more alive than she'd ever been. The day of her party she may have been aware that her friends and family were celebrating her life, but in her final moments she could already see she would soon have far more to celebrate.

Mary Griffith Chalupsky

careful what you wish for

"Why can't you grow me some lemons?" I chided my husband.

He was kneeling in our verdant garden, twisting plump tomatoes from their vines and placing them carefully in a basket. The microclimate near our home was cooled and moistened by sea breezes and nourished by near daily sunshine. *Everything* grew in our soil.

Well, everything except lemons. Our solitary lemon tree was a sad specimen among our otherwise prodigious plants. It stood by itself, as if the other, more fruitful plants had shunned it. Season after season, my green-thumbed husband tried to coax it into productivity, and season after season it refused to do anything besides cling to its scrawny, fruitless life. Trips to the library for gardening books, new mixtures of fertilizers, and visits with local gardeners notwithstanding, this year would be no different. No lemons.

"Maybe I'm doing something wrong," my husband replied, genuinely puzzled. He scratched his head contemplatively, leaving a smear of dark soil across his brow.

I knew I sounded a mite ungrateful. After all, he grew nearly everything *but* lemons: sunflowers, roses, several varieties of peppers, peaches, Fuji apples—the list went on. But I was fixated on lemons. The produce we had was nice, but wouldn't it be just *perfect* if I had a supply of lemons as well?

◌ ◌ ◌

By the next year, my husband and I had moved. To the desert.

Now, our entire garden consists of a single plant: a lemon tree. And the lemons it produces are massive! When I look out the kitchen window, regardless of the season, I can see dozens, if not hundreds, of yellow globes hanging from the tree. It's all we can do to pick them before they fall to the ground.

Now I'm the one scurrying off to the library, where I search for new recipes to use up—excuse me, *make use* of our lemon bounty. Feeling a bit like Private Bubba Blue talking to Forrest Gump about shrimp, I list every use for lemons I know: lemon shrimp, lemon bread, lemon chicken, lemon cookies, lemon pasta, lemon marmalade, lemon cocktails, lemon pie—and, of course, lemonade.

We give out packages of lemon-themed treats at Christmas, and I've created and distributed baskets with all the lemon-based ingredients for a rejuvenating at-home facial to countless friends, acquaintances, and plain old strangers. My freezer is crammed with ice-cube trays filled with fresh lemon juice—just in case someone drops by for a visit and their fresh-squeezed lemonade isn't *quite* lemony enough.

Yet even with the absence of other fruit, and the glut of lemons, life is definitely sweeter now. The old saying goes, "When life gives you lemons, make lemonade," but our move has taught me something: if I only make lemonade, I'll never use all the lemons life gives me. I have to be creative with my recipes *and* expansive with my guest list. I suppose being creative and generous is a good recipe for life, too, especially when you find yourself in the desert.

Eve Gaal

Lemon Drop

That sounds like a lot of lemons, even for *God Makes Lemonade*! Eve told me that her husband's favorite lemon entree is lemon shrimp (mine too), but that hers is lemon pasta. If you'd like the recipe, you can contact Eve through her blog (www.thedesertrocks.blogspot.com)... just don't tell her you don't like lemons! Brenda and I have an invitation to try out a recipe or two next time we're in Eve's neighborhood. —Don

a laundromat love story

*I*n the old brownstone apartment buildings near Rittenhouse Square in downtown Philly, onsite washing machines are rare as polar bears. Even when a building *does* have a washing machine, it usually lurks in a dungeon-like basement filled with broken furniture and rats' nests.

So, like everyone I knew, I had a weekly ritual: on Sunday afternoon, I'd trek to the nearest Laundromat, dragging every piece of dirty clothing I could find in an overflowing laundry basket perched atop a filled-to-bursting wheeled suitcase.

It hadn't been that way growing up. I was raised in a wealthy suburban community of sprawling five-bedroom houses and three-car garages, with nary a Laundromat in sight. The only thing I worried about was whether to buy the latest toy or gadget right away, or wait until it went on sale. Everything I needed was handed to me, and even more was piled on top of that. Driving through our well-groomed neighborhood, I certainly never had to think about doing my own laundry, or about the people who did—at least not until I moved downtown and met Al at the Laundromat.

Actually, I smelled Al before I ever saw him. He worked at the Laundromat closest to my apartment—and I use the term "worked" loosely. All of 120 pounds, and pushing eighty years old, he sat against one wall in a white lawn chair and puffed an endless supply of cigarettes while reading the newspaper. On the counter beside him, a dilapidated coffee maker churned out pot after pot of coal-black joe.

I didn't have much experience with Laundromats, true, but I was pretty sure they should smell more like a spring breeze and less like a chimney.

From the moment I met Al, I disliked him intensely. His very presence seemed to darken the Laundromat. It didn't take many weeks for my dislike to become disgust and eventually hatred. If I ran another errand while my clothes were drying, I would return to find that Al had removed my clean sheets mid-cycle with his filthy, cigarette-stained hands. To top it off, he was rude to my face. I wished he would simply go away—to where, I didn't care, so long as I never had to see him again.

If only there had been another place to do my laundry nearby. I would have done almost anything to get away from Al.

♂ ♂ ♂

One day, after leaving the Laundromat for a cup of decent coffee, I returned with an attitude. I was prepared to rip into Al for messing yet again with my clean laundry.

Instead, I found my clothes dry and folded, placed neatly in my laundry basket.

Perhaps this is Al's way of apologizing to me for everything he's done, I thought. Gracing him with a curt "thank you," I took my clean laundry home, confident he'd learned his lesson.

The next week I returned to the Laundromat to find my clothes folded again. This time Al had nothing to apologize for, so I felt like I needed to tip him, and I slipped five dollars into his hand as I left.

Thus began the next stage in our relationship—what I joked was our "dating phase." Every Sunday I'd leave my laundry drying and walk to the corner store, and Al would fold it. I began buying his favorite treats: packs of Newports, lottery tickets, and ground coffee for his machine. He called me "Baby"; I'm not sure he ever learned my name.

We didn't say much, but we didn't always need to. Al and I became fast friends, despite our differences. His small act of kindness—even if he wanted money, it was still a kindness—made me see the *person* he was. And as soon as I saw the person, we connected.

As the months passed, I would sometimes notice something as I got dressed: my clothing carried a hint of smoke from Al's menthols. The former me would have been repulsed, but the woman I was becoming found a strange sense of peace and comfort in that now-familiar smell.

♂ ♂ ♂

When my lease on the Rittenhouse Square brownstone was up, I moved five blocks east into an upscale apartment complex. It had been blessed by the Kenmore gods with a clean and easily accessible laundry room; never again would I need to schlep my dirty clothes to Al's Laundromat.

♂ ♂ ♂

Six months after moving, I was walking along Chestnut Street when I heard a voice behind me.

"Baby! Baby!"

I immediately recognized the familiar rasp of my friend Al. I spun toward his voice, only to stop cold. Something was wrong with Al. He sitting on the stoop of an apartment building, and he scarcely looked human—more like a piece of discarded litter. His body had wasted away so much that his weight matched his age. A pair of Walkman headphones was perched on his head, and one hand clutched a package of his ubiquitous Newports.

He saw the questions in my eyes. The Laundromat had closed soon after I moved, he told me, and he had to leave the attached apartment. He looked for another job, but no one wanted to hire a dirty, chain-smoking senior citizen with no education. He was homeless now, he said—this section of sidewalk was his home.

When I hugged him, I could feel every bone. I pulled back, nearly frantic. What could I do? "Come on, I'll take you to McDonald's. What else can I get you? What do you need? I could—"

He cut me off. "Baby, I just need some batteries for my Walkman and some chocolate milk."

I dashed across the street to a drugstore and grabbed batteries, chocolate milk, snack food, and a couple of packs of Newports. Then I rushed back to where Al was sitting. The things I was bringing him were completely inadequate for what he needed—it was like showing up at a four-alarm fire with a squirt gun.

I handed Al the bag, and he set it down beside him. Then he hugged me tightly. "Thank you," he said. "Thank you." Then he looked into my eyes. "I love you, Baby."

"I love you too, Al."

I was late for my appointment and had to go. Before I left, I wrote down my phone number on a scrap of paper and gave it to him, along with twenty dollars. Leaving felt exactly like what I wasn't supposed to be doing.

After my appointment, I raced home and clicked through websites, searching for any nearby shelters and soup kitchens. I copied the information onto an index card that I put in my wallet, praying I would run into Al again soon. I imagined giving him the card and watching him walk toward a church or a community center, anticipating a warm meal and a clean place to sleep for the night.

That night, as I pulled on a nightshirt, I noticed that it smelled like fabric softener—no trace of menthol smoke. It smelled too clean.

♂ ♂ ♂

I never saw Al again, even though I searched for him. Many nights after work I wandered the hallways and escalators of Market East Station and other public transit stops, looking on every bench and in every corner for a frail, eighty-pound man listening to a Walk-man. All my searching was in vain.

What did the people think who walked past Al and me that final night when I hugged him on the steps? I'm sure they saw a study in contrasts: an old man and a young woman; one impoverished, one wealthy; one black, one white. What they didn't know—what they couldn't know if they were unaware of other people's suffering, like I used to be—was that we were united by more things than separated us.

Al woke me up. Now, whenever I see a homeless person, I try to buy him or her a meal—or at least share one of the granola bars I always carry in my purse. This is truly the least I can do, since doing nothing is no longer an option. Al taught me that he was more than the sum of his negative qualities; if his smoking and rude words had kept me from becoming his friend, I would forever be poorer.

I wonder if I can say the same about myself. Am I more than the sum of *my* negative qualities? Who am I, beneath my selfishness and petty fears?

Al had three vices: Newport 100's, black coffee, and lottery tickets. Before I met Al, I didn't even realize my biggest vice: blindness. Al's were simple and easily fixed with a few dollars. Mine, however, will take a lifetime to remedy. Every time I crouch beside a homeless person, look him or her in the eye, and offer food and friendship, I'm taking a small step—just like Al did for me.

the
tree line

*P*atti, I just totaled your car," he said.

Gulp—not the words I wanted to hear right before moving five hundred miles! My poor husband. He'd been driving my car slowly around an icy corner when it slid off the road and into a steel mailbox. It was no longer drivable, so he had it towed to the mechanic.

Aaron was fine, but the timing was awful. He had recently been offered a job in Oregon, and we were moving from British Columbia to the States in less than a month. We were desperately trying to get our current home into rentable condition, and I was busy applying for visas, filling out immigration paperwork, transferring bank accounts, finding a place to live in Oregon, and packing.

This car crash felt like the straw that might give this camel a nervous breakdown.

A quick description of our cars during that time is in order. My husband bombed around in a black '94 Ford Ranger 4x4 that we affectionately called the Moose Killer. It was the complete package: 6" lift kit, bush bar, Warn winch, CB radio…everything necessary to do damage to both boggy jeep trails and our bank account. Meanwhile, I cherished my white '95 Volvo 850 wagon. (The extra-cool part was the nickname: since my name is Patti, we dubbed my car the Patti Wagon.)

Our plan *had been* to sell Aaron's truck and use my more practical station wagon to move. Unfortunately, I'd recently learned that I couldn't keep the Volvo in the United States because of an emissions regulation. So we decided to use my car to move, and then return it to Canada to sell it.

Now the Patti Wagon was nearly totaled. With money so tight, how could we justify putting more than $1000 dollars into a car we were probably going to sell at a loss? And how would we afford a new vehicle once we settled in Oregon? Trying to stay positive, I visited a large used car lot, hoping against hope that I could trade in my way-past-its-prime Patti Wagon for an American vehicle.

No such luck. No one wanted our trashed Volvo, and none of the American cars were even close to being affordable. Angry and frustrated, I headed home. Combined with the high level of stress I was already under, this latest incident caused me to question everything. Was moving *really* the right thing to do?

Two days after the crash, Aaron asked me to pick up some equipment for a last-minute home renovation, so off I went. The rental shop just happened to be located next to a tiny used car lot. On a whim, I pulled in. I'd scarcely opened my door when a man looked at my shattered windshield and crushed fender and asked, "You going to fix that?"

Nice, I thought. Like having a pimple on my forehead pointed out by the prom photographer. "Maybe," I shrugged, wondering if I should get back in my car and drive away.

The man studied the Patti Wagon. "I've got a '93 Volvo 850 that isn't running, but I'm parting it out. I'll sell you the fender if you want—it's white. And I'll install it for a hundred bucks."

Huh. One of the exact parts I needed, and at a fraction of the cost. Was this really happening? I asked him if we could get the job done right then, and he agreed.

What was he even doing at the used car lot? I wondered. Was he a customer, a salesman, or just someone who happened to be wandering by? Later, as he lay in the muddy field where his Volvo was parked, wrestling off my crushed fender and installing the new one, he explained. "I was just waiting for a sales guy. I'm looking to buy a 4x4 for work. They were going to do a straight-up trade for my truck, and give me a '97 Ford 4x4 and an '83 Volvo."

Those cars sounded eerily familiar. Mindful that Aaron and I *still* needed to unload both our vehicles and get something we could use for our move and keep in the States, I asked, "What kind of truck were you trading in?"

Pointing, he replied, "That 2002 Toyota Tundra, two-wheel-drive. I'm looking for a 4x4 for work to get up and down Hemlock Mountain."

"How many kilometers does your Tundra have on it?" I asked.

He looked up at me from the mud. "Actually, it's in miles. It's a U.S. vehicle."

This seemed too good to be true. Trying not to sound anxious, I asked, "Maybe you'd like to trade me your truck for my wagon?"

"Not straight across the board—remember, I was looking to get into an older 4x4 for work."

That's when I asked to step away for a minute. I called Aaron, and when he answered, I didn't let him get a word in edgewise. "Stop what you're doing right now and listen—drive down here and meet me. Hurry!" When I hung up, I told my impromptu mechanic the thought that had just raced into my mind: our two vehicles for his, straight up.

When Aaron bounced into the muddy field in the Moose Killer, the mechanic's face lit up. We had ourselves a deal.

It turned out to be the perfect outcome for everyone. I got rid of the Patti Wagon without having to import or sell it. Aaron and I found ourselves with a wonderful new truck we could use for the move and keep in the States. And our new mechanic friend had the 4x4 he needed, as well as a second old Volvo. A definite win-win!

After test-driving the Toyota, Aaron smiled at me. "See, honey—aren't you glad I crashed your car?" Considering how things had worked out, I had to admit I was.

Aaron was the perfect person to savor the irony of our situation: he grew up in a logging family, working in logging camps and saw-mills. He graduated from university with a forestry degree, and we were moving to Oregon to work in the forest industry. Now, a truck called a Tundra—by definition, a "frozen, treeless region"—had saved the day.

Later, as we drove in our new truck toward our new life in the States, I thought about the place where the tundra meets the for-est. In that region, known as the tree line, it isn't easy for trees to grow, and there are no guarantees—but they *can* grow. Sometimes in life we're pushed to the edge of our habitat, and all we can do is trust that we'll find the sunlight and the soil we need. And if we're patient, more often than not we will.

Patti Schulte

{ beautiful after all these years }

randma was fighting for every breath. I watched the sheets that covered her frail body rising and falling irregularly as I sat beside her bed. She wasn't supposed to live many more days. Grandpa had brought her home from the hospital, and our family was helping the hospice nurses keep her comfortable. Now it was my turn to sit with her, and if she woke, to tell her I was there— to let her know she was loved.

I watched her, and my thoughts turned inward. Here she was, surrounded 24/7 by people who loved her, but I'd given up on what I called "true love"—bouquets of flowers, moonlit walks on the beach, passionate love letters. Marrying my high school sweetheart at age eighteen led to verbal abuse, three kids, and an early divorce, along with the certain expectation that I'd never again experience love. Who would sit beside me when I was old and let me know I was loved?

♂ ♂ ♂

When I was growing up, I never thought of my grandparents as a loving, romantic couple. I rarely saw them kiss, and they weren't given to quoting poetry or spontaneously waltzing around the kitchen. They were hardworking, no-nonsense folks with very little money.

But my image of them started to change in the time I spent with my family as Grandma lay dying.

During those days, we took Grandma and Grandpa's photo albums off the shelf and began to leaf through them. In the earliest albums, my grandparents were younger than me: Grandma with olive skin, dark shining eyes, and a smile that still glowed, even from fifty-year-old snapshots; Grandpa with fair skin, laughing eyes, and an air of happy mischief. They looked perfect together...not in the flawless sense, but in the way they were so clearly meant to live their lives alongside each other.

What I noticed most in the albums was their happiness. In every picture, Grandma and Grandpa were delighted to be together, and it had nothing to do with external trappings like fancy vacations or fast cars. Actually, the opposite was true: their happiness shone all the more clearly in the context of pictures that showed their average, workaday lives. When I was a kid, I'd only seen the unsentimental facts of their marriage—where they lived, how many children and grandchildren they had, and so on—but now I was peeking beneath the surface into the heart of their love.

Grandma wasn't getting any better. There wouldn't be any miracle recovery or final burst of energy. Her life, like a fire, was slowly but surely dying out, and all that remained were embers. We sat beside her, cherishing and trying to protect the warmth that remained.

As the days passed, and I continued to study the photographic story of my grandparents' marriage, it began to dawn on me that I was seeing something beyond simple happiness. Just as my grandparents' love went beyond merely romantic love, so the decades of their marriage produced something I could only call joy. The earliest pictures revealed—through a sidelong smile, a hand resting on a knee—that they adored each other. Clearly, that adoration had increased with every passing year.

The arrival of my grandmother's fatal cancer had done nothing to change that.

♂ ♂ ♂

Grandma was worried most about leaving Grandpa. She'd been caring for him for so many years that she feared he wouldn't live long without her. Even as the last of her strength faded, she delegated jobs for her children and grandchildren to do for Grandpa once she was gone. For her, that was the hardest part of dying: she wouldn't be able to take care of him when she left.

Grandpa spent most of their savings during the last weeks of Grandma's life. He needed his wife to be as comfortable as possible, even if it meant he would have nothing left when she was gone. I think he knew that her death meant he would have nothing left anyway, money or no money, and so he poured out his savings for her just as he had poured out a lifetime of love.

I always took my turn sitting with Grandma, and I was glad to do so. But I was grateful for a break, too, when it was someone else's turn to sit at her side. One night I walked down the hallway to the bathroom, and passing Grandma's door I saw Grandpa sitting beside her bed. There was a night-light on in the room, and in the feeble glow I could see that Grandpa was holding one of Grandma's fragile hands in both of his. Grandma weighed less than ninety pounds by then, and the cancer in her lungs had almost destroyed her body. Her skin was pulled taut across her bones, and her complexion was wan.

As Grandpa held his wife's hand—how many times had he held it in their decades together?—he began to speak in a low voice that I had to strain to hear from the hallway.

"You're beautiful, so beautiful. More beautiful than ever."

With those simple words, he defined their life together—even as he redefined mine. Not long before I would have wondered how it was possible for Grandpa to look at her and say such a thing. But that night I understood it was impossible for him to say anything else.

I recently had my picture taken with my new husband; when I look at it, I see the same look in our eyes that I saw on every page of my grandparents' photo albums. It is the look of true love—and I know I will see it in my husband's eyes every day for the rest of my life. True love lasts a lifetime, and not even death can blind love's adoration of the beloved. True love sees truly what counterfeit love cannot, like the night my grandfather looked through the eyes of love at the most beautiful woman in the world.

Amber Alonso

the peppy saint

In 1952, Covell and Ruth Hart—my paternal grandparents—sold all their belongings and moved from America to Lebanon with their two young sons. They were Christian missionaries who founded and ran an orphanage for boys and girls—a first-of-its-kind at that time in the Middle East. A third son soon followed, and the family of five enjoyed their time living and working overseas.

On Christmas Eve, 1954, the Hart family celebrated the holiday with all the children in their care. The orphan children opened small presents, and everyone shared a delicious meal before ushering in the holiday with songs sung by candlelight.

Christmas morning, however, the five Harts planned to celebrate together as a family. As twenty-nine-year-old Ruth got out of bed, she collapsed to the floor, unable to move from her neck down.

Ruth had been struck with polio, a disease that affects the central nervous system. The Salk vaccine came out earlier that same year, but it hadn't yet reached Lebanon. There is no cure for polio, and Covell and Ruth understood that she would be paralyzed for the rest of her natural life. Their three children, however, were still too young to grasp what had happened to their mother. Indeed, only the oldest—my father—would retain any memories of his able-bodied mother.

Polio victims, if their diaphragms were paralyzed, were sometimes placed in iron lungs—tubelike metal cases that wrapped around the body and helped patients breathe via mechanical pumps. There was only a single iron lung in all of Lebanon. Blessedly for Ruth, its elderly occupant had passed away the day before her collapse, leaving it free for her. She was immediately moved to the hospital and placed in the iron lung, where she lived for the next three months until her thirtieth birthday.

Even though she was able to breathe on her own, without the use of an iron lung, Ruth needed to return to the States for further medical care. It must have been an amazing sight when the ambulance dropped Ruth off at the military airstrip used by the Air Force, and she was loaded by a forklift—still lying on her hospital bed—directly onto a cargo plane that would fly her to Germany and then to America.

Grandma Ruth ended up in the polio ward at the University of Michigan in Ann Arbor. She and the others were hooked up to all sorts of contraptions to help them move their limbs, but Grandma preferred to remain in her bed. Even as her body was trapped in a hospital bed, she was famous for her ebullient spirit. She even taught a children's Sunday school class, with the kids gathered around her in a semicircle. But it certainly wasn't an easy position for a young woman with small children to be in. Once her youngest, my Uncle Jim, was placed beside her for some snuggle time with his mother. Waking, he rolled off the bed and crashed onto the tile floor. Grandma watched, helpless, as he wailed on the ground. According to family lore, that was the only time during her decades of suffering from polio that Ruth cried.

During the Vietnam War, when my father served in the Navy, Grandma Ruth wrote him many letters. She would ask for a typewriter to be placed on a tray in front of her. Then, holding a pencil between her teeth, she would poke out a message, one letter at a time.

Grandma Ruth died at the age of sixty. I was only eight, but already I had memories of her that I knew I would treasure forever. When I visited her she would ask me to look in the top drawer of her dresser. There, among the neatly folded socks, I would discover bright candy suckers hidden and waiting for me—placed there, I later learned, by nurses at Grandma's request. Sometimes I would lie in bed beside her and listen to her tell stories. Her laugh was contagious—a great, rolling chortle that ended in fits of delighted snorting. Anyone passing by her room would glance in, wanting to be part of the joke.

"I've spent thirty years on my feet and thirty years on my seat," she'd say near the end of her life. In both seasons of her life, she lived with grace and aplomb, inspiring everyone around her. Polio's sneak attack compromised her body, but it could never conquer her heart and soul.

Grandma once said that when she was a missionary in Lebanon, running the orphanage, she used to think about how wonderful it would be to get to heaven and just *rest*. Later in her life, however, she looked forward to something different. "I've had my share of resting," she would say, "and now I'm looking forward to getting to heaven and jumping up and down. If you see a peppy saint there, don't ask me to sit, for I've sat long enough!"

Matt Hart

an unlikely christmas tradition

itting down at my computer, I scanned the subjects in my inbox:

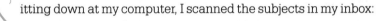

- Re: Let's have dinner soon!
- Save 30%—This Week Only
- Appointment Reminder
- Re: Story Pitch

There it was! My heart leapt as I scanned the subject line again: *Re: Story Pitch*. Finally, I was hearing back from my local newspaper's editor about my article idea. With Christmas only weeks away, this might be the perfect present.

I clicked the message, hardly daring to breathe as I read the reply. "Thank you for sending us your article idea. Although it's a great story, we have no freelance dollars available."

I paused for an instant. Then, undeterred, I fired off a reply, offering to write the article without pay, asking only for byline credit. I knew my story idea was a good one. I wanted to profile a local bakery and its loyal patrons during the holidays, focusing on the heartwarming friendships and the seasonal creations. It was a strong story with enough angles that I sensed it was feature material. It wasn't about the freelance money, which wasn't much anyway—I was willing to write it for free as a way to build my resume and develop future writing projects.

The editor's reply arrived quickly. "Legally, we can't do that. Sorry."

Now my heart sank. They wouldn't even let me write it for free? I knew I would move on to my next writing project soon—we writers are conditioned to expect rejection—but in that moment the editor's negative response stung.

What happened a few weeks later only compounded my hurt. I was sitting at the kitchen table, still groggy, while I unfolded the morning paper. Suddenly all my sleepiness disappeared. My eyes took in the feature story—*my* feature story—about the local bakery. Except someone else had written it. The editor had stolen my story idea and taken the credit. Rejection is one thing, but betrayal is something else entirely.

As I sat at the table, reading with my hand over my mouth, my husband walked in. Steve took one look at my face and asked, "Who died?" Wordlessly, I held up the paper so he could see the article. Then I set the paper down and asked sheepishly, "Do you still want to go to Camden?"

One week earlier, Steve and I had heard about a nonprofit group that was going to hand out Christmas gifts to impoverished children in Camden, New Jersey, in one of the most dangerous neighborhoods in the country. Steve had wanted our family to go help on Christmas Eve—he thought it would be a good experience for our eight-year-old daughter.

"But Steve," I'd pleaded at the time, "I can't go. I might be covering my bakery story for the paper that day, and I can't be in two places at once. We'll go next year, I promise!"

Now that someone else had written my story, however, I didn't have to be in two places at once. "Helping in Camden today sounds perfect," I said, and his smile let me know he appreciated my making the best of a disappointing situation.

Christmas Eve morning came, and the three of us donned warm jackets, filled our pockets with tissues and lip balm in anticipation of a cold day outdoors, and piled into the car. The directions led us to an abandoned, trash-strewn lot surrounded by crumbling brick buildings and rundown rowhouses.

Since this was our first time helping, we didn't know where to go. I steered us toward a portly, rosy-cheeked volunteer who was wearing a "Jesus is the Reason for the Season" pin and a candy cane–striped scarf. We introduced ourselves.

"God bless you," she said. "I'm Marilyn, and my husband Chuck is wandering around here somewhere." As we chatted, we were interrupted by the rumble of two large U-Haul trucks backing up to the empty lot. Steve headed toward one of the trucks and began unloading boxes filled with coats, socks, and underwear. Our daughter and I headed toward the other truck, from which hundreds of bicycles were being wheeled and parked in neat rows.

Meanwhile, in another corner of the lot, a volunteer cooking team was heating stainless steel vats of hot chocolate and filling long tables with pan after pan of homemade baked ziti. Soon they added a movie-theater popcorn maker to the mix, and delicious odors began to waft across the lot.

As all this was taking place, Santa rolled up in a maroon pickup truck, the bed of which was filled to overflowing with wrapped presents for the children. Everything was ready, and the leader of the event perched atop a makeshift platform and addressed all of the volunteers. He thanked us for coming, and his final words—"Thanks to all of you, these families won't be forgotten this year"—clued us in on what was about to happen.

Without fanfare, neighborhood families began to arrive. A long line formed as people waited patiently. My daughter and I took up posts near a huge pile of stuffed animals. Our job was to match each child with his or her perfect furry friend, giving a soft puppy to this child and a multicolored parrot to that one.

I remember most of that day as a series of indelible images. I watched a mother trying, without much success, to feed forkfuls of ziti to her son, who was perched excitedly on the seat of his new bike. I observed a father standing with his hands in his pockets to ward off the chill, leaning gently against his wife's shoulder. I saw children moving closer to the pile of presents, their smiles widening with each step.

At the end of the day, as we were getting ready to leave, Steve and I sauntered over to Santa and asked if he had time for a picture. "I always have time for my elves," he chuckled. We handed our camera to another volunteer, squeezed in close, and smiled.

"How long have you been coming here?" I asked Santa.

"Oh, this is about my fifth year. How about you?"

I told him that this was our first time. As the volunteer handed back our camera, Santa asked, "You coming back next year?"

I looked around the lot. Hours earlier it had been deserted, strewn with broken glass and broken dreams. Now it was filled with happy families whose Christmases just became a bit brighter. Our team of volunteers hadn't solved the neighborhood's problems. But I was discovering that we *can* start to change the shape of our communities, one family at a time. This Christmas Eve event was a beginning, but it certainly wasn't the end.

I looked at Santa. "Wouldn't have it any other way. We'll see you next year."

As we walked away from him, a set of twin girls came to stand shyly in front of him. Beaming, he pulled them onto his lap. My final image from that day is of Santa waving good-bye to us, his infectious smile spreading to the faces of the twins in his lap.

I took a deep breath. Only days earlier I believed that my Christmas wouldn't be complete without inhaling delicious bakery smells as I wrote my feature story. Now I understood I'd been looking forward to the smell of my own success. In downtown Camden a better scent captivated me. It was hope, and it left me wanting more.

freunde

Orville Willard Phillips Sr. was a prince of a man. My father-in-law was a true Southern gentleman, born and raised in Pine Bluff, Arkansas. As Hitler's panzer divisions raced across Europe, Orville met and married a spunky young woman named Heula Mae Insley. They married in the summer of 1940, and two sons—Orville Willard Jr. and Claude Dennis—soon joined the family. And that's when Orville was called by his country to fight in General Patton's army on the European front.

On June 6, 1944, more than 150,000 Allied soldiers attacked the German forces guarding the beaches of Normandy, France—a day known forever after as D-day. In the following days, Orville was one of several hundred thousand additional troops who poured into France to secure the beachheads and push inland. Just days after his boots hit the ground, his platoon was pinned down in a bunker and surrounded by German troops, and Orville and his squad mates were forced to surrender.

The captured soldiers were taken to a railroad station and crammed into cattle cars. The rail journey took more than twenty-four hours—a day without food, water, or a breath of fresh air. Necessity forced the GIs to relieve themselves inside the cattle car, and waves of nausea overtook many of the men.

At last the train stopped and the doors of the train were slid open. In the sudden light, the prisoners of war squinted painfully. However, when their eyes adjusted, they wished they could have remained on the train. "They've taken us to a prison camp," whispered Orville. German guards mocked the prisoners as they were marched off the train at gunpoint.

Orville's buddy stared straight ahead as he answered. "Yeah...and it'll take a miracle to get out of here alive."

Follingbostel was a camp for Allied prisoners of war in the German countryside. Completely surrounded by barbwire fences and guarded by a full complement of soldiers, Orville and his fellow prisoners knew escape was impossible and rescue unlikely—they'd probably die before either could happen.

Inside their barracks in Stalag 11B, each GI was given a wooden bunk with no mattress. The windows on the wood-framed buildings held no glass, and the winter wind seemed to cut into the prisoners' flesh like lashes from a whip. From towers bristling with machine guns, guards surveyed the entire camp.

One night Orville managed to ignore his hunger pains and the lice crawling on his body long enough to pray, *Lord, if you spare my life, I promise that when I return home I'll teach my boys right from wrong and take them to church every Sunday.*

A few days later, one of the German officers told the residents of Stalag 11B that he needed twenty-five farmers. Orville had grown up helping his father on the farm, and as he raised his hand to volunteer he whispered to his buddy, "At least we won't starve to death!"

Digging potatoes in the fields was hard, but it was marginally preferable to life in the main camp. After digging potatoes until his back felt as if it were on fire, Orville collapsed on a bale of straw in the rat-infested barn that was their temporary home. As he did every night, he pulled out a faded picture of Orville Jr. and Dennis. A guard approached, and Orville held up the picture and two fingers: "My two sons."

A tiny smile broke through the guard's defensive frown. Glancing around, the guard pulled a photograph from the back pocket of his uniform. *"Meine Söhne,"* he said, handing the picture to Orville.

Orville stared at the picture. "Our boys look to be the same age," he said softly, a lump rising in his throat.

"Ja," said the guard, switching to English. "You and me are not different." Then the guard paused before continuing, and when he did his voice was softer. "No winners in war. Maybe when the war is over, your boys and my boys will be friends."

For a moment, Orville's world had shrunk to the space between him and the German guard—to the space between the hearts of two weeping fathers who ached for their families. He extended his hand to the guard, and for the length of a handshake the two men were equals.

ᗡ ᗡ ᗡ

Several months later, on February 18, 1945, the same guard ran up to Orville, who was at work in the potato field. "The war is over!" he cried. "You are free!"

Orville dropped his hoe and fell to his knees. *Thank you, God,* he breathed.

The next day the International Red Cross took over management of the camp to ensure that the prisoners were returned to their respective countries and the German soldiers were disarmed and processed. Every POW was given a journal, and Orville took his and walked through the camp until he found his former guard. "Will you sign this for me?" he asked, extending the journal and a pen.

The German soldier scribbled a note inside the journal and handed it back to Orville. It was written in German, and the guard said that he would translate what he had written.

When the war is over,
and we all go home,
we will always remember our friendship.
Gefr. * *Patberg*
Marienfelde, Germany

♂ ♂ ♂

When Heula Mae threw her arms around her husband, he was fifty pounds lighter and a lifetime older. He'd experienced things that he would never be able to share with his faithful family, who had never stopped believing he was alive or praying for his safe return. Only his fellow soldiers would know what his time in the German camp was really like.

But he made sure to tell his love about the prayer he'd prayed one night on his icy bunk in Follingbostel. The next Sunday, the Phillips family sat together in a pew at the local church. It wasn't long before their pew became more crowded, as Paul Franklin and Don Bedford were born. (Those two boys grew up to be ministers, but I bet I didn't need to tell you that.)

Orville passed away on August 7, 1998. He lived more than fifty full years after being liberated from the prison camp, but he never forgot the moment he grasped his German guard's hand in friendship.

They say war is hell, so only something stronger than hell can transcend it. On a miserable winter night on a German potato farm, something did just that when two fathers were brought together in friendship by their love for their sons.

Dixie Phillips

---

* *Gefr.* is the German military equivalent of *Pvt.*

connection

Were we really going to do this *again?* My husband and I were arguing for what seemed like the thousandth time. He was drunk, as usual. He hadn't even come home until after three in the morning, and since then our argument had escalated with every passing minute. Soon we were shouting at each other, then screaming.

Pretty soon my husband got right in my face and spit profanities at me. Even then, he wasn't satisfied. So he began to hit me.

I was six months pregnant with our daughter, and our firstborn son, still a toddler, was in the next room. I wish I could say that time in my life was only a bad dream. I wish I could say it was the only time my husband physically abused me. And I wish I could say I'd tried to get help before. But we don't always get what we wish.

That night something different happened. The instant his fist struck me, it was as if a powerful voice exploded inside my head. *No!*

I raced across the room—ahead of his drunken stumbling—and grabbed the phone to dial 911. My husband was right on my heels, however, and my act of resistance enraged him. Just as my finger hit "1" for the second time, he lunged at me and grabbed the phone. He yanked it from my hands, and then he tore the entire phone right out of the wall.

Bits of plaster and paint scattered across the room. I knew I was going to pay for trying to call for help. I could only pray that my unborn daughter would be safe inside of me and that my son would have no memory of the night. The next few minutes were a blur of frenzied attacks and screaming.

Suddenly—*knock! knock! knock!*—someone was at our front door. A high-powered light shone through the window. It was the police!

My husband immediately let me go and fled the room, while I raced to the front door. I flung it open and let the two officers inside. They looked me up and down and didn't like what they saw: a pregnant woman, breathing hard, hair in disarray and with fresh bruises and welts coloring her skin. From the other room came the sound of my husband trying to clean up and hide the shattered phone.

Confused, I panted, "How did you know to come?"

The officer stared at me. "You called 911."

"But my call never went through! My husband ripped the phone out of the wall! Which neighbor called you?"

"No," he said, looking me dead in the eye, "the call came from *you.*"

As it turned out, a recent upgrade to the emergency system in my township included a new feature: any 911 call registered instantly, regardless of whether the call went through or not. The instant I dialed that second "1," even as my husband ripped the phone from the wall, help was already on the way. I just had no way of knowing it.

My sense of relief was immense. As the officers led my husband away to jail, I knew I was finally safe. However, the weeks and months that followed weren't easy. As I learned is common in domestic violence situations, I hadn't told anyone what was happening. Now I felt anxious and alone. The few people I reached out to for help seemed to blame *me*—and they implied that it wasn't fair to the kids to be without their father. I started to have nightmares that someone was breaking into the apartment, and every day I heard frightening noises.

I began seeing a wonderful counselor who helped me confront my fears. Whenever I heard a noise, she told me, I needed to get up and identify it. That was the only way to overcome my fears.

One morning I was fixing breakfast when a sudden noise terrified me. I had never heard it before—a kind of high-pitched, repeating warble—and my mind and heart began to race.

What should I do? Was someone breaking in? Trying to follow my counselor's advice, I ran into the front room, where the source of the frightening sound became clear.

It was my young son, laughing.

Have you ever had a moment where time slows to a crawl? Outside the window I saw trees swaying in the breeze, gently, like underwater seaweed. Sunlight slanted through their branches and poured into our little room, lighting up my son's face. He had his head thrown back, shoulders shaking, face split by the widest smile I'd ever seen on him.

Time resumed and I dropped to the floor next to him. Tears poured down my cheeks as I realized: *I've never heard my son laugh out loud.*

Our home had been so full of tension and fear that laughter was impossible. We all kept our heads down, our mouths shut, and our emotions locked away. We had been walking on eggshells for so long that we'd forgotten how to dance. My son was the first to remember.

Soon my entire body was shaking. Not with sobs, however, but with laughter—right along with him. It was honest, hope-filled, full-body laughter. I felt like I'd rediscovered what it meant to be alive. Maybe I had.

In that moment, I knew we'd be okay. Whatever shape our family was, as long as we had each other, we'd be okay.

The police were only minutes away when my miracle cry for help connected. With one hand on my pregnant belly, I put my other hand on my toddler's head and promised that I would never be farther away than a heartbeat.

Anonymous

what i was missing

I was trapped, and I didn't even know it.

For years I tried to convince myself I was the prototypical independent, modern woman. I was single, savvy, and having a blast. I hit the clubs, ditched the church, and chased men who I knew would never want to settle down. Almost all of my old friends were married, and most had started having kids. I could be happy being the fun aunt, couldn't I? I didn't need a spouse or children of my own, what with all the fun I was having in my fast-paced life.

One day, as I stood in front of the mirror getting ready for another night on the town, the thought popped into my mind. *I can't live a lie anymore.*

I was nearing thirty, and in my heart of hearts I longed to settle down with the right man and have children. As I prayed for guidance and wisdom, I felt like I was waking up after a long sleep, and the sun was just rising on the rest of my life.

♂ ♂ ♂

Two years later, I was back in my hometown for my younger sister's wedding, still single and still determined to chase the pure desire at the center of my heart: to find the right man and get married.

I bumped into a man with whom I had a history: he was the first boy I ever thought I loved when I was a teenager. We grew up two houses away from each other, and he was my crush for almost ten years. He was shy, and mostly he avoided me as we grew up, but he secretly enjoyed the fact that I thought he was special. As we chatted and reminisced about old times, I asked if he'd like to join me at the wedding reception. He agreed, and we made a date for the following day.

At the reception, our conversation flowed easily, and soon we were sharing intimately. I felt overwhelmed by the things he spoke about, like his love for his family and his deeply held values.

A certainty entered my heart: I was sitting across the table from my future husband. So I gathered my nerve and asked, "Do you ever see yourself married with a family, or is that something you know isn't for you?"

He looked surprised, so I rushed to clarify. "I know in *my* heart that someday I want to get married and start a family—of course I'm not saying to you, necessarily—so I don't want to go on a second date with someone who knows in *their* heart they need to remain single."

My heart was racing, but I didn't regret my bluntness. I'd spent too many years trapped in false desires to reenter that prison now.

To my surprise, a smile flitted across his face. "I get what you're saying," he said, "and yes—if the right person came along, I want the same thing."

The rest of the reception party was a happy blur.

♂ ♂ ♂

No one ever accused my husband or me of being fast movers. It took us a few years after that conversation to finally get married. We did start trying to have kids as soon as we were married, however, and now we are the parents of two children that we love more than we thought possible.

My husband once asked me why I thought we'd known each other for so long before finally becoming a couple. I told him I'd spent too many years chasing the wrong things, but that maybe, looking back, it was the perfect amount of years—the perfect amount of years to admit what I'd been missing, and then recognize him when he walked back into my life.

Dawn Coyle

more than fluff

he sun was dipping low in the sky when I finally ventured back into my beloved garden. In the three short weeks since the successful removal of my melanoma, I could already see the neglect in my usually neat rows of flowers and shrubs. Gardening in the sunshine was a singular joy, yet it was that very joy that caused the cancer on my skin.

Before stepping into the dirt, I grabbed a hat and applied a piece of gauze to protect the site where the melanoma had been removed. I'd always reveled in the feel of rich, loamy soil beneath my feet and fingernails, but now I was terrified of getting dirt in my wound. As I moved about the garden, pulling weeds by their roots and deadheading fading blossoms, I felt my pleasure wane. The sun was setting, and a large section of my garden was now neat and tidy, but my heart wasn't in it. My stiff back and growling stomach demanded that I call it quits. With my husband out of town, I had a lonely evening of self-pity and worry to look forward to.

Would I ever truly enjoy my garden again? Did my skin cancer signal the beginning of a flowerless life spent indoors?

Depressed, I trudged along the narrow path toward the garden shed to put away my tools. Suddenly a cloud of black-and-white fluff floated across my vision from behind some low shrubs.

I'd *definitely* been outside too long.

The fluff was still moving. I blinked several times and shook my head. Then I realized what I was seeing: a family of skunks. In the dusky twilight, their furry bodies and coal-black eyes shimmered. For long seconds I stared at them, transfixed. I felt as though I'd been transported to another world. Their beauty and force of life pierced my heart; I wanted to freeze that moment in time.

However, I was also aware that having skunks near my house wasn't wise. Without giving much thought to what I was doing, I clanged my tools together, hoping they'd turn tail and run far away from my property.

The adult skunks kept right on walking. The young ones turned tail, all right, but they sure didn't run! Instead they did what skunks do: pointed their fuzzy little rears toward danger. Fortunately they must have been too young to spray, but it wasn't for lack of trying. Once their message was delivered—*We'll saunter where we want, when we want, thank you very much!*—they resumed trekking across the garden. Just an ordinary family of skunks, out for an ordinary evening stroll.

Except that to me, the experience was anything but ordinary. Indeed, it was the *extra*ordinary encounter I needed to reorient my life.

My stress and sadness about my surgery faded to a faint whisper. As I removed my dirty shoes and placed them on the porch, I realized something: if I hadn't had the melanoma, I wouldn't have been working so late in my garden, and that family of skunks would have shuffled by unnoticed. In its own slow way, melanoma brought me to the exact place I needed to be. It caused me to step outside of my self-pity and into a world of wonder where a simple moment becomes magical.

I'm once again a regular fixture in my garden, although I'm always careful to slather on sunscreen and don a wide-brimmed hat. Since that evening I haven't seen the skunks, but I think of them often, with gratitude. Their waving tails and curious gaze opened *my* eyes to the things that really matter.

plain old ted

The neat, winding paths of the cemetery near my home in Florida were peaceful and serene. Although my recently deceased relatives—my father and my grandmother—had been laid to rest a thousand miles away in their hometown in Indiana, walking through this memorial garden helped me feel connected to them. Ever since they'd passed away only one month apart, I'd felt isolated and adrift, like a boat whose moorings had been cut. I couldn't seem to move past the one question burning in my heart: Why had they been taken from me so suddenly?

The cemetery was nearly deserted, save for an assortment of squirrels and rabbits that darted and hid among the headstones and monuments. I passed other people every so often, such as mourners or groundskeepers, but my only faithful companion was my grief. I just couldn't accept that my father and grandmother were gone for good. My grief was coloring the rest of my life.

Fridays were a bit different, however. Fridays I could always count on seeing a well-dressed elderly gentleman near one of the monuments. Without fail, he sat on one particular bench and read aloud from a book. As I observed him week after week, I noticed that on the monument next to the bench he always placed a single red rose and a Styrofoam cup with a straw in it.

These somewhat odd behaviors—the reading aloud, the rose, and the cup—were enough to make him stand out. For about a month I waved every time I passed by. He always waved back, and then immediately resumed reading aloud from the book.

One Friday I stopped and introduced myself.

"How do you do, Michelle?" he said politely, shaking my hand. "I'm Ted Henderson."

"Who are you visiting, Mr. Henderson?"

He smiled. "Please, call me Ted. I'm spending time with my wife Margie," he said, nodding toward the gravestone with the red rose and the Styrofoam cup. "Every Friday you'll find me here, rain or shine."

Now I was definitely intrigued. Hoping to learn more, I asked if Fridays were somehow significant.

Ted nodded. "Friday evening was date night for Margie and me," he replied. "We'd go to supper, see a movie, play cards with our neighbors—that kind of thing. It gave us a few hours together away from the kids."

Ted looked from me to the monument, took a breath, and continued.

"When Margie got sick and went to a nursing home, we still had date night. It was something we both looked forward to. I'd bring her a red rose and a chocolate shake. Then I'd read to her—the newspaper, a book, or a chapter from the Bible. Forty-nine years… that was a lot of Friday night dates."

Ted sighed. "I figure just because I can't see her anymore, it's no reason to cancel our date night. And maybe she can see and hear me still."

I was floored. The difference between our outlooks was so stark: here I was bitter and crying while I walked the cemetery, and Ted was on a date with his sweetheart of nearly five decades. This man's continuing connection with his dead wife was nothing short of a miracle. I suspected that Ted had something important to teach me.

"May I join you?" I asked.

Ted smiled. "Sure. I'd like that."

For a while we sat in companionable silence. Then I asked, "Would you tell me more about Margie?"

It was like a jolt of energy raced through Ted. He sat up a little straighter and rubbed the palms of his hands on the knees of his slacks. "Margie was the prettiest girl I ever saw—deep blue eyes, cheeks the color of peaches, and long curly hair as red as a fire truck. And spunky! I fell in love with her on the spot."

I smiled encouragingly—not that Ted needed any encouragement to talk about his true love. "She was crazy about me, too, though I never understood why. I mean," he said, shaking his head slightly, "I'm just plain old Ted."

He chuckled, but then out of his fond memories grew a melancholy shoot. "Margie passed on eleven years ago." His voice slowed slightly. "It seems like only yesterday we were newlyweds weeding the garden. When the weather was hot, we'd squirt each other with the hose."

Ted paused, and then continued, as if he'd made a decision. "Folks at church keep trying to fix me up with widows," he said. "I tell them no thanks. There's only one lady for me."

Feeling as if words were completely inadequate, I offered, "She must have been very special."

Ted took my comment in stride. "Margie loved people. She visited sick folks, knit booties for new babies, gave away most of our homegrown vegetables to the needy, and taught the kindergarten Sunday school class. Little ones were crazy about her."

"How many kids do you have?"

Ted gazed into the distance. "We had twin boys: Theodore Jr. and Andrew. Teddy played football, and Andy was our scholar. Both were as handsome as movie stars, but they couldn't have been more different. It's funny how that works. After college…"

Ted stopped, but I could tell that he wanted to finish his story, so I waited.

"After college, they enlisted in the Army. We lost them in Vietnam. They died seven months apart."

Ted's voice grew husky. "After that, a light went out in Margie. Children aren't supposed to go first, you know?"

We were both crying now, but Ted lifted his chin resolutely. "Our boys were proud to serve their country. They were where they wanted to be."

Feeling guilty, I started to apologize. "Please forgive me for stirring up painful memories."

Ted looked surprised. "Young lady, I believe the Almighty sent you to me so I'd have a chance to talk about my family. Nobody asks about them anymore. I miss them like crazy, but since they left God has never stopped giving me a million reasons to get up each day. I have wonderful friends, a beautiful granddaughter who spoils the heck out of me, and my needs are met. What more could I want?"

When he said it that way, the answer was obvious: nothing. So why was it so difficult for me to answer that same question for myself? Ted must know something I didn't.

"How did you find peace after all you've suffered?" I asked.

"When Margie died I was devastated. I moped around for months. Then one day I imagined what she'd say if she saw me sitting around in my pajamas at one-thirty in the afternoon, my hair looking like shredded wheat. She'd holler, 'Ted, quit bawling, get off your lazy behind, and find something to do!'"

We laughed, and he continued. "So I got out of my chair and started moving. It was hard, and there were still days when grief got the better of me. But I kept pushing forward through the pain—for

Margie and for me. Of course, I make an exception on Fridays… but otherwise I'm a go-getter!"

The sun was setting, and Ted looked at his watch. "Mercy, look at the time! Margie always said I talked too much." We laughed again, and then he studied my face intently. "Young lady, next time I want to hear about you. There's a world of hurt in those green eyes."

I smiled and wiped away the last trace of tears. He patted my shoulder, and then bid me farewell: "You know where I am every Friday."

♂ ♂ ♂

Over the following days I thought often about Ted. He lived every day with a simple acceptance of the hand he'd been dealt. One day a week he focused on missing his beloved, and the other six he focused on living. That was a skill I was far from mastering. I could learn something from Ted.

The next week Ted wasn't sitting in his customary spot, nor the week after that. Three weeks after our conversation in the cemetery, I read Ted's obituary in the newspaper.

♂ ♂ ♂

Ted's memorial was the best party I'd been to in years. The hall was packed with people who laughed and chatted while big band music bounced out of the stereo. At the buffet table, a friendly young woman extended her hand. "Hello," she said. "I'm Sharon, Ted's granddaughter."

When I introduced myself, a look of recognition crossed her face. "*You're* the lady Grandpa met at the cemetery! He'd be so happy to know you came!"

Shocked that Ted had told his granddaughter about me, I replied, "I liked him so much! I just wish I'd gotten to know him better."

Sharon's face lit up.

She told me all about Ted. How he was an Air Force pilot in World War II. That he was shot down by the Germans and sent to a prison camp. That he survived and eventually returned home, but as a walking skeleton because he routinely gave away his rations to other men who needed them more.

As we talked, Sharon led over me to a bulletin board covered with photographs: Ted in his military uniform, Ted and his beloved Margie holding the twins, Ted graduating from MIT, Ted at his desk at Cape Canaveral where he worked for NASA, Ted holding baby Sharon. He was a genuine hero who'd had every reason to grow bitter over the years as he lost or had taken from him the things he loved. But instead, he'd lived just like he died: with a grateful and generous heart.

On the drive home I remembered something Ted had said: *I kept pushing forward through the pain—for Margie and for me.* I knew with certainty that Daddy and Grandma would want me to do the same—and before I, too, ended up in my pajamas at one-thirty in the afternoon with hair like Shredded Wheat!

So I enrolled in grief counseling at Suncoast Hospice in Largo, Florida, and as time passed I watched the sharp edges of my grief become smoother and less cutting. It never disappeared, but I wasn't expecting it to—not since I learned from Ted's cemetery dates that healthy mourning has a precious, particular shape.

Soon after my last session, a parade of broken hearts began to march slowly through my life, each one looking for help and healing. Before I met Ted I would have had nothing to offer them. But now, as I watch God use my darkness to light the way for others, I give thanks for Ted—for "plain old Ted," whose ordinary actions taught me an extraordinary lesson.

Michelle Close Mills

sent away for good

Hunger was twisting my stomach in knots, but I knew there was no food in the house. My Swiss parents tried their best to keep food on the thirteen plates in our cabin, but things were desperately difficult. Back in the 1930s, there wasn't much in the way of jobs in Chehalis, Washington; the Great Depression had seen to that. Few people could find work, food was scarce, and there was no such thing as a social safety net.

In the backwoods area where we lived, things were even worse for my father, my mother, my ten brothers, and me. None of us had beds to sleep on, and we wore the same pair of stained, stinking overalls for weeks at a time. We were barely surviving.

One day, hungrier than I'd ever been, I crept down to the creek that flowed across the west side of our land. The creek was our refrigerator, and in it I found a glass bottle filled with milk. Glancing over my shoulders to make sure I was alone, I knelt at the edge of the bank. Below the surface of the creek, the milk shimmered and shone, drawing me. I slid my hands into the water and lifted the bottle. Creek water beaded and ran down its sides as I removed the top. I took a long, delicious sip. Then I refilled the bottle with water from the creek, capped it, shook it, and returned it to its resting place.

Later that night, one of my older brothers discovered the diluted bottle of milk. He took me out of the house and down to the creek, where he gave me a vicious beating—a pummeling I can still feel in my bones to this day.

The scarcity of food had other consequences for our family. We children, lacking any real nutrients in our diets, succumbed to numerous ailments and diseases. My younger brother and I suffered from rickets—a softening of the bones due to lack of vitamin D. Our legs became extremely bowed, and we were teased constantly.

City officials in Chehalis knew about the difficult conditions that we, and many of our neighbors, were struggling with. Thinking that it would ease my family's burden, the officials suggested my parents put my younger brother and me up for adoption. This idea was nearly unthinkable to my father, even as he recognized that he and my mother could no longer care for all of us. Subsequently, he contacted my mother's brother, who lived with his wife in Portland, Oregon. They had no children, and they agreed to take us in.

At first I didn't want to leave my home. Living on the edge of starvation in the woods was the only life I knew, and I did love my family. What five-year-old can imagine saying good-bye to her parents and brothers for good?

The matter was already settled, however. And by the third time my mother came to visit me in Portland that first year, I couldn't imagine going back. When I saw her coming, I ran and hid in my uncle's pasture, fearing that my mother was going to take me back to Chehalis.

At my new home in Portland, the doctor recommended that my brother and I be put on a goat-milk diet, and within one year our legs had returned to normal. My brother and I were being raised in a loving, safe home, and every day there was enough food on our plates. We were still helpless children, and thanks to the gracious care of our uncle and aunt, we escaped the worst ravages of the Great Depression that destroyed so many other lives.

Life wasn't all roses in Portland, however. As a Swiss girl, I struggled to fit in at school. My teacher told my aunt that I never spoke in class, and she wondered if something was wrong with me. Something *was* wrong: since we spoke a Swiss dialect at home, I'd never learned English! But that was the kind of problem that time and hard work could fix, unlike the conditions back in Chehalis.

As I grew older, I came to think of Portland as my home, and my aunt and uncle as my parents. We lived on a farm, so even though money was still tight, we could grow our own food and we had plenty of milk and eggs. I helped my uncle deliver milk to our neighborhood customers, and in school I learned about bookkeeping. When I looked into my future, it seemed like things were going to be okay.

Now I'm almost ninety, and I can tell you that the years have been more than okay: they've been wonderful! Looking back across the decades, I am so thankful for my faithful husband, my three beautiful children, and my many grandchildren. I am thankful I lived to a ripe old age when the Great Depression cut so many lives tragically short. And most of all I am thankful that my childless aunt and uncle chose to make my brother and me their children. Being sent away to live on that farm in Portland probably saved my life. There I was given something that sustained me even more than home-grown vegetables and all the milk I could drink: a loving aunt and uncle who fed my spirit and quenched my thirst for love.

Bertha Raz

mommy
and me

One day when I was a baby, I cried to tell my first parents that I was hungry. For some reason this made them mad. Instead of picking me up and giving me milk, they picked me up and shook me. A lot. I was scared and hurt, and I screamed even louder to tell them to stop. But they didn't.

I don't think my first parents loved me.

Next thing I knew, I was living in a different house. My second parents were called foster parents. They picked me up all the time, but never to shake me. They always helped me get food through a tube. They sang to me and carried me around.

My favorite person was my special babysitter. She watched me all the time. I loved when she got me ready for sleep: she would wrap me in a soft blanket, rock me gently, and sing to me and pray with me. I felt safe with her.

The doctors told my foster parents I had something called massive head trauma. They said that when my first parents shook me, it gave me lots of problems, and I was lucky to be alive. The doctors also said I would never roll over or sit up or stand on my own.

I had five operations and lots of trips to the doctor. That's a lot for a baby, but at least I always got to come home to my foster parents afterward. I could rest quietly without any shaking. And I'd get to see my special babysitter.

One night she was rocking me before bed. She told me that if God gave her someone to marry, then I could go live with them. I guess she thought that she couldn't be my mommy all by herself.

♂ ♂ ♂

When I was two years old, some people said I needed to go live somewhere called an *institution* since no one would want to be my mom anymore.

I knew *that* wasn't true! Mommy was already taking care of me all the time, even though everyone else called her my babysitter. When Mommy heard that I was going to have to go away, she got really upset—but not at me. "They can't do that to my son! They can't take him away!" Even though she was yelling, it didn't scare me. Her loud voice was full of love.

The next day she had a meeting with the people who wanted to send me away. She told them a lot of things, and after that they said it would be good if she kept me all by herself.

I wondered why it took everyone else so long to figure that out.

Four months later I went to live full-time with Mommy, even though I still got to see my old foster parents all the time. It was awesome. Her smile was the first thing I saw every morning when I woke up, and every night I fell asleep in her arms, listening to her sing. We did everything together.

♂ ♂ ♂

A few years later Mommy told me something: she said she was now officially my mom. I guess it meant that everyone else could call her that now. I thought it was funny because Mommy and me already knew that!

The doctors found out lots of things that were wrong with me. They told Mommy I had cerebral palsy, seizure disorder, and cortical vision impairment. They also said I had developmental delays, speech delays, and severe gastrointestinal problems. I didn't know what all those things meant. But I did know it was hard to do some of my most fun things with Mommy, like catching a beanbag or holding a popsicle.

Whenever we left the hospital, Mommy always took me right home to play. We sure played a lot! We played with toys and letters and cups. We read stories and played peek-a-boo and tasted new flavors. And you know what? I kept doing things that made her so proud—and my old foster parents, too. I used to drink my food through a big tube that went inside me, but now I don't even need it. I'm a spoon guy now!

◌ ◌ ◌

Every day it gets easier to understand Mommy's words. I always know what her face is saying, like when she smiles at me or kisses my cheek. But now when she says words like, "We're going to the park—I'll bring a blanket and you can eat Cheerios," I understand what to get excited about!

Remember how my doctors told Mommy I would never roll over, sit up, or stand? Doctors can sure be silly. Mommy taught me to do *all* that stuff. That's why we didn't worry when the doctors said I would never understand anything. It takes grownups a while to see what Mommy and me already know.

Oh, I forgot to tell you one other thing my doctors said. They told Mommy, "Your son will never walk."

That would have been okay. Lots of my friends can't walk, and Mommy and me can go everywhere we want in my special chair. But she always wants me to try out new stuff, so she got me my very own walker. It had tiny wheels and Mommy put my favorite stickers all over it. I just grabbed the handles and started going—and before long my legs got so strong that now I can walk by myself!

Walking is pretty tricky, that's for sure. But I feel so happy when I make it across the room with Mommy cheering me on. Sometimes

I lose my balance and fall over, but I don't mind. When I'm falling I can already see Mommy running over to pick me up and help me try again. Now I can walk at my special kindergarten class, too. School is kind of scary, but Mommy says I'll do great!

It's so weird that I almost didn't meet her because Mommy and me are the world's best team.

Tracy Healy

Lemon Drop

Tracy told us that when she takes Brandon to the store or the park, people often tell him how cute he is. Remember how Brandon's doctors gave Tracy a long list of things he would "never" be able to do? Well, being able to understand what people say to him was on that list. Yet whenever anyone tells Brandon how cute he is, he breaks into a big grin of understanding! We can't wait to hear from Tracy about the next "never" that she and Brandon blow past. —Don

covered
by love

When my husband and I moved from Philadelphia to Florida, we had to sell everything. We arrived at my sister's apartment and moved in with only what we could fit in two suitcases. We were truly beginning our lives again—and all the more because I was eight months pregnant. If we could make it for six months or so, we could get back on our feet and start a new life together as a family of three.

Two months after giving birth, I opened a letter from Medicaid. Expecting to read something about my son's delivery, I found instead a notice that I no longer had medical coverage. This was *not* the news I needed while we were trying to get back on our feet as a family. I called immediately, and learned that my son would be covered until he was one, but that I was covered only during pregnancy.

Being without health insurance scared me. At least I was healthy, we had each other, and our baby could see the doctor when he needed to. Maybe losing my coverage wouldn't be such a big deal.

Six months after giving birth, I discovered I was two months pregnant! My first thought was that this was *not* the right time to have another child. We were still living with my sister and her family, barely scraping by. Still, I couldn't help feeling joyful, despite every reason to be anxious and fearful.

At our first ultrasound appointment—again covered by Medicaid, thankfully—I lay down on the reclining chair and waited while the technician smeared gel across my belly and readied the scanning equipment. I knew the drill from my first pregnancy: next would come a black-and-white blur followed by the rat-a-tat heartbeat of my baby.

After taking far too long, the technician informed me she couldn't find a heartbeat. Gently, she told us that we'd lost the baby.

I returned to the apartment crushed. Despite the less-than-perfect timing of this pregnancy, I had already begun looking forward to meeting this second child. I asked God why this was happening, and why I was going through so much pain. It didn't seem to make any sense. Later that day, I read in my Bible something Jesus said: "You do not realize now what I am doing, but later you will understand." I tried to grab this peaceful thought and hold on to it.

Next day, the doctor called to tell me that I needed to come in for a dilation and curettage (D&C), since it would be dangerous to leave the fetus inside my uterus. As soon as I scheduled the appointment, I began to dread it. I'd heard that D&Cs could be physically painful, but I was more worried that it would make me miss my baby even more and add to the confusion I was feeling.

On the morning of my appointment, I reread the promise of Jesus and drove to the hospital. During the procedure, the doctor discovered a cyst on one of my ovaries. After many tests, it was determined that I had a rare tumor called a teratoma. "If we hadn't caught this," the doctor informed me, "it would have continued to grow until it burst—and that would likely have been fatal."

I was scheduled for surgery to remove the tumor, and the operation went smoothly. The surgical team felt confident they had removed the whole tumor, and at my one-month check up I was given a clean bill of health.

The next day I received a letter from Medicaid. After updating my records to account for my miscarriage, they had determined that I was no longer eligible for benefits—effective immediately.

Understanding flashed through my brain like lightning. If I hadn't been pregnant with my second child, I wouldn't have been insured for the last several months. If I hadn't miscarried my second child at twelve weeks, the tumor in my ovary would have never been discovered. It was only because I miscarried my child that I am alive today.

This isn't a story that brings me great happiness. After all, I lost a child, and that wound will forever be tender. But it *is* a story that makes me grateful. I'm grateful to be alive, grateful to feel the love of my husband and children every day, and, above all, grateful for the peace that fills my life.

Yamaris Rosa

ever
after

Some people think fairy tales are only for children, and that things never work out quite so well in real life. But I'd like to tell you a grown-up fairy tale about a man named John and a woman named Joni. You might be skeptical, but listen to the whole story before you decide whether to believe it—and you might just change your mind about fairy tales.

♂ ♂ ♂

In early spring, while flowers and trees bloomed across the city, John's wife walked out on their marriage of more than twenty-five years. Meanwhile, in another state thirteen hundred miles away, Joni's husband ended their marriage too.

So John and Joni were alone. Unexpectedly, painfully alone. They felt the same sense of betrayal, the same longing for healing and love, even though they lived in different states and didn't even know each other.

Except that they *did* know each other—they just didn't *know* that they *knew*.

Their paths had first crossed thirty-four years earlier in Duncanville, Texas. Joni's parents were language instructors at a summer institute for Christian missionaries preparing to move overseas and translate the Bible into other languages. John's parents were students, preparing to move to Papua New Guinea. And though they don't remember that first meeting, it was the first time John and Joni saw each other.

Three years later, and ten thousand miles distant in the South Pacific, John and Joni met again. John and his parents had been living in Papua New Guinea for two years; when Joni arrived, she joined John's senior class at Ukarumpa High School. After they graduated, John and his family returned to the States.

John and Joni didn't have any contact with each other over the next thirty years. No news was exchanged, nor were any letters or Christmas cards sent. They married other people, lived in different places, and worked different jobs.

So when their spouses both ended their marriages within days of each other that spring, neither knew about the other's loss. John and Joni each experienced shock and dismay and loneliness, as if they were living the darkest days of their lives.

Does this sound like a fairy tale yet? Perhaps not. But there's one more chapter.

As late spring turned into summer, John and Joni were still living in different states, still unaware of each other's existence. One day John decided to check Facebook, hoping to learn what had happened to his former classmates at Ukarumpa High School. That same day, Joni was also seized by a desire to reconnect with her former classmates.

And so it was that thirty years after last seeing each other in Papua New Guinea, John and Joni reconnected. A short introductory note on Facebook led to longer e-mails, and soon both John and Joni were gripped by a clear and unambiguous conviction: they were meant to spend the rest of their lives together.

Was it too soon? Some would say they should slow down. After all, they'd only been reconnected for the briefest of times. And neither had been looking for another relationship so soon after their divorce, let alone to remarry.

But John and Joni were equally certain of one thing. The Author of their story had been planning this final chapter all along—planning the time and the happenstance for them to reconnect after three decades, fall in love, and live happily ever after.

δ δ δ

And that's exactly what Joni and I are doing—living happily ever after. We now reside in Oregon, where we run a program that helps men and women recovering from addiction find stable employment and safe housing. We watch tragic stories being rewritten every day, but none ever surprise us.

After all, we're living proof that fairy tales come true.

John Shepherd

timing is everything

What made my divorce especially galling was the timing: it was finalized the day before our tenth anniversary. Rather than a day of celebration, it instead became the first day of my new life as a single mom with a five-year-old daughter.

The timing of events over the next few months didn't make things better. A month after the divorce, my father died. Three months later, I was laid off from my longtime job when the company relocated to another part of the state. And the house I'd loved was finally sold, the proceeds split as part of the divorce settlement. My daughter and I were forced to move to an unfamiliar apartment.

No husband, no job, no house, and no clue what to do next. I felt like a grapefruit that had been squeezed and squeezed until nothing was left but a crumpled rind tossed on the counter. All I could do was ask God to help me, and then take it one day at a time.

The first glimmer of good news was my new landlady, who agreed to watch my daughter whenever I went out looking for a job. Some mornings, if I needed to leave early, she would even walk her to the bus stop for school. Then, as we got to know each other, she lowered my rent so I could afford to pay it with my unemployment checks.

This was truly a gift, because I treated every day of unemployment like I still had a job. And I did, in a way—my job was finding a new job to provide for my daughter. I read the employment ads in the newspaper religiously, and went all over town looking for anything that would help pay the bills.

When my unemployment benefits were about to run out, I had gotten only one offer of full-time employment: a night shift at a home improvement store. I knew my daughter and I could survive on that money, but how could I say yes? I'd have to leave her with a babysitter every night. She'd already lost one parent—wouldn't this be like losing another? Yet *not* taking the job would leave us penniless, once the final unemployment check was spent. Having her mother around wouldn't be of much use to my daughter if we were homeless and starving. I didn't feel peaceful about the home-improvement store job, but I didn't have any other options.

Then, a week before my unemployment ran out, I was called in for an interview at a nonprofit. The good news was that it was a paid position and they wanted to hire me. The bad news was that the position would last only three months. My heart sank. If I took the job at the nonprofit, I'd soon need to start the process of looking for a job all over again.

Ultimately, I decided, my daughter came first. So I went to work at the nonprofit, my plan being to look for another job whenever I had a free moment. I'd need something lined up when the three months was over.

I liked my new job, even though it was temporary. And I continued to look for another job, but the search was as fruitless as ever. It looked as if I would soon be without employment again, or perhaps forced to work at night and leave my daughter. The day before my temporary job was scheduled to end, my supervisor called me into the office. Would I be willing to move to another position? And if so, was I comfortable working full-time on a permanent basis?

In life, timing is everything. A day before my tenth wedding anniversary, my life crumbled around me. And later the following year, a day before my daughter and I would be officially without money, a great job dropped into my lap. How great? Well, I've been working full-time at that nonprofit for a while now—almost nineteen years.

My baby daughter is now twenty-six, and if she learned anything from growing up with me it's this: don't settle for what you think you need, and wait for what you do.

Veta Shepherd

metamorphosis

Most people look forward to retirement, but it slapped me in the face. I'd spent decades working in the medical field; I knew what I did was important, and I was good at it. But the sudden onset of memory problems at age fifty forced an end to my career. Suddenly I found myself out of the workforce and cloistered at home, while all my friends continued to be productive members of society. I felt like my life had stopped while the rest of the planet kept right on spinning.

I tried to fight my feelings of hopelessness, but I didn't have any ammunition. Maybe my life *was* hopeless. I'd spend the next thirty years at home, doing nothing useful and forgetting things I used to know. Was that my destiny? Without my job or my friends—all of whom were at work still—days turned into weeks, and weeks into months. It felt as if a rain cloud was constantly over my head.

Determined not to fade into oblivion, I tried to pick up the pieces of my life. I threw myself into various hobbies, looking for purpose and happiness. I gardened for hours each day and took long walks. When the weather turned cold, I returned indoors to craft quilts and write short stories. I'd always said that "time spent under the pity tree is time spent in vain," and I aimed to prove that.

The trouble was that the branches of the pity tree cast shadows far longer than I'd anticipated. The more time I gave my hobbies, the less fulfilled I was. I couldn't just work and will my way to happiness by focusing on myself. I knew that what I needed was a wider perspective, so I decided to volunteer.

My first thought was to volunteer at the local animal shelter—surely caring for vulnerable animals would bring significance to my life. But then I realized that the number of animals I'd be compelled to adopt would exceed my fixed income. I next considered Meals on Wheels, but I worried that my memory problems would cause trouble.

At last I settled on writing. I'd always wanted to write kids' books, and this seemed like the perfect opportunity. I sat down at my desk: no distractions, no appointments, and all the time I needed to write. But I couldn't. Everything I thought of was an *adult* thought—I'd need to learn to think like a child again!

So I decided to volunteer at a local elementary school. I envisioned a quiet classroom—or better yet, the library—filled with angelic children quietly reading books and talking earnestly about life. I'd have enough material for a story in no time! Instead, I was tossed into a boisterous second-grade classroom where the noise level and the activity level were in a constant battle for supremacy.

Those first few times were certainly a challenge for a retired woman with memory problems. Yet as I continued to volunteer my time, I slowly but surely began to see unexpected things. I studied the wings of a ladybug beneath a magnifying glass with the same keen interest as the students. I watched bean seeds planted in Styrofoam cups push bright tendrils toward the light. I clapped my hands and laughed the day our chrysalis finally broke open and a butterfly began to dry its new wings.

The second graders lived in a constant state of wide-eyed wonder, and it was rubbing off on me. This was perfect!

Until the day my memory problem was found out. I was crammed into a tiny chair, with my chin nearly resting on my knees, when a seven-year-old boy looked at me curiously and said, "Why are you asking me the same question over and over and over?"

My secret was out, and in that moment my newfound *joie de vivre* almost disintegrated. I was embarrassed, of course. But more than that, everything in me was screaming that I should run and never look back. I could return to my garden, my quilts, and pretend that I'd never tried to become as a child again.

I laughed off his question, got through the rest of the day, and returned home to do some serious soul searching. Maybe I was no longer needed out there in the world; perhaps I didn't have anything left to offer, or to learn. Would anyone blame me if I retired officially?

The answer didn't come to me right away. Friends wiser than I'll ever be talked things over with me, and I did a lot of thinking. But before too long I opened the door to that classroom full of second graders again. No child would be harmed by my memory problems; I might even help to teach them that no one is perfect. And I understood that they'd already taught me far more than I could ever give back to them. They taught me that life doesn't happen all at once, but in seasons—whether you're a butterfly, a child, or a recently un-retired woman.

In my season of life, I needed to see the world through children's eyes. In their season, the only thing those children needed from me was love, and that was something I could give no matter the state of my memory.

Bea Edwards

bitter grace

My name—Marianne, which means "bitter grace"—used to leave a bad taste in my mouth. That conflict between *sweetness* and *pain* seemed to be always at the center of my life. How could I keep bitterness from eating me away from the inside out when my deepest desire—to mother an infant—was unfulfilled?

As you may have guessed, I wasn't able to become pregnant. And though my husband and I adopted a daughter, Samantha, she was three when she came to live with us. I continued to long for a baby.

The bitterness was suddenly removed from my life with a single phone call. Out of the blue, an agency I'd never had contact with asked if we would become foster parents to a three-month-old girl. "I know this is sudden," the director said, "but there is a high probability of adoption."

Hope poured over me from head to toe. This was the answer to my prayers. When I held Stacey for the first time, I knew my dreams had come true. At last I was holding my own baby.

Stacey flourished in our care. Every day I sang to her as I carried her around the house or rocked her in my arms: songs about how loved she was, songs that promised her a hopeful future. She had spent the first three months of her life in the mental hospital where her mother was institutionalized; nurses took care of her physical needs, but she had missed the intimate, daily touch of a mother. I was determined to make up for this by loving this perfect girl who had been gifted to me. I would shower her with so much love that her present and future would be transformed.

Each day I woke to care for Stacey, I praised God that grace had won the day.

♂ ♂ ♂

Before Stacey was even six months old, we were forced to give her up. We would never be able to adopt her. Stacey's mother, who already had two other daughters in foster care, had been released from the mental hospital, and she was given another chance to raise her daughter.

I had no legal rights. I was mothering her, but I wasn't her mother.

As I placed my beautiful Stacey in the waiting arms of a stranger, my face smiled. Inside, however, my heart felt like it was being crushed by icy talons. How could God let this happen to me? If God deserved thanks for bringing baby Stacey to me months before, then now he surely deserved the blame for snatching Stacey from my loving arms.

My name was complete again: Mary's bitterness had been added back to the grace of Anne.

♂ ♂ ♂

In the days and weeks that followed, I felt as if my baby had died. I grieved her loss, even as I questioned what I believed about life and my own dreams.

Yet slowly—ever so achingly slowly—I began to see what was on the other side of my veil of grief. Before I took Stacey in, every desire I had was for myself—for the perfect family that *I* wanted and thought I deserved. But she had been given to me by the Open Home Foundation, which worked to place at-risk children in safe foster homes. I wasn't the only one who longed for and deserved the perfect family. Every child did, as well.

So it was that my husband and daughter and I decided to continue being a foster family, providing short-term care for kids in desperate need of a safe respite. And so it was that two years later, a five-week-old baby boy came into our lives. His name was Zak—meaning "God remembered"—and we officially adopted him. Half a year later, we began to take care of a young boy named Cody who, while never officially becoming our adopted son, has now lived with us as our son for more than fifteen years.

If Stacey had never been taken away, I believe I would have been satisfied to raise her, sure that I had been given the baby I always wanted to have. Losing her forced me to confront the narrowness of my dream and expand my definition of motherhood. Not only that, we have been able to provide a foster home for at-risk children when they needed it most.

Sometimes, when I miss Stacey, I think about the love songs I serenaded her with. Did that love transform her future in some small way? I can never know the answer to that question. But I do know that loving her—and subsequently losing her—transformed my future. Now my name no longer seems like a contradiction. Now I appreciate the truth of *bitter grace*: that the path to joy often leads us first through sorrow.

Marianne Cornwall

the man without a face

My spirits sank as the elevator descended toward the radiation ward in the hospital basement. The two nurses who had rolled me into the elevator chatted while I sat in stony silence. *All my friends are going to prom and playing football,* I thought, *and I'm being wheeled around like a baby. What's the point of living like this?*

My life was getting worse, fast. I'd been in the hospital for almost two months. It started with a lump in my chest that grew until it was pressing on my lungs and constricting my windpipe. My first operation was a biopsy, but they hadn't been able to diagnose the tumor. What they had done was leave an open, infected hole in my chest. Next came an endless stream of specialists. Finally they were able to get a good sample of the tumor through my side.

I had Hodgkin's lymphoma.

Every night I awoke soaked with sweat, chilled and unable to get back to sleep. I'd get up and turn on the examination light above my bed, flooding my room with a stark white glare. While the light dried my sheets, I'd wander the halls. The effort it took me to breathe was a gauge of how far the tumor had spread. At first I could walk almost normally; but within weeks I was pausing every few steps, struggling to pull sufficient air through my slowly shrinking windpipe. The doctors had decided that radiation was the best course of action.

As I sank toward the basement, I felt hopeless. I knew my body was being destroyed on the inside, but now even the outside was in trouble. I figured radiation meant losing my hair, vomiting, shrinking to a skeletal weakling. I already looked like a freak. Red, green, and blue Magic Marker lines divided my jaw, neck, and upper body into zones that would soon be blasted with poisonous particles.

The elevator doors opened onto the waiting room for radiation patients. It was filled with empty wheelchairs in neat rows—and totally silent. There was only one other patient in the entire room, and my nurse wheeled me directly toward him. Six feet from the man she parked my chair, locked the wheels, and told me someone would get me soon.

I looked briefly at the slumped figure sitting across from me, nodded a quick hello, and looked away. Being friendly was the last thing on my mind. But when I glanced back a few minutes later, he was staring at me. He was heavyset, around sixty, and he was holding a cloth over his mouth. Above the cloth, I could see the same felt-tip markings that tattooed my own body covering the entire side of his face. That eye was closed, and his cheek bulged with a subcutaneous lump.

I was getting uncomfortable with his one eye staring at me, but I couldn't look away. I frowned slightly, a look that I hoped would convey my disinterest in conversation. I had enough problems of my own. That's when he lowered the cloth from his face.

Below his upper lip the man didn't have a face. There was literally nothing there.

I tried desperately to stamp down the horror rising in me, but I'm sure my expression betrayed me. I wanted to leap out of my wheelchair and run from the room, but I was frozen, horror-struck, staring into the void of his ruined features. After moments that seemed to stretch forever, the man pulled the cloth back up. He continued to stare at me until several nurses entered the room and wheeled me away.

Back in my room that afternoon, I couldn't eat or sleep. Whenever I closed my eyes, a picture of the man leapt into my mind. All I could do was stare at the clinical sterility around me and think, *It would be better for everyone if I just died.* My morning encounter had blown the last whiff of hope out of my heart.

Exhausted, I tried to keep my eyes open. I couldn't bear to see the man with no face again, or his single, staring eye. Every time I began to drift off, he was instantly with me. In desperation I cried out, "God, why did I have to see him? How much more do I have to suffer? Just let me go!"

The man inside my head glared at me with his one good eye. Then he spoke. "Kid, I'd sell my soul to be in your shoes—you don't know how lucky you are."

I felt the hospital room spinning around me; I had to grab the rails of my bed to keep from falling. There I was, I was a high-school dropout, a kid with cancer, a multicolored freak about to be irradiated. I hadn't done a single good thing with my life, and now it was getting worse. I was an absolute nobody.

And the man with no face was jealous of *me*.

That moment marked a turning point in my life. At the time I still had an infected hole in my chest. I was still days away from seeing the radiation treatments begin to beat back the tumor that was pressing on my lungs and windpipe. I was years away from regaining my health.

But I knew I still had a life to live—whatever that life looked like.

It's been thirty-four years since that fateful morning, and I thank God that I've never again wanted to end my life. I don't know what happened to the man with no face. I used to whisper a prayer for him whenever I closed my eyes and saw him; now, whenever I think of him, I realize how blessed I am.

Andy Artell

Lemon Drop

I spoke to Andy recently and he told me that he was getting ready to celebrate his thirty-fourth year of being cancer free. Looking back at his story, I can't help but think about how important perspective is. When Andy first saw the man with no face, he was ready to give up living—but now, more than three decades later, he can't imagine missing out on all that's happened since. Andy hopes his story will remind people that there's always someone worse off, and there's always a reason to hope. —Don

ten days in dallas

It was an unremarkable Monday morning in November when I picked up the phone and heard my youngest stepson's voice. He was obviously upset. Several years earlier he had been involved in a serious automobile accident, and though his recovery had been nothing short of miraculous, he still suffered from several deficits, including difficulty speaking. I had to ask him to repeat himself several times before I could understand him. When his words finally registered, the world stopped spinning for an instant and my stomach lurched into my throat.

"Someone found Jody dead this morning. He hung himself."

♂ ♂ ♂

When my husband and I got married more than thirty years earlier, I brought three children to the marriage and he brought five. Then we had two kids of our own, bringing the grand total to ten. I often joked that with so many children, we might have a major disaster at any moment.

I hadn't meant this.

Telling each of our children about Jody's suicide was agony, but I especially dreaded telling Nik, our youngest; he had always been the glue that held our family together, and right now he and his wife, Krystal, were having trouble. They'd recently decided to end their seven-year marriage, although nothing was official yet. They married right out of high school and Nik joined the Air Force soon after. Their first son was born that year, and twin boys three years later. Meanwhile, Nik was deployed to Iraq for two tours. Now the five of them were scraping by in Anchorage, Alaska. Money was tight, the boys were a handful, Nik was drinking too much, and Krystal was keeping her emotions inside while she tried to hold everything together.

Every day for the past few weeks I'd been on the phone with either Nik or Krystal. They'd given up on their marriage, it seemed. And now I had to call and tell them Jody was gone?

I finally dialed their number, my fingers trembling. Nik didn't say much after I shared the news, just a few words, lots of silence, and then he hung up. He called back later and told me the Air Force would send him home, but he'd be alone. Krystal didn't want to make the trip.

I knew I couldn't control their decision, but I felt so strongly that they all needed to come for the memorial. I prayed as fervently as I ever have for anything. I wrote notes to both Nik and Krystal, and talked to them on the phone as often as I could. Soon came a call from Nik: the Air Force was going to fly all five of them to Dallas for two weeks.

♂ ♂ ♂

In the days leading up to the memorial, as the whole family gathered in Dallas, our grief was buried beneath an avalanche of details. Jody's memory was with us everywhere we went, but there wasn't time to think about what his loss meant. Finally the service arrived, and only the strength of love the family shared allowed us to make it through.

After the service, Nik and Krystal came back to my house. Now that everything was behind us—the shock, the planning, the reunion, the service—our emotions erupted. We spent long hours crying, talking, and even raging in anger. Their boys played in the backyard with my husband while the three of us tried desperately to figure things out.

It was a tense time. But even in the furnace of those days together, I understood that we were suspended in a unique circumstance. Back home in Alaska, Nik and Krystal would have been stuck indoors because of the lousy weather, and swamped by their normal workaday responsibilities. Here they were able to entrust their kids to Grandpa, reconnect with friends and family, and process the tragedy while staying as guests in someone else's home.

At one point, while I was preparing dinner, I heard steps behind me in the kitchen. Suddenly I felt Nik's arms wrapping around me in one of his famous bear hugs. He spoke softly in my ear. "Mom— we're going to give it another try." Then Krystal was there too, and I began to cry so hard that they started to laugh at me, which only made me cry harder. The three of us hugged like our lives depended on it.

♂ ♂ ♂

Nik and Krystal celebrated their eighth wedding anniversary in February. Recently I was on the phone with Nik, and he said, "Everything is pretty good at our house right now." Something happened between them in Dallas that changed the trajectory of their lives.

A well-meaning friend recently suggested that God planned Jody's death in order to draw Nik and Krystal back together. I'm sorry, but I can't believe that. What I do believe is that God made something good out of something bad.

I guess that's what grace is—God making beauty out of ugly things. If that's true, then grace is what every marriage requires to last. Really, it's what we *all* need, married or not. Because sometimes life pulls us apart—or rips us apart—and we need something that can bring us back together.

Donna Matthews

the woman across the hall

It was May, and outside Daddy's hospital room the Tennessee day was bright and sunny.

Our hearts, however, were dark and heavy. My brother George and I listened as a doctor whispered sentences to our mother that we couldn't understand. At ages fourteen and eleven, we may not have grasped the literal meaning of the conversation, but things were all too clear.

Daddy was dying of cancer, and there was nothing we could do about it.

He'd been sick for a long time. On this spring day in 1955, he looked especially small in his hospital bed. It was like he was shrinking, and soon there would be nothing left but the clean, white sheets.

Yet Mama wasn't one to dwell in despair. On that day, just as on every other day we came to Campbell's Clinic, she turned the hospital ward into her personal forum of care and hope. While my father rested, she walked from room to room with my brother and me in tow, introducing us. "I'm Mrs. Eaves, and this is my daughter, Judy, and my boy, George. I've got another one at home, Betty Jo, and there's seven more—six grown and on their own, and little Johnny in heaven."

I'd curtsy and drawl out "Hi-dee-yah-doo" with pure Southern sweetness. After that, the first person to look up and make eye contact was instantly christened "Sweetie" by Mama, and would receive the compassion that constantly flowed from Mama's enormous heart.

Not many of the countless "Sweeties" we met at Campbell's Clinic knew what was happening to our family, because Mama was reluctant to bring up her own troubles. If pressed, she'd smile encouragingly and say something like, "We'll make a way. My husband's life verse is, 'Seek ye first the kingdom of God.' That's what we've always done, and we're not going to stop now. We're doin' what God wants us to do here, and he'll take care of us."

When Daddy died that year of metastasized colon cancer at the age of fifty-nine, Mama was forty-nine and still had three of us at home. She had never worked outside the home, having dropped out of school to care for her two younger brothers after barely finishing the eighth grade.

Mama's faith seemed to be limitless, but that didn't change the difficulties we faced at home. She was a single mom decades before anyone coined the term. We lived in a little house in Chattanooga in what locals called the Shepherd District—a neighborhood for the poorest white folk that overlapped with the even poorer black neighborhoods in our corner of the segregated South.

Even after she took my sister Anna and her four young children into our tiny home, Mama's response was the same. "We'll make a way. God wants me to take care of this family, and if I'm doin' what God wants me to do, then he'll take care of us."

There we were: an unemployed widow, her divorced daughter, and seven kids living in one of the most impoverished neighborhoods in the city. No money, no plan. Mama was undoubtedly resourceful, but we needed something to change. All we had was a growing list of questions and no answer in sight.

It wasn't long after Daddy died that the answer came from an unexpected source.

When Daddy was still in the hospital, one of my mother's favorite "Sweeties" was the lady my brother and I called "the woman across the hall." She and Mama were from different worlds. She was a professional who worked for the Veterans Administration, and she dressed like "rich people." Yet, disarmed by Mama's relentless compassion, she invited Mama into her life. The two became close the way people do when life's pain thrusts them together.

After visiting Daddy, Mama talked with her about life, kids, and what they would do if their husbands died. Once, the woman across the hall pressed Mama for details. "Mrs. Eaves, how will you pay your bills? You have no income, no job, and no training. How are you going to take care of yourself, keep your home, and care for these three children?"

Mama quickly deflected the questions. We knew she was uneasy talking about that kind of thing in front of us. Instead she said, "Oh, you don't worry about me, Sweetie, I'll be just fine. Now, I just baked some cookies. They're still warm—try one. Aren't they good?"

Just a few days before my father passed away, the woman across the hall asked Mama if my father had ever served in the armed forces. "Well, yes," my mother said, "but only a few months in World War I. He'd just finished boot camp when the Armistice was signed."

To my mother, this was just one more conversation with someone who was hurting and needed a friend—and such conversations provided the woman across the hall with the kindness and encouragement she desperately longed for during her lonely stay in the hospital. Without my mother's knowledge, the woman did some research and discovered that we qualified for veterans benefits.

Within a few months of Daddy's death, we were receiving full benefits from the Veterans Administration—benefits that lasted until my baby sister turned eighteen!

Maybe the answer to our problems wasn't so unexpected after all. If Mama was looking out for other people, as she believed God wanted her to do, was it any surprise that God was looking out for her?

Whenever adults asked Mama what she would do when Daddy died, they never seemed convinced by her reassurances. But George and I were. Mama's strength and confidence put steel in our souls, and I wondered why others had such trouble seeing what was already so clear to her.

For the twelve years after Daddy died, those monthly checks provided for our minimal needs. Not once did we go to bed hungry, no matter how many of us were crammed into that little house in the Shepherd District. Mama lived to the ripe old age of eighty-three, and she never tired of telling her children and grandchildren about the woman across the hall and their providential conversation.

Mama's strength in the face of pain seems almost like a miracle, but those of us who knew her understood that it came as natural to her as getting out of bed in the morning. Yes, her husband was dying of cancer—but she could still be a blessing to every other hurting soul in that small Southern hospital. That's simply what Mama did with pain: she took it into her heart and transformed it into a gift of encouragement, like a batch of fresh cookies; then she served that gift to every "Sweetie" she met with a smile and a prayer.

Judy Cocoris

unexpected laughter

When my husband and I got married, I told him I didn't want to have children. I'd known that for years, and I wanted to make sure he agreed with me. Little did I know that several years later, having children would be my deepest desire—and that it would both break my heart and overwhelm me with joy.

Several years into our childless marriage, I felt the weight of my heart beginning to shift. After years and years of leaning one way, I began to notice myself thinking about babies. Where was this coming from? It felt like a huge life change. After all, I'd pictured my future—holidays, vacations, career—a certain way, and that way never included kids. Yet my new desire for babies also felt natural. Almost inevitable. As if I were an apple tree, and nurturing fruit was in my DNA, but it had taken a certain number of years to mature. Suddenly, I couldn't wait to be a mom.

Except I couldn't get pregnant.

Once it became clear that this wasn't just a short interruption, but a real issue, my feelings flared. I was angry and confused. Why had I started to long for children, only to discover I couldn't have any? Had I been right before to picture myself childless?

My doctors determined that we should start fertility treatment, but on the day treatment was to begin I found out I was pregnant already! Life was beginning to feel like a roller coaster, but this latest change was welcome news, to say the least. However, the ride didn't let us off: two weeks later we learned that the baby was in my fallopian tube. Losing that baby began a dark season. I felt as if I was being taunted and teased by life.

Four months later, against all odds, I became pregnant again. This time I carried the baby almost all the way to term, and despite an early birth and a five-week hospital stay, we found ourselves at home with a beautiful baby daughter. When she was sleeping, wrapped snugly in a blanket, we'd look at her in awe. We'd come so far in such a short time: from thinking our future would be childless by choice to studying the perfect, miniature features of a girl we knew we would love forever.

When we were ready to have another child, I was still labeled infertile by my doctors. We began trying for another baby, but a heartbreaking year passed without conceiving. To make matters worse, from the age of two my daughter prayed every night for a younger brother or sister. We didn't know what to tell her, other than *We'd like that, too, honey. We're trying.* The trouble was that our efforts didn't seem to be getting us anywhere, and neither did the doctors'.

I didn't want to complain. After all, we had a gorgeous daughter, among countless other blessings. But why was my heart filled with an almost constant longing for another child if I couldn't become a mother again?

My husband and I had talked over the years about adopting a child from Ethiopia. We even started to fill out the necessary paperwork, but something inside of us told us to stop. Perhaps this wasn't the right time, or perhaps there was something better waiting for us and our family. But what? And why not adopt? We knew from our research that there were countless children in Ethiopia who needed a new home.

Just as we decided definitively that adopting a child from Ethiopia wasn't the best decision, we got a phone call from a family we knew in another city. In the course of their work with college students, they'd met a pregnant girl in difficult circumstances who wanted her baby to be adopted. And for some reason, the family we knew decided to call us.

I hung up the phone feeling confused and shocked and hopeful. Might this be the baby for us? The more we talked and prayed, the stronger we felt that this baby was meant for us.

The birth mom was ecstatic that her child would have a loving, stable home, and we knew that the sad chapter of our infertility was being rewritten. We were able to be part of the pregnancy from the twelfth week. We were there for the ultrasound when the technician discovered the baby was a boy. And we were in the delivery room when Isaac entered the world.

What would have happened if the call had come after we'd given up on having another child, or if we'd been pursuing foreign adoption—would we have said yes to Isaac and his birth mother?

The name *Isaac* comes from the book of Genesis in the Hebrew Scriptures. Abraham and his wife Sarah want to have a baby, but they think they are too old to do so—until God promises otherwise and then delivers on that promise. When Isaac is born, his parents are old enough to be grandparents, and the sound that echoes from the birthing tent—laughter, which is *Isaac* in Hebrew—is the only possible response. All children bring joy, but perhaps it is the unexpected child that brings the greatest joy of all.

Jody McComas

making lemonade in jail

*I*t was New Year's Eve, and I decided to ring it in by robbing a supermarket.

It was late. My friends and I had been partying pretty hard already, and we were drunk, out of beer, and flat broke. Hoping to remedy the situation, I staggered across the street and into the nearest supermarket. I grabbed the closest six-pack of cheap beer and tried to walk out with it.

Unfortunately—or perhaps fortunately, as hindsight would have it—the cashier decided to stop me.

Well, *that* wouldn't do. Who was he to stop me from getting free beer? I decided a little persuading was in order and pulled out my knife. At the same time I noticed a pack of cigarettes on the counter that another customer had just paid for, so I took those as well. It was shaping up to be a great New Year's Eve.

Except that in the light of day, my simple—and simply dumb—idea to shoplift beer turned into two felony counts of armed robbery and one count of assault with a deadly weapon. The presiding judge sentenced me to six months in jail so I could "think about what I was doing with my life"—far less than the six years I should have received, but pretty hard time considering the ten bucks' worth of beer and smokes I'd taken.

Still, six months was no problem. After forty-three arrests and nearly seven years spent behind bars already, it was hard not to laugh when I received my sentence. I'd been in and out of lockups from a young age. The family that adopted me as a young boy was abusive, and I ran away constantly, which turned out to be perfect training for my jackrabbit life of crime. I'd escaped from boys' homes, fire camps, juvenile hall, mental hospitals, and even jails. Running was my default response to difficulty.

And I was constantly running from my worst enemy: myself.

So there I was: twenty-five years old and washing dishes in yet another jail. I actually enjoyed life in jail, from the drugs to the fistfights. You might say I was committed on principle to a life of lawlessness. That is, until the day a deputy sheriff came and told me to pack up my gear, pronto. Turns out I was carrying hepatitis from my years of intravenous drug use, and the authorities didn't want me spreading it around.

To isolate me, they sat me at a desk at the front of the jail. The only thing on top of it was an ancient manual typewriter. The deputy then handed me a handwritten list containing the names of each prisoner who had entered or exited the prison that day.

I took one look at the long list and protested, "But I don't type!"

The deputy shoved the list back into my hand, saying, "You do now."

The following days were an exercise in frustration. I defined the "hunt and peck" method, though I spent way more time hunting than pecking. Whenever I made a mistake—which was often—I'd curse up a storm before applying Wite-Out and then blowing on the paper until it dried.

By the time I was released from jail, four months later—two months early, for good behavior—I could type up a storm. I was still hunting and pecking, but now I was like a tornado. For once in my life I knew how to do something useful, and do it well. I'd always had stories running around in my head, but let me tell you, I hadn't spent much time reading and writing during all those years of crime!

Remember how the judge told me to "think about what I was doing with my life"? Well, I did. And I realized that deputy sheriff had given me an incredible gift. He thought he was just keeping the rest of the inmates hepatitis-free and knocking out some of his busy work at the same time, but he changed the direction of my life.

It's now thirty years since I first sat before that beat-up manual typewriter. Since then, I haven't touched drugs or seen the inside of a jail cell. But the best part isn't what I've avoided. It's what I've been able to do. Now I make my living as a screenwriter—typing! Nearly fifty of my screenplays have become television shows or movies.

Just before I was released from jail that final time, I ran into someone I knew when I was a teenager, and he gave me the rundown on all our childhood friends. Sweatdog: life sentence. Bam-Bam: double life. Preacher: life with no parole. Kay-Kay: life sentence. Butterfield: double life. Dirtdog: death sentence. Those kids never made it out, and since then I've never stopped thanking God that I did, thanks to a lazy sheriff and the surprising gift of an old typewriter.

Dave Gist

third time's the charm

eople in my family just don't have children out of wedlock. Being single parents is not in our family DNA. So when I found myself pregnant at twenty-two—still in college, unmarried, and in a dysfunctional relationship with the baby's father—I felt like a failure. Even if I hadn't been disappointing my family, there was still the fact that I simply wasn't ready to be a mother. There was no way that anything good would result from this pregnancy.

So I began secretly planning to have an abortion. Getting rid of my baby would eliminate my problems, I told myself, and I could get my life back on track. I went to the nearest clinic—a two-hour drive from my college town—but was told that because of how far along my pregnancy was, I needed more money. Undeterred, I continued working for two more weeks, saving enough for the abortion.

On the morning of the day I was scheduled to revisit the clinic, I lost my purse, and along with it all the money I'd saved over the previous six weeks. Still undeterred, I saved six weeks' worth of money again and rescheduled the procedure.

The morning of my third appointment, after driving for nearly two hours, a small voice inside told me to exit the interstate for some reason. As I drove down the off ramp, my reliable car suddenly shut off. I coasted straight into a parking space at the restaurant at the bottom of the hill.

This was getting suspicious. Every time I tried to have the abortion, something happened to interfere. Was I meant to keep my baby, even though I had so many good reasons not to?

I wandered away from my broken-down car, lost in thought. Soon I found a tree stump and sat down on it. Anger welled up in me: at myself for getting pregnant, at my child's father for not supporting me, and now at God for sticking his nose where it didn't belong. I looked up at the sky and told God how things really stood: his interference notwithstanding, I was *not* going to have this baby. My mind was made up.

As I sat on the stump, crying and telling God that my plans were final, a beat-up pickup truck rumbled to a stop in front of me. An old man rolled down the window and said, "Baby, get in—you need to eat something."

I was so absorbed in my tempestuous thoughts that I opened the door and climbed in, not even considering the fact that I was getting into a car with a strange man! He drove me right across the street to a trailer park, stopping in front of an aging but neat single-wide. An older woman, whom I assumed was the man's wife, opened the door to greet us. After inviting me in, she said I could use her phone to call someone to pick me up. After I made the call, she reminded me that I needed to eat something, and before I knew it I was sitting at their kitchen table with a heaping plate of soul food in front of me. Hungrily, I tucked into the food, and as I ate I began to weep. Unfazed by my tears, the woman talked to me in a soothing voice about how good God had always been to her family.

◌ ◌ ◌

Later, back at my place, the bizarre nature of my day slowly revealed itself to me. Why had I exited the highway just before my car broke down? How had the old man found me, and why had I trusted him? Why had his wife been so insistent on feeding me, and how had she seemed to know just what I needed to hear? It was almost as if they had been...expecting me.

One thing I knew for sure: my child was meant to be born. My plans to abort it had been thwarted at every step, and as I reflected on the whole process I understood that larger concerns were at work than my own convenience.

For the first time trusting that something good might come from my pregnancy, I released my fear and shame and told my friends and family about my baby. Until then, I hadn't told anyone. As I began to live openly, I ended my painful relationship with the child's father.

The decision to be honest—both about my pregnancy and about the fact that God seemed to want this baby to be born—set in motion a series of healing, healthy events. My ex-boyfriend began to treat me well and even look forward to the birth of his child. I got a new job as a general manager at a clothing store, which provided enough money to have the baby. And I received a settlement claim from a former employer—a check large enough to purchase all the clothing and supplies I needed to set up a nursery for my child...and for the exact amount my abortion would have cost. It seemed like every circumstance was confirming that I was meant to become a mother.

♂ ♂ ♂

Six months later I gave birth to a healthy boy. Six months after that, I put my baby in the car and drove to the exit where my car had broken down one year earlier. I wanted to find the couple who had fed me soul food that day, introduce them to my beautiful son, and thank them for being part of my transformation into the mother I was meant to be.

I exited the highway and drove slowly past the restaurant where I'd parked my car. There was the stump where I'd told God to butt out of my life. And just across the way...

Something was wrong. I quickly pulled my car off the road, feeling lightheaded. Across the street from the stump was an empty field. There was no trailer park in sight.

I got out of my car, opened the back door, and unbuckled my baby from his car seat. Carrying him in my arms, I walked slowly through the field on that side of the road, still having trouble absorbing what I was seeing—or, rather, what I *wasn't* seeing. No trailers, nor any evidence that this area had ever been inhabited. It was as if the couple, their beat-up truck, and their single-wide had never existed.

♂ ♂ ♂

As I write this story, these events—which happened eighteen years ago—seem no less incredible than that year I learned what happens when God interferes. My son is now a tall, handsome young man attending Morehouse College, and raising him has been the greatest joy of my life.

I don't know what life holds for him, or for me, but I do know that God had plans to give my son and me a hopeful future—that he planned, through my unplanned pregnancy, to prosper us. Considering how well things have turned out, now I'm fond of telling God to interfere with my plans anytime he wants.

LaTosha Brown

the stolen radio

he week after I got my first real paycheck as a full-time teacher, I traded in my jalopy for a shiny new car. It was a treat to drive after years of clanking and clunking around town. I felt proud that I could afford it because I was making a good living doing something I loved.

No car stays shiny and new for long, however. Several years after I started teaching, I married a soldier, and a few years after that he got out of the army and went back to college. We were happy, and my car was still puttering faithfully along, but money was tight. We figured that if we could avoid any major financial surprises for a bit longer, things would get easier.

Then one day my car started acting up. It was the only way I could get to work, so ignoring the problem wasn't an option. When I took it to the mechanic, however, I was shocked to learn that the repairs would cost several thousand dollars—almost as much as my car was worth! The timing was terrible. Once my husband was out of school, we'd have some extra money to put toward a repair; why couldn't my car have waited until then to start giving me trouble?

We decided to take a few days to think it over. It wasn't that we expected a cheap and ingenious solution to materialize overnight; we simply couldn't figure out where we were going to find the money.

The next day I drove to school, feeling discouraged. In the calm of the early morning, I tried to regain a sense of hope and possibility. I knew we would make things work...somehow. Besides, I couldn't think about my car issue. In a few minutes I'd have a classroom full of students to teach.

As I turned the key in my classroom door, I thought about the day ahead. I loved looking out across the neat rows of desks, seeing my students working diligently, heads down and pencils racing across their papers. My secret weapon was a portable stereo I'd brought from home—when I needed my students to get some serious work done, I'd pop in some classical music and watch their thinking shift into a higher gear.

I swung open the door and noticed immediately: my portable stereo was gone. Someone had stolen it.

On any normal day, the theft of my stereo would have been unfortunate but I would have adjusted. That day, however, it seemed so much worse. Because of the repairs my car needed, I was as concerned about our finances as I'd ever been. Having to replace my classroom stereo with my own money added insult to injury. And a bigger worry snaked through my mind: was this theft the second event in a chain of bad luck? Would I be able to handle the next thing that came my way?

With a heavy heart, I trudged down the hallway and notified my principal. He filed a report about the incident, and as we were finishing up, he asked if I had a picture of the missing stereo. Because I'm an organized person, I assured him that I had the user's manual filed at home and would bring it to school the next day—if my car could manage to get me there!

That evening, I quickly located the missing manual. Without really thinking about what I was doing, I began to leaf through the rest of the papers in my file cabinet. There didn't seem to be anything of importance, and my mind started to wander. I almost flipped right past a nondescript letter when suddenly my brain registered what I was seeing.

It was a long-forgotten recall notice for my car—a recall notice about a problem that, until a few days earlier, hadn't been an issue with my car. Feeling lightheaded, I quickly read the notice and digested its meaning: the manufacturer would fix my car for free.

When I started having trouble with my car, the notice about that recall didn't even cross my mind. If my classroom stereo hadn't been stolen, I would have never had a reason to sift through those old papers. The notice would have remained forever forgotten, and who knows how we would have managed to scrape together the money to repair my car. Thank God for whoever it was that stole my stereo!

The next day in my classroom, my students probably wondered why I smiled whenever I looked at the empty spot on the shelf where my stereo used to sit. They had no idea how thankful I was that it had been taken from me.

Melanie Elliott

will you dance?

*K*nock *knock knock.* I sat in my bed, legs hugged to my chest, and waited. Maybe whoever it was would go away and leave me alone. My head was throbbing and my palms were beginning to sweat.

Knock knock knock. Knock knock knock. This time there was a voice, and not even my locked door could disguise its passion. "Let me in. Please. I *must* tell you something."

I knew Sam wouldn't leave. When he set his mind on something— like the previous weekend, when he'd dragged me onto the dance floor in front of everyone—he never changed it. He might knock all night long.

I crossed the room and cracked the door. His eyes, gorgeous and blue as ever, looked at me. As I opened the door wider, a hopeful smile lit his handsome face. What was he doing in my room? I was a depressed, bipolar exchange student plagued by migraines and enough insecurities to keep a team of psychologists busy for years. What could Sam—tall, popular, handsome Sam—possibly see in me?

Nothing. That was the answer I told myself. Which is why I nearly collapsed in shock when Sam told me that he loved me.

Nothing could have prepared me for that moment. It was as if his words had flung open a window in the dark room of my life, and suddenly everything was flooded with light and air. Would I walk with him to that window, hand in hand, and look out on a wide field of possibility? Would I trust him to lead me into a brand-new life?

My long silence was answer enough. He saw in my eyes that my answer was no. Sam's eyes searched mine. Then they dropped. He began to leave, but turned back almost instantly to face me again, asking a single question—a question that changed my life.

"Why do you hold back?"

♂ ♂ ♂

I had moved halfway around the world, looking for answers, only to learn that everything I needed to know was right in front of me. Sam, in asking me to let go of my fear and love him, held up a mirror to my pain, forcing me to recognize what I had become. I didn't have the bravery that night to tell him that I loved him, but his words transformed the following months and years of my life, like ripples from a stone dropped into a still pond.

Why did I hold back? Before Sam stepped through my door that night, I thought that changing my life meant *becoming* something, or someone, different. But slowly I began to understand that change starts sooner than that, as soon as we let ourselves begin to dream. The desire for change is, in itself, the first step toward changing.

Why do we hold back? I see people around me every day who are only half living—they live with fear, or regret, or they live the way they are expected to by their parents. I recognize these half-alive people because I used to be one.

Sometimes we think that dreams need to be acted out on the grandest stage the world can offer. If we dream of cooking, we need to attend a culinary institute in France. But sometimes the perfect stage is right in front of us. Why not check out Julia Child's cookbook from the library and start by making dinner for your roommate?

Why did I hold back? Because I feared my own dreams. As Sam's question turned over and over inside me, I allowed myself to see the things I really wanted: to travel, to write, to act. And as Sam's question continued to change me, I saw that the soil in which to plant my dreams was right in front of me.

Back home, I joined a community theater, wrote about my adventures in Europe, and traveled the streets of my community, finding adventure wherever I looked for it.

I will never hold back again. Not after Sam. The story he told me transformed the fearful, unstable girl I was into a dream-chaser and a life-taster. Now I tell my story every chance I get, hoping it can transform someone else's life. I've lost touch with Sam over the years, but not with what he stood for: the willingness to fling wide the door of your dreams and step into possibility. If I see him again, I know he will be proud of who I have become.

full circle

My baby girl was due any day, and I had the waddling gait to prove it. I was glowing, gleaming, and in constant awe of the child that rolled and twisted inside me. Every morning I awoke knowing I was one day closer to meeting her.

My Nana felt the same way: the fact that she already had many other grandchildren and great-grandchildren did nothing to lessen her excitement over the coming of my new girl. Nana knit incessantly, always pink, stockpiling handmade outfits and blankets for my little one.

Just after dinner, I reached down for my purse and heard the *pop* that I knew meant my water had broken. My baby was ready to come into the world, and I was ready to meet her.

Eighteen hours later, early in the morning, I was spent—ready to go home, ready to be done. Ready to call it quits. My doctor had been in and out of my room, called away often by emergencies elsewhere in the hospital. Finally I was told to stop pushing. My baby was stuck in the birth canal; the doctor would have to make the final decision about what to do.

Finished pushing, and waiting for the doctor's return, I watched the clock on the wall. The second hand seemed to have slowed to a crawl; the minute hand moved like a glacier.

Finally the doctor returned and told me forceps would be needed to pull my girl from the birth canal. *Forceps.* The same metal tool that marked this same date—June 9—in Nana's life with indelible ink on her heart.

♂ ♂ ♂

Twenty-seven-year-old Nana was overflowing with excitement at the prospect of meeting her first child. The nursery was stocked with dozens of hand-knit outfits and blankets. Looking out the front door of her farmhouse across the fields bathed in early morning light, she smiled and rubbed her belly. Her son—she knew the child inside her was a boy—would begin the next generation of family farmers. He, like his family before him, would work the soil with strong, capable hands beneath the summer sun.

When labor came, it lasted all day and into the night. Eighteen hours. Fruitless pushing led her doctor to call for a pair of forceps, with which he pulled her baby into the world on June 9, 1944.

Tiny William lived for only two days after being delivered brain-dead. Nana watched him lie in his hospital bassinet: back arched, mouth open but refusing to eat. His body had been fatally bruised and battered by the very tool that gained him entrance to the world.

♂ ♂ ♂

My doctor held up the metal forceps and told me he was going to pull my baby out. The awful symmetry was almost too much to comprehend: what was in store for me and my baby girl on this day, so like that day sixty-four years past? I pushed, the doctor pulled. I twisted, he rotated the forceps.

Finally, out came my girl. Her tiny body was perfect.

My mother wiped the mascara stains from her face as she handed me the phone. It was Nana. I could hear the hitch in her breath as I told her about our family's latest addition, who had just been saved by forceps on June 9, 2008.

The death of William was always like a missing measure from our family's song. Only God knew the particular notes that would complete that song—notes that took more than sixty years to be composed and performed. Now June 9 is a day on which our family hears the song as it was meant to be, in all its harmony and beauty. Sometimes healing takes the briefest instant, and sometimes it takes a lifetime. When Nana first held my daughter, her smile was like the summer sun, and I knew that she was finally healed.

Molly Murphy Chorman

a new song

*J*walked quickly toward my office, praying I wouldn't run into anyone in the hallway. I knew what was about to happen because I'd already experienced it twice that morning. I reached my office, stepped inside, and locked the door behind me. Collapsing in my desk chair, I buried my face in my hands and sobbed. The grief felt so heavy that I had trouble breathing.

Several weeks earlier, my wife had miscarried. We already had four healthy children who had arrived without incident, and we expected the fifth pregnancy to go the same way. At our twelve-week ultrasound appointment, however, the technician couldn't bring herself to look at us. We soon learned our baby was dead. Instead of driving home with a black-and-white snapshot of our growing hope, we drove home alone in devastating silence.

We were good at raising healthy, happy kids, not at coping with this unexpected pain. We choked through an explanation as our other kids listened, trying to be honest about what had happened and about what we were feeling. The emotional hurricane that blew into our lives over the next few days destroyed our happiness, our clarity, and our peace, even as it threatened to uproot our faith. Every hour was a new struggle. One moment we wanted to be alone, sitting in silence with our grief, and the next we resented our friends and family for not calling or coming over.

As the weeks passed, we stumbled into a state of equilibrium, even if it was still filled with hurt. We began to learn how to shrug off thoughtless remarks, and to humbly accept the genuine love and support that people offered us. We discovered that responding to others' hurts was more natural after first learning how to deal with our own. And most importantly, we were able to celebrate the life of our unborn baby by giving her a name: Hope.

♂ ♂ ♂

Several months later I traveled from my office in Connecticut to my company's Manhattan branch for a planning meeting. Expecting the hustle and bustle of the downtown office, I was surprised when I walked into a conference room that was somber and nearly silent. One of the men working there, I learned, had just found out that morning that his sister had miscarried twins. I swallowed and asked where he was.

I found him sitting alone in the video studio. The room was dark, and I could scarcely discern his sobbing shape. I pulled a chair beside his and he looked up at me, his face a mask of grief. When I asked if he needed to talk, he poured out the story, and after listening I told him my story—about how the weight of loss had threatened to choke the life from me.

In moments, both of us were weeping in earnest. Speaking in short bursts as I cried, I told him that even through everything that had happened to my wife and me during the last few months, we'd sensed that God was holding on to us—that he hadn't let go yet, and we thought he never would. He won't let you go either, I told him, or your sister.

As I stood to leave the room, the man dialed his sister's number. "Hey," I heard him say, as fresh tears streamed down his face, "I need to tell you something that someone just shared with me."

Healing is never a denial of sorrow or pain. Like a small child with a cut knee, we heal even while we're hurting, and certain scars will never leave us. As I was driving home to Connecticut that day, I thought about how in my deepest pain a bird called Hope came to perch in my soul. I heard her sweet song even above the storm, but it wasn't until I sat in a darkened room with a crying friend that I understood her message is always meant to be shared.

Jay Cookingham

death of
a dream car

*I*f you live in central Oregon, you know there's nothing better in the summertime than floating the Deschutes River in an inner tube or raft. The river, whose headwaters begin at a lake on the eastern slope of the Cascades, winds its way downhill before flattening out and lazing right through downtown Bend. And when it's hot outside—on those long days of summer when the sun doesn't set until after nine o'clock—the Deschutes fills with floaters of all shapes and sizes.

Late one afternoon I was floating the river with some friends. Back home in Sisters, half an hour away, my mother gave in to my brother's pleading and allowed him to borrow my car.

There are two things you need to know about that decision. The first is that he already had a car: an '89 Honda Accord that seemed to have more rust than paint and enough miles on it to get to the moon and back. He'd actually tried to use his that day, but it was so low on gas that he changed his mind as he headed out the driveway.

The second thing is that if I had been home, it would have been tough for my brother to get his hands on my '02 Audi A4. It was my dream car, and no one touched it without my permission. It had automatic everything, leather seats, a sweet stereo, and enough horsepower to go as fast as I wanted it to.

But I was miles away, blissfully floating the river, soaking in the sun and scenery, and laughing with my friends—oblivious to what my brother was up to. His fuel tank was nearly empty, and he needed to get to and from a meeting in town. So he borrowed my car, with my mother's blessing.

Something else about this story: thanks to his crazy schedule, my brother was running on very little sleep. By the time he headed for home, it was dark and he was fighting to stay awake. While speeding in a 25 mph zone, he nodded off at the wheel.

My brother woke moments before hitting the rear end of a parked semi trailer. In a split second, he swerved, and my Audi responded immediately to his frantic maneuver. The swerve carried the driver's side of the car—and my brother—several feet to the left just before impact. The sharp steel bumper of the trailer sliced through the right front end of the car and came to rest inches from the passenger headrest. The Audi's engine was forced backward into the car's cabin, and it wrapped around my brother's body without ever touching him The airbag deployed, and my brother's body was enveloped by it while the car was destroyed around him.

The damage to the car's body was incredible, a total loss. And that's what was so incredible about what happened. Because if my brother had been driving *his* car—with its lower height, lighter weight, and lack of airbags—it would have been his *body* that was a total loss. Instead, he was taken to the hospital and treated for minor injuries; my car was taken to the scrap yard.

Looking back on that day, I'm grateful that I wasn't consulted about whether my brother could borrow my car. I know that given the choice, I may have refused—and I'm so glad I don't have to mourn that decision. Instead, my dream car was sacrificed for a far greater treasure: my brother's life.

Sammy Jacobson

Lemon Drop

The morning after my son Cavan's accident, I walked outside and looked at his car—the one he'd *almost* driven the day before. As I looked at it, the realization hit me: no airbags. I began to weep…what if my wife, Brenda, had refused to let him take his sister's car? She would have lived with a lifetime of regret and pain. As parents we can't always know what impact our choices will have on our kids. Sometimes it's the smallest decisions that make the biggest difference. —Don

this room

ecades ago, this Room echoed with the pitter-patter of Mary Janes as a little girl, dressed in her Sunday best, pirouetted before the mirror before traipsing off to church with her parents. It watched as she practiced twirls and pliés after ballet class and admired while she tottered about in her mother's high heels. The Room smiled as the girl sat down at her desk, before she even learned to read or write, and invented poems and songs for her parents and her God.

The Room oversaw a willful child on time out, instructed by her parents to think about what she had done. And it contained both the sweet dreams and nighttime terrors of an imaginative child who envisioned monsters lurking beneath the bed, waiting to catch her.

This Room cringed at the arrival of a real monster, too: a teenage fiend who visited nightmares upon the young girl that haunted her even when the sun was shining. Too young to understand exactly what the boy from her church was doing, she was still old enough to be forever changed by her memories of his abuse.

This Room, in the following years, presided over the funeral of the girl's self-esteem. It mourned, along with her parents, the injustice of lost innocence. Late at night, it listened—along with the girl—to the sobs of her mother and father down the hall, when they thought she was long asleep.

This Room breathed an uncertain sigh of relief when, as months grew into years, the girl and her family pushed through the difficulty and began to heal, together.

This Room delighted, as the years passed, to hear the girl laugh once again as she talked on the phone with boys and read notes from girls. It swelled with pride to see the girl try on prom dresses, experiment with makeup and hairstyles, and begin to dream about her future.

This Room put on a brave face when the girl packed her bags for college, and it opened its arms wide a year and a half later when she returned, done with school and ready to work.

This Room held its breath while the girl—now a young woman—talked on the phone late into the night, her face lighting with a joy that only her future husband could conjure. It protected the girl's wedding gown, which hung next to the full-length mirror where she could see it when she fell asleep. It imagined how the girl would look with the train gathered behind her on that beautiful, dreamed-about day.

♂ ♂ ♂

Seven years later, this Room wept silently the first time the girl came home with her brand-new baby boy. It could tell by her night terrors that the year of lost innocence still haunted her, that her new role as mother reminded her of all it was possible to lose, and that full healing was still to come.

♂ ♂ ♂

Now this Room holds twin beds with polka-dot comforters and tiny chairs for two young visitors—beloved grandchildren who fall asleep to bedtime stories and who wake up to breakfasts of pancakes and sizzling bacon. This Room sighs with joy to see Grandpa unroll his sleeping bag between the two beds, the better to tell stories as his precious little ones get ready for sleep. This room grins at the kisses Grandma showers on her two grandchildren before tucking them in at night.

And remembering all the long, wrenching years, this Room rejoices in kept promises: that good ultimately triumphs over evil, that healing sometimes walks with slow, patient steps, and that no Room can contain all the hope of lives redeemed by love.

Nicole Swort

the
hummingbird

osh was the perfect boyfriend for our teenage daughter, Stephanie. She was impulsive and unpredictable, brimming with life; he was tender, thoughtful, caring—and handsome, too. Secretly I believed he might be the right man to settle down with Stephanie one day.

We loved having Josh around. I was an avid gardener, and he helped me care for the menagerie of animals that flocked to our lush backyard. Josh took it upon himself to maintain the hummingbird feeders that dotted the landscape, religiously cleaning them and refilling them with sweet nectar..

Over time, Stephanie's impetuous spirit tested the limits of Josh's pragmatism. The young lovers decided they needed to spend some time apart, and Josh stopped coming to our house. Soon after, Stephanie learned she was pregnant.

After receiving counseling about her options, Stephanie decided to keep the baby and not return to high school. When she told Josh, he reacted badly. He wasn't ready for the responsibility of raising a baby, and he certainly didn't want to get married. Josh pleaded with Stephanie to give the baby up for adoption. When she refused, the distance between them widened and bitterness took root. Each assumed the other was making a selfish choice. It seemed the couple would be unable to reconcile before the baby was born.

Josh and Stephanie weren't the only ones having trouble. My husband and I found ourselves on different sides as well. He believed that Josh and Stephanie weren't ready to be parents, and he encouraged our daughter to pursue adoption. After all, even though she was close to graduating, Stephanie was choosing not to finish high school, and soon she would be a single mom without a job or a degree. But Stephanie was passionate about keeping the baby, and it seemed to my maternal instincts that her passion would be just what she needed to become a wonderful mother. Our household was constantly on edge, and there was no solution in sight.

Three months before the baby was due to be born, tragedy struck. Josh was driving home from work late at night when he lost control of his car and ran off the road. He was mostly uninjured. However, he had taken some medication before leaving work that caused him to become disoriented. Unable to restart his car, he left it and wandered deep into the woods. This was in February, and the temperature was plummeting. Before anyone could find him, he died of exposure, only a few miles from the warmth and safety of his parents' home.

The guilt hit me like a hammer. The lingering resentment I'd felt about his relationship with Stephanie haunted my every thought. Regret, anger, resentment, denial—the circle spun on and on. I tried to anticipate the birth of my first grandchild with happiness, but it seemed all I could do was wallow in grief.

At last Stephanie's baby was born. Ava Grace let out her first lusty cry in a birthing room filled with mothers and aunts from both families. We had spent the last three months weeping for Josh; now our eyes welled with tears of joy. Josh's mother told us that Ava Grace was the spitting image of Josh as a baby, and all of us felt that some of his spirit was living on in his daughter.

Home from the hospital, I returned to my hummingbird feeders. In honor of Josh's memory I cared for them lovingly, watching the bright birds flit from feeder to flower.

One day Ava Grace was in the kitchen with me, resting in her carrier, when I heard a persistent tapping at the picture window. After ignoring it for a while, I looked up to see a stunning red and green hummingbird hovering outside, rapping the window with his long, curved beak. *Tap. Tap. Tap.*

He showed no sign of stopping. I'd seen birds fly into the window before on accident; startled, they'd immediately fly away. But this bird was different. He didn't seem to want to leave, and he wasn't agitated. He simply hovered, and tapped, with persistent regularity.

A sudden thought flew into my heart, but I dismissed it immediately. Surely I was imagining things. Yet still the bird hung shining in the air. *Tap. Tap. Tap.*

On instinct, I stepped over to Ava Grace and turned her carrier around so she could see the hummingbird. Almost as soon as I did so, the bird stopped tapping. He didn't fly away, however, but continued to dart around the window, almost as if he was searching for something.

I looked down at Ava Grace. Her blond hair only accentuated the piercing blue of her eyes, and she seemed to have taken notice of the shimmering shape on the other side of the glass. Picking her carrier up, I walked toward the window, hardly daring to breathe. Even as I drew closer, the bird continued to dip and spin, unafraid.

Finally I held the baby in front of the window. The hummingbird was frozen in midair, his thrumming wings the only sign of motion, his eyes locked on the baby. If not for the window, Ava Grace could have reached out and touched him.

For a moment that seemed outside of time we held this pose, the unlikely trinity of grandmother, baby, and bird. Then, in an iridescent blur, the hummingbird streaked away, leaving only the afterimage of his gleaming plumage. It was a wordless farewell compressed into a single shining second. Suddenly, the dam holding back my emotions shattered into a thousand pieces, and I wept for the father and daughter who would never meet.

When my flood of tears finally slowed to a gentle trickle, a new sense of peace was planted inside of me, a sense of peace that would grow deep and strong in the coming weeks and months. Josh didn't live to know his daughter, but I believe he was given the grace to see her happy face that afternoon. As sad as I will always be that Josh's life was cut so short, my encounter with the hummingbird helped me understand the gift that is mine to receive every day of my life: a child's face brighter and more beautiful than any flower in the world.

John and Lisa Leonard

lion's den

andra Martz, the editor of *When I Am an Old Woman I Shall Wear Purple,* was coming to Pittsburgh, and the agency I work for had booked her as a speaker for our company's anniversary gala. While in town, Sandra would be hosting several invitation-only writing seminars for local authors, and my employer—knowing that I write—wrangled an invitation for me. I was thrilled and grateful, and immediately wrote it down on my calendar.

Soon, however, I discovered a problem: the seminar was being held in the prestigious Pitt Club at the University of Pittsburgh. For any normal person, that wouldn't be an issue—but I'm not a normal person. I'm a rabidly proud Penn State alumna, and no self-respecting Nittany Lion would *ever* set foot in the Pitt Club. It would be like Wile E. Coyote and the Road Runner sitting down to watch a movie together.

However, there was no gracious way to back out. My employer had given me this invitation as a gift. If I tried to explain my reasoning for not attending the seminar, I'd hear something like *Are you really going to let a silly college rivalry get in the way of a great writing workshop?* The problem was I knew such sentiments were true— yet I *still* didn't want to go.

As the day of the seminar drew closer, I began to feel nervous and afraid. Would I be kicked off the local board of Penn State alumni? I had my excuse ready: "I was forced to go by my employer, and I hated every minute of it!"

The day of the seminar, I dressed in a carefully chosen ankle-length dress of blue and white: the colors of Penn State. Feeling like a secret agent sneaking behind enemy lines, I took what seemed like a deserted route between my car and the Pitt Club, constantly looking over my shoulder to see if I was being watched. Had I been sitting atop an iceberg in my bathing suit I wouldn't have been any more uncomfortable.

Inside the club I found my seat. The other attendees looked vaguely hostile, as if they might sniff out my allegiance at any moment and pounce. What was I doing there? I was sick to my stomach and wondered if I should leave. No writing advice was worth sitting in that room for a moment longer.

Then the woman beside me looked over and smiled. "Hi, I'm Debbie. What kind of writing do you do?" I told her that I published devotionals, to which she replied that she was a Christian as well. Her friendliness started to melt my trepidation, and we chatted amicably. Soon, Debbie's friend Melanie arrived. The three of us hit it off, and almost before I knew it the two-hour seminar was over.

That was sixteen years ago, and I honestly don't remember what Sandra Martz talked about at that workshop. I'm sure it was wise and inspirational, but I was too distracted to pay attention—too surprised by the realization that I'd just met two women who would change my life. Since that day, Melanie has become one of my dearest friends and even helped me critique my novel. Debbie started a writers' group that Melanie and I joined, a creative forum for writers.

Today I consider myself the writer and person I am in part because of two ladies I met at an event I absolutely did *not* want to attend. Don't get me wrong, I'm still a proud Penn Stater—*that* hasn't changed. But I'll forever be grateful for the day I entered the Pitt Club against my better instinct, and found that sometimes intuition is trumped by providence.

Kathy Irey

heavenly harvest

The tentacles of the Great Depression were far-reaching and cruel. Daddy had a job, and we had a house, but even our family—like many other families in rural New York—suffered. Haggard mothers, already weary from preparing meager meals of beans and cornbread, posted hand-lettered signs: *Will iron 3 baskets of clothes for 50 cents.* Worried husbands carefully carved out thick layers of cardboard or scrap linoleum to insert into the ever-thinning soles of their work shoes. Barefoot children sucked on pieces of salty ice left behind when the ice truck pulled away, pretending it was their dessert.

With seven children to feed, Mother and Daddy fought desperately to stay above water. They told us every day that God would keep providing for us, but things never got easy. Fortunately, Daddy had a green thumb. His garden allowed Mother to stock the shelves in our cool, dirt-floor cellar with home-canned fruits and vegetables. She prepared imaginative, though often meatless, meals for her hungry brood. And before we ate, Daddy always bowed his head to pray. "Our gracious, loving, heavenly Father, we thank thee for these provisions for our bodies. Use them, we pray, to make us stronger so that we may serve thee better." We all said "amen" together.

As the months passed, my father's take-home pay from the Lehigh Valley Railroad withered from nearly $2 an hour to $1.50. When it hit $1.28 an hour, my mother knew something needed to be done. She'd already cut every corner and trimmed every bit of fat in the family budget. At this rate, we simply wouldn't have enough money to put food on the table.

She and my father had a talk. Both of them were exhausted: he from another endless day in the rail yards, she from managing the household and us kids. Mother reminded him that the bank was threatening to foreclose on the house, and then she raised a possibility. What if we stopped giving our offering at church, and instead committed half of the garden to help feed the pastor and his family? This would loosen our budget just enough to buy things we needed but couldn't grow, like milk and clothing.

Daddy resisted. He looked forward to the moment every Sunday when he was able to drop our offering in the church collection plate. He came from a proud generation, a generation as faithful and generous as it was hardworking.

However, Daddy knew Mother was right. On Saturday, he swallowed his pride and walked out into the garden. It was far enough into spring that there was little chance of a killing frost, even in upstate New York. It was time to plant. He used his hoe to draw a line down the center of the plot. With twine and sticks, he marked out the rows in each half and meticulously planted seeds in anticipation of the coming harvest.

Every evening after supper, Daddy carefully weeded and watered every row in both sides of the garden, satisfied that he would produce a crop that would provide for his family and for the pastor's.

As the days lengthened and warmed, harvest time approached. Unfortunately, there was a serious problem. For some unknown reason, the two halves of the garden were now distinguishable by more than the center dividing line. The pastor's half was flourishing prodigiously, and every plant was beginning to bow beneath the weight of ripe fruit and vegetables; meanwhile our half of the garden was scarcely surviving. We'd been counting on a rich harvest to see us through the coming months, and so far all that our half was producing was withered leaves.

Daddy worked tirelessly to save the family's vegetables, using every tool and trick he could think of. And as he toiled in our half beneath the baking summer sun, the pastor's half of the garden continued to run riot. The pastor's promised tomatoes grew so large they threatened to snap the vines from which they hung, and his green beans shot taller than the stakes to which they were tied.

Mother and Daddy had a decision to make, and everyone wanted to tell them what do to. Friends and relatives said that God would *surely* understand if our family claimed the preacher's half of the garden. We'd planted it and cared for it, after all. And God knew that we children desperately needed the nutritious food. My parents wouldn't think of jeopardizing our health for the sake of a silly promise, would they?

After much prayer and soul-searching, Mother and Daddy decided to keep their promise. They would still give the pastor's family the produce from the healthy half of the garden. At dinner they told us that God would keep providing for us.

The pastor, unaware of the backyard drama, began to receive bags overflowing with cucumbers, succulent tomatoes, and long, waxy green beans. Daddy kept their porch stocked with bags of beets, bushels of golden corn, and piles of pungent onions. Each time he dropped off a load of produce, Daddy felt grateful that he was able to give something to God's work in our town, despite his falling wages and the difficult times.

Not long after the produce began to flow from our garden to the pastor's kitchen, something happened that changed our family. Daddy never asked for help from others, but he did ask for God's provision every night, and that's exactly what we began to receive in bushels and basketfuls. Neighbors, friends, and even strangers started leaving food on *our* front porch. These providential gifts usually arrived at night; in the morning we'd wake to yet another offering of nutritious food.

We would always remember that as the summer our half of the garden hardly produced a thing, and we gave the pastor's family everything in the other half—yet our cellar shelves brimmed.

The following fall and winter were hard for everyone, but we made it through. I couldn't count the number of hungry or homeless folks who enjoyed a hot meal at our table, and we always had enough to share. My parents' generosity produced a bountiful harvest that fed people far beyond our family. Daddy always taught us that God would provide, and that was the year we learned that lesson by heart.

Mariane Holbrook

made a mother

little girl, six or seven, carries a doll in her arms as she pads down the hallway toward her playroom. Her mother, who is walking toward her, starts to ask the girl a question but is gently interrupted. "Mama, shhhh—Dolly is sleeping already. I need to take her to bed."

The girl's voice is low and tender, so as not to wake her doll. Her mother nods, smiles, and lets her pass. Through the open door of the playroom she watches her daughter kneel beside the toy crib and cover the doll with a soft blanket, then whisper something in her ear and tenderly kiss her plastic forehead.

ᕁ ᕁ ᕁ

When I married my husband, Nathan, just six days before my twentieth birthday, my childhood dream of motherhood seemed about to come true. After we settled into our new home, Nathan and I began trying to start a family. It wasn't long before we conceived our first child, but the pregnancy ended in miscarriage three months later. We began trying to get pregnant again, but this time many years passed with no result.

Fast forward, and I began to experience some discomfort in my abdomen—discomfort that gradually but steadily became pain. After consulting several doctors, I was diagnosed with endometriosis, a condition that prevents pregnancy. We decided that I should undergo a surgery to scrape out several cysts in my ovaries. As I awaited my surgery date, the pain in my abdomen increased. When the surgical team began the procedure, they discovered that the disease was far more widespread than had been thought, and the surgery took much longer as they struggled to identify and remove all the growths.

After the surgery, my pain disappeared. Life began looking up. We were still young, and I was enjoying my work with the kitchen staff at an extension campus of my alma mater. Nathan and I hoped we could begin trying to start a family once again.

However, three months after the surgery, mild abdominal pain returned. Over time, the pain increased, and my doctors weren't optimistic about treatment. It seemed that if surgery didn't work, there weren't many more options for me. The pain naturally made us assume that the condition preventing me from getting pregnant was still with me. My dream of having a family was looking more like a fantasy.

As I talked to my mom one night, she suggested that I look into alternative treatment options, since I was experiencing so much pain. One day, when I was at the store buying my homeopathic medications, I spotted a young, pregnant mother stooping to hand something to her young daughter, who was smiling up at her. The scene pierced my heart. *When would it be my turn?*

Whenever a friend announced she was pregnant, I celebrated with her, but it was always bittersweet. The new treatment quickly alleviated most of the pain in my body, but my spirit continued to ache.

◌ ◌ ◌

I tried to appreciate everything good in my life, pray about the bad, and enjoy my job. I was cooking and leading in the kitchen at work, and one Sunday, as I prepared a meal for a summer camp, I met Meaghan, one of the teenage staffers. I recognized her from our church. She'd attended the camp a few summers before, and now she'd returned to work.

As we prepared the next meal, she told me about her home life: how her parents sometimes abused her, and how she'd been in and out of foster homes. Before coming to camp she'd been staying with friends, but she wasn't sure where she'd live when the summer ended.

When I got home from work that night, I told Nate about Meaghan. Both of us felt like we wanted to help her, but we weren't sure how, so we called the youth pastor at our church.

"Wow, it's great that you're responding so quickly to my request," he said.

Since both Nate and I missed church that morning, we asked him what he meant. He explained that he'd made an announcement during the morning service that he knew of a teenage girl in need of a home. How had we known about Meaghan if we hadn't been at church?

Well, God can work in mysterious ways, and we certainly didn't need to be in church to get the message about Meaghan!

During the next week, Nate and I thought and prayed about her. We talked with people who knew her at church, trying to understand what she really needed and what would be the best way to help her. Then we met with Meaghan. After talking things over, and allowing ourselves time to make a decision, we decided together that Meaghan could come live with us when her summer job ended.

We certainly didn't have any long-term expectations. All we knew was that right then, in that season, Meaghan was meant to be part of our family.

ó ó ó

It's been almost two years since Meaghan moved in with us. At first things were awkward as my husband and I got used to sharing our space and she got used to our expectations and the everyday realities of sharing a home.

But family life grew steadily better. In the two years that we have been a family, we've made countless memories together: taking hikes, sharing picnic dinners, treasure hunting with our GPS, and trying out—and tasting, of course!—new cookie recipes. And those are just the adventures that really stand out. Every day we get to live life together as a family, and in the normal, ordinary realities of life we find ourselves content and grateful.

Now we refer to Meaghan as our "unofficial adopted daughter." Her biological family still lives nearby, and they communicate from time to time. All of us are glad for that, even though the relationship is seldom smooth. Meaghan is saving money for college; she hopes to be a doctor, and Nate and I support her wholeheartedly. Life still has some bumps for me, too. I still have endometriosis, and continue to take homeopathic remedies. They help, but I'm not cured.

I don't know if I ever will be able to have children of my own. What I do know is that I'm a mother *now*. It's taken me years to discover the truth about family, but it's a truth that has changed my heart forever: families are not always born; sometimes, they are made.

Karen Earls

held
by love

*I*t had been fifteen years since my last seizure, and I was beginning to think I'd never have another one. My husband and I were living in a small town in Kansas, and we loved the ordinary rhythm of our lives, from quiet meals to worshipping at our church to seeing friends at the market.

Then one night, I had a massive grand mal seizure. All the old uncertainties and fears came flooding back as we drove to the hospital. The doctor tried to put us at ease by assuring me that everything would be back to normal the next morning. My husband and I returned home, shaken, but certain that God would take care of us.

We almost forgot about the incident—until the following week when I had two more major seizures that kept me in the hospital for three days. More tests were run this time, given that the seizures were happening in quick succession after a fifteen-year reprieve. The additional tests didn't offer the doctors a better picture of why I was suffering, so once again I was sent home and told that everything was "normal."

Back in my own house, I was on edge. Soon I began suffering from headaches that made my skull feel like it was splitting in two. The medication I took only made things worse—I began to experience vivid, terrible hallucinations. An ambulance had to take me to the ER, where the doctors decided I needed to be admitted to the mental ward. Thankfully, I don't remember many details about that awful time, but the flashes I recall are bad enough. Nothing could be done to reduce my torment, and while the doctors waited for my medication to wear off, I had dark and violent visions.

When things were back to what the doctors called "normal"—which included a headache, the possibility of a severe seizure at any moment, and our still-heightened levels of stress and fear—I was released. To compound matters, the cost of all this medical attention was far beyond our means, so now we had yet another problem to worry about.

Back home, I gradually began to feel better—thanks in large part to the faithfulness of our church friends. We were showered with cards, thoughtful phone calls, and delicious meals. It started to seem that everything was becoming normal again—*actually* normal!

That's when I had two more major grand mal seizures during the night. My husband and I were at a loss. From the depths of our hearts we cried out, "Why, God? Why?" Yet somehow we knew that we needed to stay positive and keep trusting, to continue to be faithful no matter how difficult things became. Every day, despite the fear and uncertainty, we spent time together, praying and reading our Bibles and speaking with friends from our church. It seemed like the only thing we could do.

One Sunday, soon after these latest seizures—and the latest additions to our overwhelming medical bills—the youth director from our church asked if he could bring the kids over to our house. We wouldn't need to do anything, he assured me, other than be ready for a surprise.

Later that day, cars parked outside. The youth director came to our front door and told us that the kids had decided to egg our house.

It had been a few years since I was a teenager, but I was pretty sure I knew what "egging a house" meant—and certain that I didn't want it! He quickly alleviated my concern, however, by explaining that they wanted to bless us with dozens of plastic eggs. My husband and I watched as the kids filled our front yard, carrying baskets brimming with decorated eggs. We were given the eggs, and many hugs as well, and then they left us so we could go inside and open the gifts.

It was like Christmas and Easter and Thanksgiving all rolled into one glorious hour. We opened egg after egg, twisting them apart to reveal a stream of blessing that seemed like it would flow forever. The kids had filled the eggs with notes of encouragement, hopeful verses from Scripture, sincere promises to pray for us, and even small folded bills to use for our medical expenses!

We were overwhelmed. How could such a wonderful thing have happened to us?

The youth director had an answer. Throughout the previous weeks and months, while we suffered through my seizures, mounting medical bills, and mental anguish, our church had been doing more than just dropping off meals and praying for us. They'd been watching, too. And what they saw was a couple who continued to hope and trust and love, despite having every reason in the world to do the opposite. We'd inspired them, he said.

Our tears began to flow. We knew that if we'd inspired anyone, it wasn't because we were courageous or strong, but simply because we knew our only hope was to remain faithful to each other and God.

When every last egg had been opened, and it seemed a thousand hugs had been given and received, the kids said their good-byes, leaving my husband and me in our living room. We were by ourselves, but not alone; we were completely surrounded and held up by love.

Later, a shocking thought occurred to me. Could it be that my seizures were a blessing, since they'd led to such a beautiful outpouring? I would never wish my condition on anyone else. But for myself I have come to a place of acceptance. Without my seizures, my husband and I never would have been "egged" with such a miraculous gift.

Whenever I hear a story nowadays about how the youth of our nation are in trouble, or going down the wrong path, I think to myself: *They must be talking about kids in some other city. Just like an egg, every kid in my town has a heart of gold.*

Barbara Caywood

steps to forgiveness

One day it all became too much—my father's abuse, the vile names he called me, the constant fear. I recorded a suicide message on my cassette player so my mother would know what happened to me. I set the tape on my desk, grabbed my hunting knife, and walked alone into the nearby woods. I found a secluded spot where it would be hard to find my body. After getting high on pot, I rolled up my sleeve and placed the blade of my knife on the tender skin of my left wrist. I could feel the cold metal blade like a heavy weight. It would take only the slightest pressure to push it through my skin, and once that simple act was accomplished, all of my problems would slowly fade into nothingness. I was all alone in the world.

Then I heard a voice: *No.*

In my surprise, I almost dropped the knife. I quickly scanned the forest around me, but all I saw were trees. Still, I had *definitely* heard a voice telling me not to cut my wrist.

Too shaken to continue with what I planned, I sheathed the knife, went home, and destroyed the tape. Unfortunately, I wasn't finished trying to destroy my life.

If my young life was like a jigsaw puzzle I was trying to piece together, my father's goal was to scatter the pieces and grind them beneath his heel. His cruelty was as normal to me as the sunrise. The insults he spat at me crushed my spirit, his fists bruised my body, and when I was twelve he began to abuse me sexually as well. I grew callous in an effort to protect myself; if I couldn't feel, I couldn't hurt. Drugs and alcohol became my favorite means of escape.

Several months after my suicide attempt, I was in the same secluded woods with my buddies. They chanted, *Three, two, one...go!* and I cracked open a can of cheap beer and began to chug. Two of us were racing to see who could drink the most in one minute. Foam ran down our chins as we shotgunned beer after beer, the yells of our friends spurring us on. Just as someone yelled, *Time's up!* I slammed down my sixth can. I was the winner.

I stood up to celebrate my victory, took two steps, and fell flat on my face. My wasted friends figured I had simply passed out from drinking too much. I was very much aware, however, yet unable to move or speak. I could feel the dirt and twigs pressing into my face, and the hands of my buddies awkwardly picking me up and carrying me to a nearby cabin we were using. They threw me on a cot so I could "sleep it off," but I wasn't passed out. I was dying.

I felt the life leaving my body, like a sheen of water evaporating as the sun hits it. The sensation began at my feet and traveled up my legs, and even in my addled state I realized that when it reached my head it would be the end. When the death creep reached my chest, I heard a familiar voice. It didn't belong to any of my friends—they were all passed out or drinking outside the cabin. It was the same voice I'd heard in the forest several months before.

Is this the way you want it to end?

It wasn't. Even though I'd been ready to kill myself, I knew I didn't want to die there, surrounded by people who didn't really care about me and reeking of cheap beer. I cried out silently inside myself, *No, Father! No!*

Then everything went black.

♂ ♂ ♂

I woke the next morning. I was alive, clearly, but I felt completely sober as well. I looked around the cabin at the snoring, stinking shapes of my buddies. Then I packed up my sleeping bag, walked out the door, and never looked back.

ơ ơ ơ

A few months later I was leaving for church with my neighbors when I heard, through the open window of our house, the panicked yell of my mother. I knew by the sound of her voice that she was in trouble. I walked back into the kitchen and was instantly met by a rain of blows from my father. The minute he saw me, he forgot about my mother.

Surprised at first, I took a few of his punches. But I managed to deflect the next few, and outright block the dozen after that—and then I realized something transformational. I was my father's physical equal.

He realized it too, and that understanding kindled a fresh rage in his eyes. I was far past the point of backing down, however, and I screamed, "You can't hurt me anymore!" In a show of power, I turned my back on him and began to stride up the long flight of steps to my room.

Unwilling to give in, my father followed me, calling me every vile and hurtful name he could think of. He knew that his physical mastery over me had suddenly ended, yet he still sought to dominate and control me in other ways. As I climbed the stairs, my anger started to boil over. The words spitting from his mouth were truly terrible, and each insult caused my fists to tighten. "One more word and you're *done*," I said in a low voice. I reached the top of the stairs as I said that, and for the first time in my life I felt a measure of power over my abuser.

My father had more than one more word. I knew that if I turned and hit him, he would fall down the steep stairs, perhaps even breaking his neck. The temptation was growing with every word he hurled at me, and I was losing control.

The breaking point came when he accused me of doing something vile with my mother. "That's *it!*" I spat. I planted my back foot and began to pivot, centering the whole force of my body behind my fist for a punch that would silence my father's mouth forever.

At that exact moment, as the powerful punch steeled in my body, I heard the familiar voice again. In a microsecond it spoke to me and said, *Forgive him—and tell him I love him.*

Everything happened so fast that I didn't have time to argue. By the time I finished my pivot toward my father, my fist was unclenched and open—and so was my heart.

"Dad, I forgive you," I said, "and God loves you."

My father paused for a long moment, mumbled a few more choice insults under his breath, and retreated down the stairs.

♂ ♂ ♂

That happened thirty-eight years ago, and every day I taste the fruit of that forgiveness. I've been married to my best friend for nearly three decades, and we have seven children—what we like to call a small nation!

I wish I could tell you that my father and I reconciled after that encounter on the stairs. The truth is that we never did. Losing him was painful, and the pain taught me that while reconciliation requires two people, forgiveness takes only one. That day I was miraculously given a second chance at life—a chance to leave victimhood behind forever. My father didn't *deserve* to be forgiven, but my lack of forgiveness would forever imprison me. The choice to forgive my father unlocked my chains—the same chains that almost dragged me to my death as a teenager—and set me free to hear my true name. I was no longer—am no longer—named by the insults of my father, but by my true identity as a husband, a father, and a man with hope and a future.

Jay Cookingham

Lemon Drop

Jay's story reminds me that forgiveness brings a certain kind of freedom. But recently I learned something else from Jay: when his story took place, the laws didn't often protect the victim in domestic violence cases. If Jay had knocked his father down those stairs, and his father had been seriously injured or killed, there's a good chance Jay would have been sent to prison or a juvenile detention center. Sometimes forgiveness gives us literal freedom, too! —Don

tsunami

The first discernible change on the beach in Phuket is how the incoming waves hesitate in their journey toward the sand. It is as if something is pulling them back, something they are powerless to resist.

♂ ♂ ♂

On the other side of the world it is Christmas day. At my sister-in-law's house, a steady snowfall blankets the trees, the driveway, the hedges outside the window. Inside, I sit alone in front of the fireplace. I'm meant to be celebrating the day with my family—eating, drinking, and laughing—but my worry for my faraway daughter leaves me gasping for air. *Please,* I plead in silence, *stay on the Phuket coast. Don't go to the Full Moon Party.*

♂ ♂ ♂

On the beach in Phuket, tourists and locals alike watch the ocean, wide-eyed. They put on sunglasses to get a better look in the glare; they unpack binoculars and cameras from their beach bags. The normally tranquil water is roiling and troubled, as if it doesn't know which way to go. Now it is receding: like a great inhalation, the water is being sucked out to sea, exposing dozens and now hundreds of yards of sloping wet sand. Fish jump and flop, drowning in air, while flocks of birds fly inland.

♂ ♂ ♂

I shiver and move closer to the fire. I can't get warm enough. With my feet tucked under me, and my arms wrapped around my knees, I fix my eyes on the red lights blinking on and off on the Christmas tree. *Blink. Blink. Blink.* I understand, bit by bit, that I am looking at them as if from deep underwater. That must be why the lights are shimmering and waving. Suddenly the weight of all the water filling my sister-in-law's living room presses down on me, crushing my chest with its pressure. I can't breathe. I feel my lungs fill with water.

♂ ♂ ♂

In Phuket, far out at sea, a new thing emerges: it is a wall of water, built brick by wet brick from each tiny wave it sucked into itself. At last high enough, and fortress-strong, it begins its inexorable trek toward the shore, forever crashing and forever rebuilding itself. Soon the dark dots on the white sand resolve into figures of tourists and locals: most still taking pictures, a few beginning to step back, to turn, to run.

♂ ♂ ♂

Sitting on the couch by the fire, I travel in my mind's eye to the Full Moon Party on an island in the Bay of Thailand. I am a bird, winging my way northeast across the island from Phuket. Hundreds of kilometers distant, I see the island lit up like a torch in the night: a wild, sprawling rave. Twelve thousand people dance below waving coconut palms and the warm open sky. The pulse of the music reaches me even at my great height, and I taste tendrils of narcotic-laced *smoke. Please don't let her be there; please let her be on the Phuket coast.* My husband comes to find me. When he looks into my face, the line between his eyebrows becomes a canyon. "I can't breathe," I gasp. "Take me to the hospital."

♂ ♂ ♂

My daughter sends an e-mail across the world; as it races through fiber-optic and network cables at the speed of light, it emerges as a poem:

> I'll write more
> in a couple of days,
> Mama, but I wanted to tell you
> we're safe.
> There's been an earthquake
> and tidal wave here in Thailand,
> but we're okay.
> Just wanted to let you know
> so you don't worry. We left Phuket
> three days ago. For the Full Moon Party.
> I'll write more
> soon.
> Love ya.

♂ ♂ ♂

The next morning when I wake, my lungs are no longer full of water, no longer being crushed by a great weight. My husband turns on the television and we watch news footage of the ocean rising up and covering Phuket. I read the e-mail from my daughter over and over, letting its medicine soak into my mind, my heart. My daughter left the Phuket coast for the party before the earthquake struck. *She is safe*, I think with joy. *Blessedly, disobediently safe.*

Cathy Kozak

can i call you mom?

School was almost out for the year and my four kids were looking forward to summer break. For me, however, vacation just meant more work. Since my divorce five years earlier, I'd been a single parent to my four kids. I lived in Kansas and their father lived in Florida, but he may as well have lived in Fiji for all the help he was with the children.

One hot day, my oldest son, Paul, came tripping home from school with the sole of his sneaker about to fall off. As I watched him walking awkwardly up the driveway, I had a painful realization: I simply couldn't provide properly for my kids on my own. I was doing my best, but they deserved so much more. The flapping shoe wasn't a big deal by itself, but it was a warning flag I finally paid attention to. Since I was already working as hard as I could to give the kids what they needed, there was only one other option.

I phoned my ex-husband and asked if he would consider taking the two boys—Paul, eleven, and Anthony, eight—so that between our two homes the four children could all enjoy a better quality of life.

A week later, I did the hardest thing I had ever done: I drove my two sons to the airport and put them on a plane to Florida. For the sake of my boys I put on a cheerful mask, telling them how much fun they'd have living near the beach, visiting Disney World, and seeing their father more often. Yet all the while I felt as if my heart were going to explode inside my chest. I'd provided *everything* for them during the last five years, and sending them away was the loneliest failure imaginable.

I watched my sons walk side by side down the jetway, getting smaller and smaller. When they turned the final corner and were lost from sight, I staggered to a nearby chair and collapsed. My cheerful mask cracked and fell to the floor as sobs shook my body. But even as I wept, I knew I couldn't stay there. My girls were waiting for me. I cleaned up, drove home, and began the next stage of my life with a smile pasted on my face.

♂ ♂ ♂

The years apart from my sons were achingly hard. I still had my wonderful girls, but our family was smaller than it was meant to be. There were frequent moments of happiness, but no lasting joy. I missed the daily events that shaped the boys' lives in Florida: sleepovers, baseball playoffs, first dates, prom night. It was as if our family were a body, and when the boys moved to Florida we lost an arm and a leg. The girls and I staggered through life together, longing to be whole.

♂ ♂ ♂

Six years later, in 1992, my two boys moved back to Kansas. It was wonderful to have them home, yet something was missing. Even though we were together again, we couldn't make up for those six missing years.

Paul was only home briefly before enlisting in the Navy. He hoped to serve for several years, earn a degree at the University of Kansas, and then return to the Navy as an aviator. Coming from a military family, I supported his decision with all of my heart. I couldn't help feeling like I'd regained him only to lose him again, however.

Paul left home for service on the aircraft carrier USS *John F. Kennedy*, and I continued to do what my remaining three children needed me to as they navigated their turbulent teenage years. Then came the day every military family dreads. An officer stood on my porch, hat in hand, and informed me that Paul had died while on duty at Falon Naval Station in Nevada. When the officer left, I discovered there were no words left inside me. Pain was a ratchet that tightened down with a force I never knew was possible.

When eleven-year-old Paul flew away to Florida, I knew our relationship would never be the same. And when twenty-year-old Paul died, I knew I would never regain those missing years.

With two memorial services to attend for Paul, I struggled just to stay functional. In the midst of my fog of grief, a previous employer gifted me with a tree that I could plant in Paul's memory. I chose a hill outside the Military Science Building at the University of Kansas. Paul's request to transfer to college had been approved by the Navy, though he didn't live to fulfill that part of his dream.

The tree was planted, but I didn't have time to think much about it. With three other children needing me to be strong, I dug deep—and prayed that I'd have enough strength to make it through each day.

♂ ♂ ♂

I began to date Ken in 1999, when my three kids were out of the house and on their own. Ken had spent the better part of that decade raising four kids as a single dad. We lived several hours apart, and in order to see each other we took turns driving to each other's home. I happened to be at his house on New Year's Eve, 1999. After watching the fireworks on television, neither of us felt comfortable with me driving home because of the Y2K scare. Ken told me I could sleep in the bedroom of his youngest son, Donovan.

The next morning, I woke at 4:30 a.m. to what I am convinced was a message from God: *Look around this room.* As my eyes focused in the dim light, I could see basketball trophies, hand-drawn pictures, baseball posters, toys—all the things a normal boy of eleven would have in his room. Just as I began to wonder what I was supposed to be seeing, it hit me: a boy of *eleven*. I began to weep before the rest of the message arrived, telling me that I would marry Ken and become Donovan's mom.

Filled with a sense of joy that was like a combination of a warm blanket and angel's wings, I stepped into Ken's living room. Ken and Donovan were talking quietly, unaware of my presence. Our relationship was just beginning, and I kept my revelation to myself and waited. Everything would happen in the right time. The new millennium had just begun, and on that first day of January I knew a new season of my life was beginning, too.

Later that summer, just before Donovan began middle school, Ken and I were engaged. In September we were married, and I moved into a new house with my new husband and my new son.

♂ ♂ ♂

I would be lying if I said the transition was smooth. Donovan and I had our fair share—or maybe more than our fair share!—of altercations. Every time we disagreed or fought, the question arose: What possible blessing were Donovan and I to each other? It wasn't easy for him to accept me. After all, he had the volatile emotions of a teenager coupled with the stressful transition of having a step-mother around. But I continued to do what a mother does: I made cookies, cheered at his basketball games, pinned on his corsage on prom night, and made sure his laundry was picked up.

In other words, I did everything I never had a chance to do with Paul.

In 2006, Donovan sent me a letter from boot camp. He'd recently joined the Marines—a decision that was harder for Ken to accept than it was for me. Expecting that Donovan wanted to commiserate about the trials of boot camp with me, I opened the letter and began to read.

> Carla, I was thinking a lot before I left and since I've been
> here. I meant to say something before but didn't get the

chance. I've never really thanked you or told you how much I've appreciated you these past years.

You've been such a wonderful mother to me that I wish I could just call you Mom.

You do so much for me in a motherly manner that I've never had before, I didn't know how to respond. Basically you're amazing and I love you more than you can know. I can't wait to see you in three months and give you a big hug and say this in person.

Love, Donovan

I could hardly read the words for the tears in my eyes. I had been Donovan's mother ever since I married Ken, of course, but it had seemed through the taxing years that the affection was largely one-way. Now I knew otherwise. And in Donovan's asking to call me Mom, I saw the fulfillment of a promise made years before as I looked around his bedroom.

Donovan has since finished his four years in the Marines and is currently serving with peacekeeping forces in Kosovo. He plans to return to the States soon and move to Lawrence, Kansas, where he's been accepted as a freshman at the University of Kansas.

When he moves to Lawrence, I know I'll make the trip with him and help him unpack and settle in. I'm sure I'll give him a few more kisses and hugs than is seemly, and he'll smile, half with embarrassment and half with genuine affection. But after he's moved in, I'll have one more thing to do before I leave campus. I'll walk with Donovan to Paul's tree on the hill outside the Military Science Building and take a picture. Then I'll say a prayer of protection over the son who now calls me Mom, and a prayer of thankfulness for the years of love I've shared with all my children.

Carla Wicks

we love you

San Francisco, summer of 1967. Something new was in the air, a youth movement that seemed to be changing everything. I was fresh out of college and working downtown at the international headquarters of a bank in the engineering department, but the new music styles of electric guitars beckoned me to the Fillmore Auditorium and Haight-Ashbury, where the hippie revolution was blooming like a field of wildflowers. The more I hung out with these free-spirited folks, the more I realized that their lives were headed in a different direction than mine. While I was enmeshed in corporate competition and financial gain, they were chasing spirituality and community. And their *music*—I was an accomplished saxophone player, but my melodies had been silenced in the world of electrical engineering.

The hippies' quest awoke something at the core of my being, something that had been lying dormant beneath my pressed suit and well-shined shoes. I understood that there was more to my life than living and dying, more than trying to make it through another day just like the day before. I began hanging out with the hippies whenever I could, hoping to find what I was missing.

I found it one day on the radio. A Rolling Stones song came on called "We Love You," and as its lyrics washed over me a profound insight soaked into every part of my being: there is a love flowing through everyone and everything. *We love you. We love they.* Somehow, in the backseat of that car, listening to Jagger and Lennon and McCartney sing those mysterious lines as we cruised through the streets, I knew that the thread of God's love passed through us all.

I was so changed by the beauty of this experience that I decided to devote my life to seeking and trying to understand love and God. I quit my corporate job at the bank and started playing music again. In the following years, I played in some bands that were selling out concerts, like The Elvin Bishop Group and Sly and the Family Stone. I was living my dream.

But the hippie movement had a dark and decadent side, too. Even as I was selling records and making a name for myself, I was drawn to what proved to be the empty ideals of "free love" and illicit drug use. This led to a vicious spiral: the more women I was with and the more alcohol and drugs I used, the more I suffered—and the only way I knew to cope was to do more of the same.

My dysfunctional lifestyle hit rock-bottom one day. I'd had a child with a woman, and when she broke up with me and left with our child, I decided to end my life. The pain was simply too intense to medicate or dull any longer, and death seemed to be the only way out.

Without a plan yet for how to commit suicide, but preparing to do it soon, I found myself wandering through my old haunts. I drifted into Tower Records, and out of habit headed to the bin of 45s to check on my sales. There were hundreds and hundreds of records, all packed in tight rows so that their labels and titles couldn't be seen.

In that massive, multicolored stack of records, there was exactly *one* place where the pile was parted. My eyes were drawn to the record in that gap: "We Love You" by The Rolling Stones. Chills raced up and down my body as I stood in Tower Records, reading this message to me from God. I was loved, and I needed to live.

And I did. I lived past that night, that week, and that year. Because of that record-store miracle, I knew there were other things planned for me, and I wasn't willing to miss out on them. Since that day at Tower Records, I've been privileged to be a part of world-class bands, compose and record music for movies, perform on television shows, release CDs, and write many books. But as wonderful as all those opportunities have been, there is an even bigger reason I'm thankful to be alive: every day I live gives me another chance to discover more of the thread that unites us all and share my discoveries with others.

Dennis Marcellino

the magic of a sister

My younger sister, Meagan, was born with neonatal leuko-dystrophy, an irreversible condition in which portions of a baby's brain degenerate, resulting in progressive loss of strength, appetite, vision, and the ability to develop normally. Her prognosis was grim—but we didn't know precisely how grim until our younger brother, Jacob, was born with the same condition. I was only fourteen years old at the time, and I had to confront the fact that both of my siblings would likely die young.

Jacob lived to the age of two, as doctors predicted. Meagan, how-ever, continued to defy the odds, celebrating birthday after birthday. We knew she was sick, of course, but it began to seem that she might keep right on living. Even though her illness cast a shadow over our family life, there were still many moments of brightness.

When it came time for me to leave for college, I picked a school about an hour from my family in Colorado so I could get home quickly if need be. It wasn't only to be close for emergencies, either: I wanted to be a consistent part of Meagan's life, able to watch her grow up.

After I graduated from college, I grew restless. I decided to move to California and try to start a new life. Meagan was still living and growing; I couldn't stay at home my whole life, could I? Besides, I could always move back. I kissed my family good-bye, whispered words of love in my ten-year-old sister's ear, and drove toward my new home beside the ocean. I told myself that if I was supposed to come home, my sister would send a sign.

The first sign arrived shortly after I settled in California. A longtime friend from back home called me to say she was expecting a baby. I longed to be near her through her pregnancy, but I told myself it wasn't a sufficient reason to move home.

The second sign came later that same week—on September 11, 2001. As I watched the Twin Towers crumble, I knew in my heart that I should move home. I sensed the impermanence of life in a way that cut to my soul. I decided nothing was more important than living near my family.

Back in Colorado, I moved in with my pregnant friend and got a job with a company that provided in-home caregivers to sick patients. I had a single client: my sister, Meagan.

In the weeks and months that followed, I spent every day with my favorite person in the world. Together, Meagan and I planned her upcoming eleventh birthday party. We traced her hand with markers on bright stationery and sent personalized invitations to all our friends and family. It was going to be the biggest bash she'd ever had.

The morning of her party, Meagan became very sick. My parents and I discussed whether to cancel the evening's festivities. We sensed that Meagan might be nearing the end of her time on earth, and we wanted to give her friends and family a chance to say goodbye. So we went ahead with our plans.

It was heartbreaking to open the door to guest after guest, their faces alight with joy, and tell them the birthday girl wasn't doing well. Sadness overtook the day like waves washing over sandcastles at the seashore. But each guest put on a brave smile and came inside to offer Meagan words of love and appreciation. Perhaps we party best when we understand what we might lose.

Late that evening, after the final guest had departed, I walked quietly to my little sister's side. I enfolded her in my arms and whispered our favorite song, "You Are My Sunshine," in her ear. "You'll never know," I sang to her, my voice thick with love, "how much I love you."

It's okay if you need to leave us, I told her. You're going to be okay. We're all going to be okay.

Early the next morning, while it was still dark, my phone rang. My sister had died during the night, my mother told me.

I wondered if Meagan knew, somehow, that I needed to be home with her. Had she called me back to Colorado so I could care for her during those magical, final months? So we could say good-bye?

◊ ◊ ◊

Several years later, I was engaged to my future husband. I knew I needed to face my fears and have genetic testing done. I had to find out whether I was carrying the same abnormal genes that had struck Jacob and Meagan.

I was.

My husband's test, however, was inconclusive. This meant we had no definitive way of knowing whether our children—should we choose to have children—might be struck with neonatal leukodystrophy. After an exhausting season of prayer and searching, we decided to trust that our love could bear the weight of whatever happened.

Ten months later we were pregnant, and nine months after that I gave birth to a daughter, Adalayde Jane. She is the textbook definition of health.

When I hold Adalayde Jane in my arms, I often think of my sister, Meagan, and the years I spent watching out for her. Now I know she is watching out for me—and for her niece. When I sing "You Are My Sunshine" to Adalayde Jane, I picture Meagan listening with a beautiful smile, and singing along.

Christina Newell

not by accident

A small town on the interstate in South Carolina was our chosen rendezvous. My sister was driving up from Florida with our mother, and my husband and I were driving down from North Carolina to meet them. We were looking forward to bringing Mom back to spend a few months with us.

When it was time to leave, my husband, Jerry, and I filled our travel mugs with coffee, climbed into our minivan, and headed down the highway.

I was driving, which I always do; Jerry lost his vision to diabetes years ago. About twenty minutes into our trip, we were on the outskirts of Charlotte on Interstate 485. As I scanned the road in front of us, I noticed two things. The first was a flock of Mylar balloons drifting across the sky. There were dozens of them shining in the sunlight, and after I described what I was seeing to Jerry, I quipped that someone's wedding or anniversary party was going to be without balloons that day. The second thing I noticed was that the brake lights ahead of us were beginning to wink on and off like Christmas lights. I wasn't the only one watching the balloons—a so-called gawkers' block was developing.

I tried to keep my eyes on the road, even as I continued to sneak quick glances at the balloons. Suddenly the brake lights on the small car in front of me lit and stayed lit—and seconds later the car smashed into the back of the small truck in front of it, destroying its hood and front fenders.

I instinctively slammed on my own brakes, quickly checking to my right and left to see if I could swerve into another lane. No luck. We were slowing, but would it be in time?

"What's going on?" my husband asked, bracing himself against the sudden deceleration.

"We're going to hit her, we're going to hit her!" I cried as I continued to mash the brake pedal to the floor. The small car in front of us had rotated slightly after mangling its front end on the truck, and both the truck and the car were stopped. A moment later, we came to an abrupt but smooth stop as well, thanks to our antilock brakes. Our coffee hadn't even spilled! At the instant we stopped, our front bumper lightly tapped the small car in front of us, like a quick kiss on the cheek after a first date.

In the sudden silence, I asked my husband if he was okay. "I'm fine," he said, "but what's wrong? What happened?" I briefly recounted what had happened. While I spoke, I saw the driver of the truck make his way to the shoulder. The woman in the car in front of us, however, remained in her vehicle. Was she injured? Unconscious? I told Jerry I would be right back and climbed out.

As I walked toward the driver's door of the small car, I could see her car was totaled. Through the window I glimpsed the woman still gripping her steering wheel tightly with both hands and staring straight ahead. She seemed frozen in shock.

I tapped on her window. "Are you okay? Miss, are you all right?" She slowly turned to look at me, and as she did her stoic mask dropped and she began to sob. Then she pulled her hands from the wheel and covered her face, still sobbing.

"Can you get out?" I asked. She pulled the handle on her door, but the crumpled metal only opened a few inches. Her whole body was shaking with violent sobs.

I walked to the other side of what used to be her car and tugged on the handle of the passenger door. It opened smoothly, and I leaned over into the car so I could see the woman's face. "Can you climb over here? Get your purse and come out on this side."

The distraught woman still didn't move. Instead she wailed, "What am I supposed to do? I've never been in an accident before!"

I glanced back at Jerry, still sitting safely in our van. Then I looked again at the woman. In a tone that I hoped sounded both firm and friendly, I said, "First you need to get out of this vehicle. Come on— I'll help you. Climb over. Bring your purse."

I took her hand and helped her crawl across the seat, and then I pulled her to her feet outside the passenger door. The whole time she was repeating, "I'm so sorry. I'm so sorry!"

I led her to the side of the road, and as we walked she blubbered, "I hope it's not too bad." Obviously she hadn't noticed that the front of her car looked like a wadded-up gum wrapper!

An off-duty police officer pulled up behind my van and switched his blue lights on. Then he hopped out and rapidly checked every- one for injuries, called the authorities, and collected our driver's licenses. The young woman blurted, "It was my fault—all my fault!"

I quickly cut her off. "Shh, dear, be quiet. Stop and think before you talk at the scene of the accident—everything you say is important." She nodded obediently, but by then she was shaking so badly that she couldn't stand on her own. I wrapped an arm around her to help support her.

The events of the next few minutes are familiar to anyone who's ever been in a traffic accident: I pulled our vehicle to the shoulder, the Highway Patrol took statements from us, First Responders cleared the debris from the highway, and a flatbed tow truck arrived. As we watched, the driver tried to decide how to lift what was left of her car onto his truck.

By then the young woman was making calls: her boss, her mother, a friend. As she dropped the phone into her pocket, she realized that

I was getting ready to help Jerry back into the van and leave. She wrapped both arms tightly around me. "Oh, thank you, thank you! I don't know what I would have done without you! I'm sorry you got in an accident, but I'm *so* glad you were here!"

While I hugged the young woman back, I realized something strange. Despite the delay and the fright and the hassle, I too was glad I'd been there. This was a new experience for me: being glad I was in a traffic accident! But it was almost as if I'd been that girl's guardian angel, placed there at just the right time to help her navigate a traumatic experience.

I will probably never see that young woman again, but the one time we met was the one time we needed to. I like to think that a kind person might stop to help my young daughter if she is ever in a similar accident. If so, I have a sneaking suspicion it will be someone like the young woman I helped: someone who understands the value of gentle words and a strong arm to lean on. Who knows? Perhaps it will even be a woman who was herself helped though a tight squeeze years before on I-485.

Jean Matthew Hall

katie's gift

*J*n 1985, Kathryn Alice Burchett was born into our family. We were overjoyed to welcome our first daughter into a home with two boys. My wife, Joni, and I had both secretly wanted a girl, and Katie's arrival thrilled us. She would be daddy's special girl and mommy's little partner.

We anticipated that she would light up our lives. What we couldn't know was that Katie's life would be both more tragic and more incredible than we could ever imagine.

The way the doctor announced Katie's birth told us something was very wrong. Whispered orders and urgent instructions flew around the delivery room. Moments later, our happiness was shattered by the knowledge that something was very wrong with our baby girl.

Katie had a terminal neural tube birth defect. Her condition, known as anencephaly, meant that her brain had not developed normally in the womb. A large portion of her brain was simply missing, and she was not expected to live beyond a few days. The delivery room doctor summed up Katie's condition in cold terminology: "Her condition is not compatible with life."

Not compatible with life? His words didn't make sense to us. The daughter we'd dreamed about was right there with us, alive.

Our shock and grief were as deep as they were sudden. Katie would never enjoy a normal life, even for the tiny number of days she was expected to live. There was no cure, no hope for even modest improvement. I still recall nearly every agonizing word I choked out as I relayed Katie's condition to our friends, family, and—most painfully of all—our two young sons. The day she was born, we had to start thinking about her death.

Katie would never open her eyes. She couldn't smile. She lacked the ability to regulate her own body temperature, so her room temperature had to be constantly monitored. Part of Katie's condition was an area of exposed tissue at the back of her skull that never healed and had to be covered regularly with sterile dressing.

Despite all this, Katie confounded the doctors by living. She refused to let go of life.

Joni's devotion to Katie shone like a beacon in those dark days. She insisted that we bring Katie home with us. I worried about the effect that caring for Katie at home might have on the boys. Truthfully, I was probably more concerned about the effect on *me*. But Joni would have it no other way, so I showed husbandly wisdom by agreeing to bring our daughter home.

Soon, little Katie had established her place in our family's routine. She responded to her mother's touch and learned to drink from a bottle. She even grew a little. We took her on a family camping trip. For one precious summer, Katie was a faithful fan at her older brothers' baseball games.

A lot of people, including some close friends and family, thought our decision to bring Katie home was a mistake. Some made hurtful remarks. A kid at school taunted our oldest son by saying his sister didn't "have a brain." (No doubt something the classmate had heard at home.)

One time we dressed up the troops and went to have family pictures taken, only to have the photographer insist that Katie open her eyes. Even when we explained that she physically could not open her eyes, he refused to take our picture; he argued that the lab would not develop any pictures in which eyes were closed.

One Sunday morning, a friend called to tell us that Katie wasn't welcome in the church nursery. The other moms feared that Katie might die in their care and traumatize a volunteer worker. They also worried that the opening at the back of Katie's skull might generate a staph infection. If they had come to us with their concerns, we might have been able to allay some of their fears. But the decision was made without our input, and we could no longer take our baby daughter to church.

When Katie was three months old, Joni decided she wanted to have another baby. I wasn't sure. What if the same birth defect manifested itself again? Even so, we decided to trust God, and soon Joni became pregnant. We celebrated Katie's first birthday at the end of Joni's second trimester, and just three months later a healthy baby boy joined our family. Katie couldn't see Brett, but she could feel his soft newborn skin.

Life grew even more hectic. My work as a television director required me to travel, and Joni was at home with Katie and three boys aged eight, five, and brand-new.

One evening in May 1986, Joni and I made plans to get away for an evening. We had a nurse come stay with Katie and Brett, and we took the older boys to a friend's house.

Late that night after picking up the boys, we pulled into our garage and started to get out of the car. Suddenly two men wearing black masks and brandishing guns burst into the garage, screaming at us not to move.

They forced us into the house. One of the gunmen held the boys, Joni, and the nurse at gunpoint. As Joni prayed fervently in the living room, I experienced a supernatural calm—believe me, it was not of my own doing. The leader walked me around the house and threatened to harm my family if I didn't reveal where things were stashed. He demanded cash and grew angry when I told him that all our money went to pay Katie's medical bills.

Our oldest son, Matt, heard the exchange. "Mr. Robber," he said, "you can have my piggy bank." They actually took it.

All the while, Katie slept quietly in her room. Both intruders seemed to be terrified of her. Perhaps they thought she had something contagious, since we had a nurse in the house. Whatever the reason, they steered a wide path around her room and never threatened her.

Before they left, the robbers forced us into a bedroom and jammed the door shut from the outside. But of course, the bedroom those rocket scientists locked us in shared a common bathroom with Katie's room. As soon as they left I went through Katie's room and outside to my car phone (they had cut our phone lines) to call the police.

Soon the ordeal was over, and we began to regain some of the calm that Katie never lost. Some of our possessions had been taken, but the things that matter most to a family—our lives, our love, and our hope—remained beyond the grasp of the thieves. Aside from some tough talk and waving pistols, they didn't harm us in any way. It was as if they were operating under a "steal but do not assault or maim" directive. We found out later that the two gunmen did far worse things to other victims before they were caught, including sexual assault. We were the exception, and I'm convinced that Katie's presence spared our family of those terrors.

Some people wonder about Katie's purpose in living fourteen months, since every medical opinion maintained she would die within a few days of birth. In my heart I'm persuaded that there are many reasons our baby girl stayed with us for so long, reasons bigger than I will ever comprehend fully.

But I will always be convinced that Katie lived as long as she did for two particular reasons. First, so that her brother Brett could join us and for a season we could be a whole family. Even though it was short, we will treasure that time for as long as we live. And second, to be our guardian angel during that robbery. Katie's severe physical abnormality, coupled with her almost otherworldly serenity, so unnerved the robbers that they abandoned their hyperviolent pattern of behavior.

Just weeks after the robbery, Katie's heart began to fail. On June 4, 1986, on a warm summer morning, Katie died with her family at her side.

From the time she was born Katie could never smile; her only facial expression was a tiny frown or grimace. But when Katie's life began to ebb away, a feeling of peace entered the room like a comforting breeze. As her courageous spirit finally left her tiny body, a wide smile lit her face for the first time. I will always believe her smile was a response to the heavenly escort whispering, "Well done, little one. It's time to come home."

Dave Burchett

kyle's legacy

*I*t was late summer in Atlanta, Georgia. Outside, the night sounds of distant traffic and droning cicadas filled the darkness. My three grown kids all lived in different cities, and I was living by myself. It was a night like any other.

A knock suddenly woke me from a deep sleep. *There is no way I'm going downstairs to get that,* I told myself. *It's probably just some neighborhood kids playing ding-dong-ditch.* In the silence that followed, my mind began to play tricks on me, and a spark of fear flared in my heart.

After several minutes, even as my fear continued to grow, I decided I was being silly and selfish. What if one of my friends was in trouble and needed my help? I climbed out of bed, hunted down my cell phone, and tapped it on.

Three new messages.

Two were from my daughter and one from my cousin; all instructed me to call my daughter right away. I punched in the numbers, and her words fanned my spark of fear into a blaze.

"Mom, are you alone?"

It was a strange question that did nothing to calm my fear; she knew I lived alone, and it was the middle of the night.

"Mom, I'm really sorry you're alone—but Kyle is dead."

The words every mother dreads seemed to stop my heart. A wave of shock instantly flooded me, washing away fear, pain, confusion—everything. I was entirely numb.

"He died of a heroin overdose. Kyle was with his friends, and this afternoon they found him dead. The police and coroner couldn't find your contact information, so they came to me."

The silence of the house was overwhelming. I could feel my heart beating again, but why couldn't I feel anything else? Kyle *couldn't* be dead from a heroin overdose—he was always so scared of that stuff. There must have been a mix-up, a mistake.

"Mom. Mom, I'm so sorry."

♂ ♂ ♂

By the next morning I was flying across the country, back to my hometown. I would try to console my other children and the rest of my family, try to learn what had led to my son's death—and most difficult of all, I would try to step into the coroner's office and identify Kyle.

As the miles passed below me, one question ran through my mind over and over: *What on earth happened?* Kyle was a delight from the day he was born. He was beautiful and kindhearted, equally likely to tease me or to pull me into a hug. Kyle loved guitar jam-sessions with his brother and sister, and sports and campouts and picnics had always filled his life with laughter and adventure. Recently he'd even moved back home with family. He was saving money so that he could visit a locally sponsored school in Uganda; he had expressed interest in spending extended time there helping however he was needed.

Even as I moved through the next several days on autopilot—visiting the coroner's office, meeting with my family, planning the memorial service, viewing Kyle's body and saying good-bye to him, picking out the casket, preparing to speak at the funeral—the seed of a passion took root in my heart.

I spoke about Kyle five times in the month following his death: at his memorial service, to my church's youth group, once at the high school, and twice at the middle school. Each time I spoke, I sensed that there was nothing more important I could be doing than using Kyle's death to try to save other lives.

After each session, I met with kids who knew Kyle and were reeling from his death. *If it could happen to Kyle, it could happen to me,* they seemed to be thinking. During the honest and heart-wrenching talks I had with kids and parents, one theme played constantly in the background: a lot of great kids are living dangerously, and their friends are keeping it secret. Any of Kyle's friends who were with him that fateful night could have saved his life, but a kind of unspoken pact silenced each of them. Kids tell themselves they're being a good friend by keeping their mouths shut, and no one wants to be a pest or a snitch. Yet sometimes silence is deadly.

As this passion—some might call it a calling—took hold of my heart, I began to understand that Kyle's story could serve as a wake-up call. It would challenge kids to break the code of silence and get help for their friends. That's how Just1x (Just One Time) came to be. The program isn't just about confronting students who are living dangerously—involved with alcohol, drugs, sex, eating disorders, cutting, and so on. It's also about challenging the people who *know* good kids living dangerously to get help for their friends.

Speaking for Just1x is never easy. In front of strangers across the country, I play the actual 911 call from my son's death. Not a single day passes that I don't miss Kyle desperately. Losing him is the hardest thing that has ever happened to me. But I was able to see very quickly that his death didn't have to be repeated in other lives. Just1x is Kyle's legacy. It makes losing him just a little bit easier, and it makes choosing life just a little bit more important.

I was his mother—the one who watched over him and kept him safe—but throughout his life Kyle was always *my* fierce protector. Now his story is helping to protect others, and for that I will be forever grateful.

Penny Whipps

Lemon Drop

I went for a long motorcycle ride after my nephew Kyle's memorial service, and as I rode, I did some soul searching. I felt guilty about not always loving Kyle and his friends enough. I felt like I'd sort of folded my arms across my chest in disapproval instead of giving those guys a bear hug of acceptance. Now, through Just1X, Penny Whipps opens her arms every day to hundreds of hurting kids. That's just one of many reasons I'm so proud of my little sister. —Don

finishing well

The Pacific Crest Olympic Triathlon, held every year in central Oregon, may not be the famous Ironman Triathlon in Hawaii, but it's plenty difficult: roughly a mile-long swim, a twenty-eight-mile bike ride, and a six-mile run. Thousands of athletes from across the country gather to compete for course records, cash prizes, and trophies.

I wasn't "in it to win it," but finishing *was* a big deal to me. This particular race was on my bucket list, and I was doing everything I could to get ready for it. Plus, my friend Joel—who lived two hundred miles away—had signed up, too. We promised to cybertrain together in the months leading up to the triathlon.

As race day drew closer, it seemed like I was training constantly: running and swimming on my lunch break, biking in the evenings, hitting the gym when I could. I was determined to finish the triathlon, even if the thought of three and a half hours of intense racing made my stomach twist itself in knots. This race wasn't going to beat *me*. No way, no how.

Before I knew it, race day had arrived. Joel and I had trained as hard as we could, and now our efforts would be put to the test. We were ready: legs marked with our race numbers, wetsuits zipped, goggles tightened and checked. I was in a starting group before Joel's, but we planned to meet up after the finish and compare stories.

And then—almost before I knew what was happening, the starting gun went off.

The swim felt good. I paced myself well over the nearly one-mile course, and emerged from the cold water right on schedule. I located my bike, shook off a cramp, gulped some energy gel, and hit the pavement spinning.

As I rolled through beautiful mountain passes dotted with thick stands of ponderosa and juniper, I let myself relax. I was doing great, and with less than half the bike leg to go, the steepest section of the course was already behind me.

That's when the pedal fell off my bike and clanked across the pavement behind me. Since when do pedals fall off bikes? I braked to a stop and tried to think. A few turns of my Allen wrench and I had the pedal reattached. That was easy! I hopped back on and began to pedal, only to discover that I'd put the pedal on crooked. Now one of my legs was bowed, and I felt like a clown on a mini-bike.

I wasn't going to ride the next ten miles like *that*, so I stopped once again and reattached the pedal. This time I aligned it correctly, and I was on my way. Until it fell off again half a mile later. Seriously? A spectator helped me fix the pedal, while I repeated through frustrated tears, "I just want to finish the race!"

Repair completed, I remounted my bike and began to ride. I tried to compose myself. I still had a race to finish, and I'd known it wouldn't be easy. Things began looking up—until my pedal fell off again one mile later.

That's when I realized this wasn't going to be the race I wanted; it was going to be the race I was given, and I had to choose whether to accept that. I'll be honest—it seemed like a lousy gift!

Over the next ten miles my pedal fell off eight times, giving me plenty of chances to become proficient at putting it back on. I began to feel like one of those NASCAR pit crews who can swap four tires in five seconds flat.

With two miles to go, the pedal fell off for the final time. I could tell it wouldn't go back on for anything. Was this the inglorious end to my hard-fought race? All I'd wanted was to finish, and now it looked like not even that would be possible.

But this was my big race, and I wasn't dead yet. I hopped off and ran the final two miles of the bike leg, clomping along in my bike shoes and wheeling my now useless bike beside me. At the bike/run transition area, I ginned up a bit of hope. I still had it in me to keep going, despite being forty-five minutes behind my target time.

As I ran, I started to savor the atmosphere. The route was lined with cheering spectators who sprayed the runners with refreshing water pistols. Children ran alongside the course, giggling and clapping. Someone even offered me a beer! I knew that the finish line was getting closer with every stride, but I also felt fatigue creeping into my arms and legs. *Almost there,* I told myself.

With only half a mile to go, I looked ahead, aching to see the Finish banner arching overhead. Instead—and I had to blink hard to make sure that in my weariness I wasn't imagining things—I saw my training buddy, Joel!

Somehow, among the thousands of racers and across the more than thirty miles we'd raced—or jogged while pushing a bike, in my case!—we'd been reunited just before the end. I was so happy to see him that I forgot how tired I was. We ran the final section together, side by side, and crossed the finish line to the proud cheers of our friends and family.

As I devoured a post-race feast of Red Vines, pretzels, pasta, fruit, and bagels, I realized I could already look back and laugh. I was delighted to be wearing my finisher's T-shirt—doubly delighted, in fact, because I'd finished such a different race than the one I'd set out to accomplish.

I guess that's what life is about: learning how to handle mid-race changes and finding help along the way. It helps if the pedal doesn't fall off your bike, but for most of us, at some point it will! When it does, I discovered, you have to finish the race you've been given—not the one you *wish* you were in. And the finish line? It's even sweeter if you cross it with a friend.

Dana Jones

june
bug

The year was 1993, and I was on the prowl at the University of South Carolina. I had everything I needed for a good time: youthful energy, a healthy appetite for self-indulgence, decent looks, and off-the-charts charisma. My entire life was about the next hookup, the next party, the next way to prove I was living the dream. I was racing down the highway, but I was less worried about where I was going than how fast I could get there. Faster was always better.

One summer while I was working as a lifeguard, two coworkers introduced me to a stunning coed. Her looks blew my mind, and all I could think about was how to impress her. So of course on our first date I started leaping over parking meters downtown.

Now I've got to warn you: there are some gory details ahead, but stick with me—it's a story worth hearing.

So I was leaping parking meters, and my date was laughing, and all was going well—except that I didn't see the No Parking sign on the other side of the final parking meter. I hit its thin, metal edge with my legs splayed, instantly slicing open my scrotum. (Told you things would get gory.) There I was, writhing on the sidewalk in front of my date. Let's just say she wasn't very impressed.

If you want to know how dumb I was during those years, this will tell you everything: a minute later I got up, kept drinking, and acted like nothing had happened. Party on!

The next morning I woke up with a lightning storm of a hangover. That was par for the course. What was out-of-bounds was the bloody, black-and-blue slash between my legs. Turns out I hadn't dreamed the part about doing the splits on sharp metal the night before. Even in my sorry state, I realized I had two choices: treat it like a simple cut that would heal on its own; or call my dad, tell him about my stupidity, and ask him to take me to the hospital.

You can probably guess which option I chose.

That Saturday was pretty hellish, but I got through the day by pretending nothing was wrong. Night couldn't come fast enough, and I went to bed hoping that a good night's sleep would fix everything.

The next morning I could barely walk. Still, there was no way I was going to call my dad, so I limped to work at the pool. I consoled myself that at least I could remain stationary all day—I was scheduled to guard a group of chaperoned eighth graders learning to swim in a three-foot-deep pool.

An hour into my shift—an hour that felt like ten as I tried to ignore the waves of agony radiating from my crotch—a five-foot eighth grader decided to stop swimming halfway across the pool. He sank straight to the bottom and did a credible impression of a drowning victim.

I probably don't have to tell you what happened next. I was a world-champ egotist, and I suddenly recognized this as my chance to Save a Life and Be the Hero. The second I hit the water, my agony dial cranked up a few notches. The pool chemicals stung my open wound, but adrenaline carried me to the drowning boy's side in seconds. I reached underwater and pulled him to the surface. He was flailing and sputtering, and I could see his eyes were filled with terror. That's when he kicked me.

The next thing I knew, I was flopped in the locker room like a dead fish, and my coworker told me he needed to examine my you-know-whats. Then his face went whiter than a sheet—he looked like he was going to vomit. I propped myself on my elbows and looked down. What I saw was psychologically scarring: my testicles had retreated into my body, leaving a flat flap of ragged skin that used to be my scrotum.

Okay, if you've made it this far, that's as gross as things get. When I saw the shape I was in, even I knew it was time to call my dad and head to the hospital.

Three different doctors gave me three different opinions. The first told me I would lose both my testicles and never have children. Needless to say, I requested a second opinion. The second doctor told me I'd definitely lose the right one, and I would probably never have kids. And the third doctor—hey, it never hurts to ask—told me they *might* be able to save my right testicle, and I'd probably never have kids.

♂ ♂ ♂

I wish I could tell you that my forty hours of hell turned my life around, but that would be a lie, and I try not to do that anymore. In fact, the opposite happened. Once I healed, the thought occurred to me: If I can't have kids, I can be even *less* responsible about hooking up!

So that's what I did. I spent the next seventeen years doing absolutely nothing productive with my life. You would *not* have wanted to know me.

Now, flash forward to the end of that debauchery. I was thirty-four when I got a call from a woman I'd been with a while back. She told me that five weeks earlier she'd given birth to a baby girl. She figured that since I was the father, I'd want to know.

Screeeeeech! The car of my life had been careening ahead, and now I had whiplash. I said three words to myself that I never thought I'd say: *I'm a father!*

So my daughter came to live with me. At night, I'd place her on the bed next to me. It was summertime, and the evenings were warm. She'd sleep there on her back, her knees pulled up to her chest just like a bug. I'd lean over and touch her tiny fist with my pinky, and she'd grab my finger in her sleep and coo.

I was no longer in bed with my latest fling every night, but with my baby daughter. I had a lot of time to think. And I realized that whatever else happened, we were in this together, me and my June Bug.

♂ ♂ ♂

It wasn't an instant turnaround. It took four years for June Bug and me to pull the car off the highway to hell and start motoring down a different road.

But I know there's no going back. That old me-first highway is closed forever. After all, I can't think as much about what *I* want when forty pounds of high-energy craziness is drawing on the wall with her crayons! Or when it's just the two of us, snuggled up before bed, and she asks for one more story.

June Bug is five now, and I've had plenty of time to reflect on my wild youth. I've come up with a formula that describes my life before thirty-four: $D = (Y*C)^2$. That stands for Disaster equals Youth times Cockiness, squared. It's a wonder I didn't screw things up even more, given that in my youth I possessed more than my fair share of cockiness.

I'm starting to rework this formula; I decided that those first three decades don't determine the rest of my life. For way too long I was flying down the straight and narrow—problem was, that road went the wrong direction, and the only place I was speeding toward was nowhere.

Then one summer day my sweet little June Bug crawled into my life. Now the road ahead is full of curves and detours. And what I'm learning—what my darling daughter teaches me every day—is that those winding country roads are where real life happens. The highway doesn't offer much by way of a view; it's on the scenic route you see everything worth seeing. So now I just roll down the window and enjoy the ride, with June Bug at my side.

James Scott Hensley

empty
coke
bottles

om and Dad tolerated what they thought of as my strange and unnecessary affection toward the poor. I'd chat with the down-and-out that frequented our street and try to get them some food or cash or a blanket whenever I could. But when rugged men from the squatter's camps started hanging out in our neighborhood, my parents urged me to be more careful. With so many new beggars around, my parents thought that my acts of mercy would make our house a target for troublemakers—or worse. Post-apartheid South Africa was free, but it was also chaotic.

One summer morning, the typical sounds of neighborhood life floated through the window: birds wrestling for seed out back, dogs barking in the street, and kettles signaling that the morning caffeine was nearly ready. My Saturday was brimming with possibilities, and I had only one tiny chore. My father planned on spending most of his day reading and smoking his favorite Camel cigarettes, much to the disgust of my mother, and it was my job to fetch the paper and bring it to him.

As soon as I heard the delivery motorcycle, I headed outside toward the front gate. Swinging it open on rusty hinges, I tasted the acrid smoke of the motorcycle's exhaust as it sped to the next home. I grabbed the paper and some mail out of the box and turned to go back inside. My chore was already halfway finished, and the rest of the day would be mine.

"Please, boss. Please."

The pitiful voice came from a man crouched in the shade of a scraggly oak tree. His lips were cracked and raw and his stooped shoulders told me he'd spent many years paying a cruel tax collector named Poverty. I stopped, newspaper and mail in hand, and looked into his eyes.

"Please help me."

His eyes were desperate, and they seemed as deep and dark as a mine shaft. I hesitated. My father's words came into my head— *Don't pay attention to beggars outside our house, Luke, for it will only bring us problems*—as I stared at the man beneath the tree. Dad's wasn't the only voice I heard in my head; similar advice from my pastor and friends and church came to mind. I should mumble an apology and move on. This man was probably more trouble than he was worth.

The voices in my head seemed to be talking about beggars in general, yet here in front of me was this *particular* beggar, this man speaking directly to me through his cracked and raw lips. He was in anguish, and he was pleading with me to help.

Just as I was about to tell him that I had nothing to offer, I heard a new voice in my head, strong as thunder and lovely as a field dressed in wildflowers. *He raises the poor from the ashes and seats them with princes; he upholds the cause of the oppressed and gives food to the hungry, setting them free.* That new voice was like a rushing river filling an ocean of hope, and I suddenly knew what to do.

I crouched down beside the man. "I don't have money," I told him, "but I can bring you food and water." My words kindled light in his eyes. As I jogged back to the house, I ransacked my mind for ways to help him. Food was easy: oranges, pears, apples, bananas, and a loaf of bread, along with some bottled water. But what else could I do? I glanced through the doorway at Dad's desk, which often had spare change scattered across the surface, but then it was empty. Still thinking, I struggled out the front door carrying two full shopping bags.

The sun glinting off an empty Coke bottle distracted me. As it shone through the thick glass, the sunlight painted the wall of our house with tiny rainbows. There were six more Coke bottles collecting dust on the patio, and each one would fetch a redemption value at the local market. Knowing they would be hard for the beggar to carry, I snatched my sister's backpack and piled the empty bottles into it. Something about their ordinariness inspired me, and I thought of all the ways that a small amount of faith can yield a bountiful harvest.

I opened the front gate and knelt at the man's side. I asked him his name, and then I asked Henry if I could pray with him. He seemed delighted, so I placed my open palm on his chest, over his heart. "God," I prayed, "you own the cattle on a thousand hills. Provide a job for Henry, restore his life, and give him money. Lots of it."

I opened my eyes to see Henry watching me, and smiling. I gave him the bags of food and the backpack of empty Coke bottles, reminding him that he could cash them in at Eric's Deli and get enough money to eat that night. I watched him shuffle painfully down the street, stooped beneath his new burdens, before I turned back to my house.

I was vaguely disappointed. It was great that Henry had provisions for a few days. But soon he'd be fighting the same battle all over again. I'd half expected the empty bottles to turn into gold, or for coins to start shooting out of my ears. But that hadn't happened, and now Henry was gone from my life.

◌ ◌ ◌

"Luke! Wake up, Luke! Someone's at the gate for you! Get out of bed!"

Mom's voice shocked me from sleep at six the next morning. What in the world was she talking about?

"An old man has been yelling for you at the front gate for the last ten minutes. Get *up!*"

Somehow I knew it was Henry. I raced out the door half-dressed and sprinted to the front gate. I saw Henry on the other side, jumping up and down. A grin lit his face.

"Boss Luke, I have some wonderful news! Wonderful news!"

I flung open the gate and we stood eye to eye. His story came tumbling out so fast that I could scarcely understand his words.

"After you prayed for me yesterday I went right to Eric's to swap those heavy bottles for money. Just as I was leaving, an *umlungu** tapped me on my back. He was so excited to see me. I recognized him because he had a nose I could never forget: it was my old boss from five years ago when I worked at the West Bank power plant."

I had no idea where his story was going, but he was so happy that I begged him to continue. "Your old boss? What did he want?"

Henry continued. "Five years ago I hurt my legs at work and the company forced me to leave. The insurance promised a payout, but after two years of fighting I gave up. That's when I had to move to the streets."

Henry became even more excited, practically hopping up and down. "Then my old boss Clive told me the insurance came through, and I could collect $3000!"

I could hardly believe what I was hearing. *Three thousand dollars from a bunch of bottles?*

Henry's voice softened, and his eyes became moist. "Boss Luke, I didn't know what to tell him. I fell to my knees and wept, thanking Jesus, while all the people in the store just stared at me. And then—"

---

* *Umlungu* is slang for a white person.

Henry's voice broke. He swallowed, smiled, and continued.

"—and then Clive told me there's a new job opening for me at the power plant. I could train people to do my old job, and I could sit in an office without hurting my legs. I'm going back to work!"

Henry's eyes were shining like diamonds as he finished his story. "Jesus saved me, boss, thanks to those empty Coke bottles and prayer!"

Both of us were crying by then, and we embraced each other. He began to sing an old African folk song of thanks to God, and I joined him. The fronts of our shirts were getting soaked with tears, but neither of us cared as we stood singing together in the street. Around us the neighborhood was waking up, and people were starting to stare. What was an old black bum doing singing with a white kid at six in the morning?

Only Henry and I knew what was really happening: we were giving thanks. Seven empty bottles had become a new life for this broken-down man, and neither Henry nor I would ever doubt again that God can use the smallest, driest vessel to provide life-giving water when it's needed most.

Luke Beling

yellow is the color of love

I knew Daddy was real sick. I was fifteen, so Mama and Daddy were trying to put on a brave front. I could tell, though. Cancer had made his body rail-thin, and every day when Mama and I visited he seemed even weaker. But he always made an effort for me.

Daddy called me his Baby Doll. He tried to sit up and tell me jokes and stories, but the radiation made him groggy. Not even the fresh flowers he loved—bunches of irises, or yellow roses, or gerbera daisies—could cheer up that room. I couldn't understand what was happening. How did my strong Daddy wind up in that hospital bed?

Being adopted by Mama and Daddy was the best thing that had ever happened to me, and I couldn't cope with this. My emotions were like a ticking bomb, and one day they just…exploded. I couldn't sit around watching my father die! So I ran away from home.

I was gone two days—two days away from Daddy's side, during which time my every thought was about him. I finally decided to return. I had to get back to the hospital. He needed me. Without going home, I went straight to Daddy's room, not knowing what to expect.

His hospital room was stark and smelled like disinfectant. Surrounding his bed were my aunts. They all stopped talking when I entered, and I noticed then that my father was sitting up in bed. He was smiling. My aunts stepped back as I walked forward. I began to cry as I leaned over my father and kissed his hairless head.

"Daddy, I'm so sorry for hurting you. I'm back, Daddy."

He strained with the effort of wrapping his thin arms around me. In my ear he whispered, "Baby Doll, I love you. I forgive you, and I'll always love you, no matter what." I cried into my father's neck, and felt the almost childlike weight of his arms on my back. When I felt his body shift, I pulled away gently from his embrace. As I wiped snot and tears from my face with the back of my hand, I saw that he was looking out the window beside his bed. He raised his arm and pointed.

"What is it, Daddy?"

"See there, Baby Doll?"

I looked outside the window and saw only the parking lot. "Where, Daddy?"

"Outside the window." He smiled. "Angels. Waiting for me."

♂ ♂ ♂

Two days later, Mama and I buried Daddy. We stood side by side in front of his casket. Atop it was a spray of roses, their petals the color of spring sunshine.

♂ ♂ ♂

The pain of losing my father darkened everything. I began to rebel, no longer caring what my future would look like. I became depressed, cut off all contact with my friends, and refused to go to school.

The one-month anniversary of his death was approaching, and it was the same date my parents had adopted me. When Daddy was alive, he threw a party every year on that date to celebrate. There would be no more parties; that day would forever after be a day of mourning.

I stayed away from Mama. I tried to keep so busy that I wouldn't have time to think or feel.

On the morning of the one-month anniversary, I was sitting alone in my room when Mama knocked on the door and asked if she could come in. We had barely spoken since Daddy died.

"What do you want?" I asked, my voice filled with anger.

She stood still. Her eyes were the only part of her that moved, and she searched my face for a long moment. "I thought we could ride to the cemetery today."

I wanted to scream. But a tiny part of me realized that Mama needed to go, and that realization made me understand that *I* needed to go, too. I needed to see my Daddy. I stood from my bed and crossed the space between me and my mother. I hugged her tightly, and then we walked slowly to the car.

On the drive to the cemetery, Mama stopped at the florist's shop. I looked at her, puzzled. "Your daddy left something for you," she said. "Go inside, and I'll wait here."

Inside, I told the woman at the counter my name. She walked into the back room and returned with a bouquet. It was one dozen yellow roses, and a card was attached. With shaking fingers, I opened the card. It was a small square of paper, but it contained the world, wrapped for me and written in my father's script:

> Baby Doll,
> I'm no longer with you on earth,
> but remember I'm always in your heart.
> I love you.
> Daddy

♂ ♂ ♂

Recently, as I was admiring a fresh-cut yellow rose, a friend asked me, "Why do you love yellow roses so much, when your favorite color is purple?"

I brought the flower to my nose and breathed deeply. "Because," I said breathing again, "yellow is the color of love."

Debra Elliott

the gunshot that changed my life

*L*ate afternoon sunlight colored Rosalyn Lake copper. This far east of Portland, Oregon—twenty miles or so—I could almost imagine I was out in the Canadian wilds where I grew up and worked as a logger. In Portland I was in commercial construction, and at age twenty-four I never tired of spending every day outside. I figured I'd be working outside the rest of my life, enjoying the unique satisfaction that comes from making a living in the open air.

Work was the farthest thing from my mind that chilly November afternoon, however. I was there for the mallards.

My decision to hunt was impulsive. I'd had a new stock put on my shotgun, and I wanted to try it out. My wife, Brenda, and I had invited some friends over to find out who shot J. R. Ewing on *Dallas*. I had a couple of hours to kill before they arrived, so I stuffed a few shells in my jeans, whistled my dog Big Boy into the car, and took off without thinking to tell Brenda where I was going. I'd never hunted Rosalyn Lake before, but I knew I'd be back in time.

As I circled the lake, Big Boy whined and plunged in and out of the water. Eagerness is a fine trait in a gun dog, to a point, but a retriever needs to learn to hold still as a statue until the time comes to bring back the game. Ducks can spot any movement—and when they do, the hunter won't spot the ducks again. I whispered sharply to Big Boy, urging him to stay still. I kept my eye on a pair of ducks, sure they would be spooked by my dog before they were within range.

Behind me, Big Boy refused to settle down. Foolishly, I grabbed my gun in one hand like a tennis racket and made an impulsive sweep behind me, hoping to scare my dog into silence.

I learned later that a cross-threaded screw in my new stock gave way and allowed the trigger guard to depress the trigger. At that moment, a stunning burst of sound shattered the stillness. It felt like a gigantic fist slamming into my body, just above my right hip. I was hurled into the water. As I crashed into the shallows, an unthinkable realization burst across my consciousness.

I've shot myself.

I should have died about ten seconds later.

When a twelve-gauge shotgun fires a single shell loaded with #4 shot, it projects 150 lead pellets in a slowly expanding cloud. At forty or fifty yards, the pellets fan out to cover an area ten feet across, but at close range all of the destructive power is packed into a nearly solid mass that will tear a fist-sized hole in almost anything. The human body is no exception, and such a hole was now blasted into my right side.

Incredibly, the shot didn't go all the way through my body. The mass of lead pellets pummeled its way inside, tearing away muscles, nicking one kidney, and damaging my liver. It missed my spine, however, and there was no exit wound, through which I surely would have quickly bled to death.

That was why I was still alive, and able to think.

It was also why I was still able to feel pain, and the pain was indescribable. The doctors later told me that one pellet was carried by my bloodstream completely through the chambers of my heart and into one of my lungs. I was in such agony that I became nauseated and unable to breathe. At that point I pleaded: *God, if you're going to take me home, do it quick—or else help me with this pain!* The moment that thought left my heart, the pain lessoned just enough that I could bear it. I took that as a sign that God was with me, and I might actually make it back home.

Trouble was, I was still lying in cold water as night fell, and I had a giant hole in my right side and massive internal damage. I tried to fire the three-shot SOS signal that hunters use in emergencies, but my sluggish reload of my two-barrel gun made it impossible. I tried to stand, but my right leg gave out. I dragged myself out of the water before trying to stand again, but all I could manage was an agonizing crawl.

Somehow I kept crawling until I reached a tree. Big Boy stayed with me, puzzled and troubled, and for the first—and only—time in his life, my rambunctious dog lay down quietly beside me. I collapsed beneath the tree, watching the light fade from the sky. A pale moon glowed above the dark waters of the lake, and I could feel the temperature dropping. How long did I have? I knew people would start looking for me soon, but they didn't know where I was. I thought of how much I loved Brenda, and promised myself that I would hang on until morning—with God's help and Big Boy's warmth.

By eleven-thirty that night there were many people looking for me, but a thick fog was rolling in as well, blotting out the moonlight.

By midnight friends and family had searched all my usual hunting spots without success. Brenda's father, in an effort to distract her, suggested she search Rosalyn Lake, even though I never hunted there. Along with Eric and Jeri, the two friends we'd invited that night, Brenda eased the car through the dense fog. Suddenly something glimmered in the darkness: my car. Eric leaped from the car and shouted my name at the top of his lungs.

Incredibly, I was still conscious, but my throat was almost too dry to speak. I sucked water from my parka and, using the last of my strength, gasped out a reply and a faint whistle—and those desperate sounds managed to reach Eric's sharp ears.

The moment I saw Eric's form emerge through the mist was the moment I stopped my slow descent into death. The rest of the night was a series of small miracles that I'll never be able to explain or forget.

Brenda and our friends found a farmhouse and called the local volunteer fire department. As an ambulance raced to the scene, my body temperature dropped to ninety-four degrees. I was carried out of the woods and a medical helicopter was called. Despite the dense fog, it found a place to land near the lake—a marvel that would be repeated at the hospital when the briefest of holes opened in the fog above the helipad.

Finally, as day began to break, I emerged from surgery. For the first time Brenda cried, perhaps aware—now that I was expected to survive—of what she'd nearly lost.

Today I can walk, take my horses into the mountains, and even ride my mountain bike in the beautiful high desert of central Oregon where I live. But something was taken that day on the shore of Rosalyn Lake: never again would I be able to earn a living with the strength of my body. As I recovered after the accident, I felt a sense of loss, as if my identity had been ripped away. How would I provide for my family? What job could possibly give me the satisfaction that logging and construction had provided?

One day a friend told me something that changed the course of my life. "Don, all your life you've used your body."

As I agreed with him, fresh sadness filled me. Before I could say anything, he continued. "Now God is giving you the opportunity to use your mind."

I don't know if you believe in God, but I know without a doubt that my friend's message changed my life for the better. I would have been happy working with my hands for the rest of my life, and that road is an honorable one.

But that day another path opened up before me. I began to work in publishing, and in the years since the accident I have been privileged to work with some of the wisest, most encouraging authors in the world. Now, twenty-five years later, I see that my hunting accident molded not just my career, but my character. Apart from the pain of that accident—the physical pain of the gunshot and recovery, the emotional pain of a reshaped life—I would not be the man I am now.

As I stood on the shore of Rosalyn Lake so many years ago, I was expecting a satisfying afternoon outdoors. Instead, I nearly died—and in the process received a life as satisfying as it was unexpected.

Don Jacobson

twin chances

It was three in the morning when nausea punched me in the stomach. I sat bolt upright in bed, panting, trying to understand what was going on. My stomach clenched with greater revulsion than I'd ever experienced, yet I felt no physical pain. It was as if I was being squeezed in the fist of a phantom giant.

Something was seriously wrong. I got out of bed and padded into the baby's nursery, where my nine-month-old slept soundly in his crib. For a moment I felt relief, yet even as I gazed at his peaceful form the nausea returned. I picked him up and cuddled his warm, pliant body to my chest. Feeling a sense of menace that frightened me to the very core of my being, I decided to carry my sleeping son back to bed with me.

Just as I entered my bedroom, the phone rang. I closed my eyes and my head fell to my chest.

Still carrying my baby, I walked into the kitchen and picked up the phone. My brother-in-law Eric's voice sounded like it was coming from the bottom of the deepest well in the world. "Your sister's been in a car accident—they're airlifting her to San Antonio."

"How is she?"

My own voice sounded like a stranger's. Why was it suddenly so cold, and why was I kneeling on the floor? The giant was squeezing my chest even tighter.

His voice came from the well again. "Not good. They don't know if she'll make it."

♂ ♂ ♂

My identical twin sister's only memory of that night is waiting for the jaws of life to free her from her mangled car. It is a memory that feels nearly endless.

She was pinned in her car for hours while emergency responders searched for her, found her, and then began the excruciating task of extracting her body from the wrecked car without killing her. She almost died waiting. Her chest was crushed, and she was conscious for every second of the rescue. Her pain moved from raging to unbearable, and then it became simply incomprehensible. She hadn't known a human body could register such pain without passing out.

I arrived at the ER in San Antonio just after my sister. A doctor put his hand on my arm to stop my headlong rush. He held my eyes in his for a long moment.

"We don't know if she'll make it," he said. "There's nothing you can do right now."

Why did people keep telling me that? The menace had arrived, claws out, and crushed my sister's body like it was a soda can. And something broke in my body, too—in me who had spent a lifetime twinned to the body that now lay shattered and dying in a white room down the hall.

♂ ♂ ♂

Everyone thought she would die. She didn't, but sometimes we wondered if it was okay to wish that she would.

They couldn't perform certain operations for almost two weeks because of her failing lungs. I sat beside her bed, listening to her ask over and over if she was going to die. If she could die. I told her she was going to make it—you're going to be fine, I'd say, and dance with Eric again before you know it—and then ten minutes later she would ask me the same question.

How she survived is my sister's story, not mine. I hope she can tell it to you one day, because it will transform you as it has me. Her story involves breathing machines, pain that kept her awake through long nights, permanent nerve damage, and a battle with addictive painkillers. She'll tell you about riding a motorized scooter, then a wheelchair, then walking into her office on crutches to cheers and tears. She'll show you pictures of her husband and three children.

My sister fought to live, tooth and nail, for days and weeks and months that added up to years. When death wanted to come and claim her, she kicked it to the curb and it turned tail and ran. That's her story.

The story I tell isn't about the miracle of her recovery. It's about a different miracle, a miracle that's taken me the years since my twin sister's accident to understand. We're at the park, sitting on a bench while our children race up steps and launch themselves down a twisty tube slide. It could be a Tuesday morning in March or a Saturday afternoon in June. It could be balmy or threatening rain. But the constant is this: my sister, my ever fixed mark, sitting beside me, alive.

While our children play, we trade tips on how to get them to finish their homework and how to prepare vegetables they will actually eat. We compare gray hairs. We sit in companionable silence. And as the day warms or cools, begins or ends, we talk about the latest fashions or the deals we've seen around town.

The miracle is that we are growing old together, just as we were meant to.

That almost didn't happen. Life is sweeter now, even as I realize it is more uncertain. Perhaps it's *because* of the uncertainty that it's sweeter. Perhaps that's why we talk about the latest style in summer shoes—because life is too short for sisters *not* to talk about shoes, and souls, and everything in between.

Some miracles happen instantly. But I suspect most happen incrementally, moment by moment, so slowly that we can't see them until we look back across long years full of pain. I've seen a redwood seed—it's half the size of a pencil eraser. I've seen a full-grown redwood tree, too, and I can't comprehend how high and wide its towering body is, nor the staggering depth of its roots. I've seen a seed and a tree, but I've never seen a redwood *grow*—yet that doesn't make me doubt the miracle for even a moment.

My twin sister fought for her second chance at life. My second chance was given to me as a gift, and every time I see my sister I unwrap that gift like it's the first time, more grateful for God's grace than ever before.

Alisa Wagner

afterword

ometimes I wonder if our world doesn't pay enough attention to hope.

Love can change the world, and faith can get us through tough times. But sometimes we act like we can live without hope. I don't know about you, but the times I'm best at loving and being faithful are the times I'm also filled with a sense of hope. Reading these stories has filled me to overflowing—and made me even more grateful for those sweet moments in life.

Have these stories got you thinking about the lemonade moments in your life? Well, now's the chance to tell your story of unexpected sweetness in the midst of sour circumstances. We've already collected more stories than we could use in this book, and we're planning on working on the God Makes Lemonade™ series for a long time, so visit www.godmakeslemonade.com right now and share your story.

We're looking forward to hearing from you.

Don

If these stories encouraged you,
you can:

Like us on Facebook at
www.facebook.com/godmakeslemonade

♂ ♂ ♂

Visit our website, where you can tell us your story at
www.godmakeslemonade.com

contributors

Alisa Wagner and her husband, Daniel, enjoy raising their three amazing children: Isaac, Levi and Kiki. Alisa's identical twin sister, Crissy, is her ministry partner, doing all aspects of ministry that writers usually dislike. Alisa blogs at www.FaithImagined.com.

Amber Alonso resides in sunny Florida with her husband and four children. Amber's passion is assisting other parents who have children with special needs. Her goal is to create an environment for children where every child/person is treated equally.

Andy Axtell was diagnosed with third-stage Hodgkin's in 1976. He went through three operations, forty-plus radiation treatments, and six months of chemo. He is thankful to be cancer free for thirty-four years now, and counts every day as a blessing from God.

Ann Bardell is the wife of an engineer, mother of four grown children, and a proud grandma. Ann and her husband are beginning their first year as blackberry farmers in Eastern Washington. Her mother-in-law is almost eighty and still lives with her husband out on their remote ranch.

Anne Forline lives in South Jersey and is a freelance writer, homeschooling mom, and co-director of an after-school program. She and her family volunteered with New Covenant Ministries, Inc.: www.streetministry.us.

Barbara Caywood, a former missionary child, grew up in the Sudan and Egypt. She began going to boarding school in Alexandria, Egypt, when she was in the fourth grade. She met her husband at Sterling College in Sterling, Kansas, and after graduation taught in different elementary schools in Kansas. She retired in 2009.

Bea Edwards lives in the spectacular mountains of western North Carolina. She spends most days with her rescued pit bull/boxer/best friend, Sophie, digging in her flower garden and writing children's books. She draws inspiration and encouragement from Philippians 4:8.

Bertha Raz was born in the mid 1920s to Swiss immigrants Arnold and Elsie Blaser. She graduated from Commerce High School in 1942 and married Paul Raz in 1951. They raised three children together. One of her favorite memories is the trips she and Paul took traveling around the U.S. and to Europe to visit relatives in Switzerland.

Billie Criswell is a writer and columnist from the Delaware Seashore who has been published online as well as in print. She has just completed her first book, *The Child Question*.

Bryana Jordan has two boys, Charlie and Jace. After serving nine years in the military, she currently attends college full-time. She also owns and operates a website dedicated to helping others save money, www.couponsoncaffeine.com.

Cammy Jacobson was raised in Central Oregon and attended college at Multnomah University in Portland, Oregon. She recently moved to Santa Barbara, California, where she plans to finish her schooling and pursue a career in communications.

Carla Wicks, a Kansas native, lives currently in Texas. She is married, mother to eight grown children, has an adopted granddaughter who is seven years old, and is grandmother to eight others. Her hobbies include freelance writing, reading, and scrapbooking.

Carol Statton has always had a heart for those who are struggling or suffering. She enjoys mentoring youth both in a workplace environment as well as through youth group experiences.

Cathy Kozak is an acupuncturist and writer who lives with her family on the shores of a cold mountain lake in the wilds of the Pacific Northwest. She is at work on her first novel, *A Thousand Tricks*.

Christina Newell is a stay-at-home wife and mother in Denver, Colorado. Inspired by her daughter, she makes one-of-a-kind baby items and blogs about her daily musings as a wife and mother at www.barefootintheburbs.blogspot.com.

Dana Jones is married with two young children, Bailey and Sam. While most of her world revolves around library story time, nap time, and play dates, she dabbles in graphic design, gardening, and couponing.

Danielle Sharp, besides being an avid gardener, is a retired educator who enjoys world travel, reading, hiking, knitting, and volunteerism. She's also an advocate for annual mole checks.

Dave Burchett is an Emmy Award–winning sports television director. Dave and his wife, Joni, faced the heartbreak of finding out that their daughter's life would be very brief, beginning a journey that resulted in Dave's first book, *When Bad Christians Happen to Good People*. You can follow Dave's blog at www.daveburchett.com.

Dave Gist is a screenwriter living in North Hollywood, California.

David Michael Smith hails from the "Diamond State" (Delaware), where he lives with his wife, daughter, and son. His grandfather, Oscar Bailey, now 102, continues to garden, but now as a "consultant" from his wheelchair. David has been published in *Chicken Soup for the Soul, Guideposts,* and *Cup of Comfort.*

Dawn Coyle is very happy that she finally got the courage to listen to her heart and follow Christ's teachings.

Debra Elliott began writing as a way to release the pain and hurt following her father's death in 1976. She has managed to get through many painful obstacles in life through writing. Her words were written to heal, but in healing herself she has also helped to heal others who are hurting.

Dennis Marcellino is a former member of many top bands, as well as a best-selling solo artist. He has been a guest on television shows including *The Tracey Ullman Show* and *American Bandstand,* played sax and sang lead on two songs in *Sweet Bird of Youth*, and written eight books. More information at www.DennisMarcellino.com.

Dixie Phillips and her husband, Paul, have been honored to serve the Gospel Lighthouse Church in Floyd, Iowa, for thirty years. They have four grown children and four grandchildren. Read more about Dixie's writings at www.floydslighthouse.com.

Donna Matthews is a retired RN living in Wister, Oklahoma.

Eleanor Steele Porath is an eighty-four-year-old grandma who published her first book at eighty-one, and thereafter had great joy as a motivational speaker sharing her story of fear to faith. Her life is living proof to never give up hope: that all dreams are possible. Her hobbies are gardening and Bible study.

Emily Vazquez lives with her family on Vancouver Island. She cares for her three small children—Daniel, Carolina, and Victoria—and also enjoys writing, gardening, and jogging. Next year, Lord willing, Emily will begin homeschooling.

Eve Gaal was born in Boston but has spent most of her life in California. Besides publishing in many places, she enjoys volunteering for a literacy program at The Mecca School near the Salton Sea, teaching second graders how to read. She also enjoys cooking, reading, swimming, and riding her green bicycle with her best friend and husband, Steve.

Gina Graham and her husband live in the sunny South. Her most important job is keeping her three teenage boys happy, fed, and productive. Visit Gina at www.ginagraham.com. She hides a heart symbol in all of her art and often draws a Scottie dog in her illustrations.

Heidi Petersen, PhD (University of Colorado, Boulder, 2006), has expressed herself professionally as a writer, hair stylist, paralegal, college instructor, healing arts practitioner, spiritualist minister, and real estate investor. Her motion is propelled by her existential quest to grow. Currently, Heidi lives just northeast of Boulder with her two cats, Ginger and Poncho.

Jaclyn S. Miller is a freelance writer from Indiana. She is working toward a career in children's writing.

James Scott Hensley lives in Greenville, South Carolina. He graduated from the University of South Carolina, Columbia, and lives life with his June Bug.

Jay Cookingham is a freelance writer/poet as well as a graphic artist. He writes a blog (www.soulfari.blogspot.com) geared toward men and their role as fathers and husbands. A father of seven, Jay has been happily married to his wife, Christine, for twenty-nine years.

Jean Matthew Hall lives in beautiful North Carolina with her husband of forty-three years. She enjoys spending time with her children and grandchildren, and leading a ladies' Bible class at her church. She also enjoys raising her own vegetables, reading, and writing. Jean is the chairperson for Write2Ignite (www.write2ignite.com).

Jody McComas has been married to her wonderful husband, Matt, for ten years and is the blessed mom of two children. She and Matt have worked with college students for the past nine years and currently live in Portland, Oregon.

John and Joni Shepherd are the co-founders of Shepherd's House Community and John is the founder of M25 Ventures, Inc., which work together to help recovered addicts become business owners and productive employees. For more information, visit www.m25ventures.com or www.shepherdshouse community.wordpress.com.

John and Lisa Leonard live in Atlanta, Georgia, and have been married for more than twenty years. They have two children and three grandchildren, several wonderful dogs, and the occasional foster cat. John is the author of *Divine Evolution,* and a number of his short stories are included in the anthology *WAGin' Our Tales.*

Judy Eaves Cocoris grew up in Chattanooga, Tennessee, one of ten children. She attended Tennessee Temple College, majoring in music. Judy serves as executive administrator at Church of the Open Door in Glendora, California.

She loves to travel, read and sing. Judy has three children and nine grandchildren whom she adores.

Karen Earls lives in Owen Sound, Ontario, Canada, with her husband, Nathan, and their "unofficial adopted daughter," Meaghan, on the property of Word of Life Fellowship Canada, a Bible college and camp where she is the kitchen manager. They enjoy the outdoors, and are surrounded by many hiking trails and waterfalls.

Karen R. Hessen is an inspirational writer and speaker, a retired mail carrier, and a former nurse, innkeeper, health educator, and nonprofit administrator. She has two adult adopted children. She and her husband, Douglas, split their time between homes in Forest Grove and Seaside, Oregon.

Kasey Van Norman is the founder and president of Beautiful Adventure Ministries, located in College Station, Texas, where she lives with her husband, Justin, and her two children, Emma Grace and Lake. To learn more about her ministry, check out www.kaseyvannorman.com.

Kathy Irey is lifelong Pittsburgher. She is a freelance writer and social worker serving adults with physical disabilities who live independently in their own homes. Among her passions are water slides, wave pools, women's history, and Penn State. Her heroes include her parents, Abraham Lincoln, and Susan B. Anthony.

Keri Phay is blessed to be wife to Mike and mom to Emma, Caleb, Halle, and a baby girl on the way. She spends her days homemaking and homeschooling, and would someday like to have a little plot of land and a big garden. For now, she is content watching her kids chase the basset hound, turtle, and rabbit around the backyard.

Kim Anthony is an author and speaker who resides in South Florida with her husband and two children. She serves on staff with Athletes in Action, where she works with wives of professional athletes, coaches, and executives. To learn more, visit www.miamipros.com.

Kimberly Sutton lives near Houston, Texas, with her husband, Rick, and three children. She has a degree in journalism and has worked for more than twenty years as a youth pastor, church planter, missionary in Paraguay, and Teen Challenge rehabilitation teacher. For more information about New Life Women's Center, the organization featured in this story, visit www.creativeoutreach.com.

Krista Matthews is the mother to four children—three daughters and a son. She has spent over twenty-five years in corporate America in various marketing and sales roles. She also works with women to increase their confidence in pursuing financial freedom. In her spare time she enjoys networking, traveling, and cooking.

Lisa Lane is now a dispatch operator, raising her son and doing her best to provide him with a good life, and a good example. She still struggles with depression and bouts with bipolar disorder, but she has never again thought about taking her own life. She hopes her story will help others who are struggling.

Loretta Nemeth is the director of communications for the Byzantine Catholic Eparchy of Parma and editor of its newspaper, *Horizons*. The widowed mother of five, she has tried to live her life following Father Vic's example of being sensitive to the needs of other people.

Luke Beling is a native of the rainbow nation, South Africa. He has a heart for the poor, lonely, and forgotten. His dream is to minister among the poor with the compassion and love of Jesus, and then write about it. Currently he and his wife reside in Rochester, Minnesota, where he coaches tennis, teaches English, and writes.

Mariane Holbrook is a retired schoolteacher who lives with her husband, John, in Kure Beach, North Carolina. She enjoys playing the piano and painting her favorite birds. She is the author of two books, *Prisms of the Heart* and *Humor Me*. To learn more, visit www.marianholbrook.com.

Marianne Cornwall was born in New Zealand but now lives in Central Queensland, Australia, and loves her three children to pieces. Marianne sells real estate, has a passion for writing, and loves walking her dogs on the beach.

Mary Griffith Chalupsky has always had an ambition for writing. Born during the Depression and raised with only the necessities of life, she married young and, with her husband, raised a large family. A multitasker, she helped her husband farm while attending college, working a full-time job, and volunteering in her community.

Mary Louise Tancraitor Wilson, aka Mary Lou Wilson, was born and raised in Swissvale, Pennsylvania, a suburb of Pittsburgh. She is the mother of four, grandmother of six, and great-grandmother of two. She now lives in Pinehurst, North Carolina.

Mary Potter Kenyon lives in Manchester, Iowa, with her husband, David, who is now her best friend, and four of their eight children. Her writing has been featured in magazines, newspapers, and anthologies. She blogs about motherhood, writing, and saving money at marypotterkenyon.wordpress.com.

Matthew Hart is married with four young children: Katie, Alex, Will, and Maddie. They live in Moline, IL, where Matt delivers home medical equipment. A Christian since age thirteen, Matt credits his grandmother, Ruth, as his hero in the Christian faith and looks forward to dancing around heaven with her one day.

Melanie Elliott lives in Bentonville, Arkansas, with her husband, Rob, and their kids, Cade and Hollie. She was a public school teacher for eight years and has been a full-time wife and mom for eleven years. She is also the author of the book *Why Am I Conservative? 24 Topics for Kids or Anyone.*

Michelle Close Mills is a freelance writer from Florida, but her most rewarding job is proud wife and mother of two grown children. Michelle maintains there is a special place in heaven for those who rescue fuzzy buddies from animal shelters. She enjoys singing, coffee dates with loved ones, and often has her nose in a book.

Molly Murphy Chorman is married and has one daughter, Lucy Louise. Molly loves the simplicities of nature, gardening, running, and reading all after a day of teaching high school business students. She loves her home on family farmland in Delaware and longs to watch her daughter grow under the same summer sun.

Nicole Swort is happily married with three young children: Isaiah, Brandon, and Arabella. While being a homemaker is her joy, she also enjoys writing, crafting, and photography.

Patti Schulte studied theatre design at Columbia College of Chicago, and then ventured out to British Columbia to study makeup artistry for film. Writing has always been a favorite hobby, as she hopes to one day publish a children's book. Patti and her husband, Aaron, are settled in the beautiful state of Oregon.

Penny Whipps founded Just1x (Just One Time) in 2009, after her son Kyle died of an accidental heroin overdose. Penny travels to schools around the country, giving a forty-minute presentation that consists of two short videos, including the actual 911 call of Kyle's death, and a passionate call to action. For more details, visit www.just1x.com.

Rick Wages has been married to his high school sweetheart, Kim, for thirty-seven years; they have four children and three grandchildren. Rick makes a living building homes, selling roofs, and making friends. In Loganville, Georgia, he's best known as "Santa" at parades, schools, and hospitals.

Robin Hewitt is now married to her best friend, Doug, and is a grandmother of eight. A full-time writer, she still finds time for an occasional beer and burger with Linda, and to enjoy a bowl of Brucie's chicken soup. Anna Zurawski, aka "Ma," is on the sunny side of ninety and still making the noodles.

Ron Fazio Jr. grew up near Philadelphia and attended the University of Maryland, where he played football. After a brief stint in the NFL, Ron moved to New York in 1988 to pursue an acting career. Now a PA, Ron lives in North Carolina and enjoys life with his wife and three daughters.

Sara DuBose is an inspirational speaker and author of four novels and one nonfiction book. She currently travels as a speaker and may be contacted at www.saradubose.com. Sara and her husband live in Montgomery, Alabama. She is the mother of two daughters.

Sarah Fuesler continues to reside in the Philadelphia area, where she is a full-time student and works as a tutor. In 2008, she was introduced to Al, a man who would forever change her outlook on living and loving. Her hope is that she can bestow the gift given to her on others.

Sharie Robbins lives in La Canada, California, with her husband, Quinn. They have three children: Anthony, 23; Ashley, 23; and Justine, 21. Quinn and Sharie have been married for twenty-five years and are celebrating the wedding of their oldest daughter in September 2011.

Susan Rickey lives in far northern California with her husband and two children, Eli and Jenny. They still like to take trips together, though none have been as monumental as their trip to Haiti.

Terri Elders, LCSW, lives in the country near Colville, WA. Her stories have appeared in dozens of anthologies, including *Chicken Soup for the Soul*. She serves as a public member of the Washington State Medical Quality Assurance Commission, and in 2006 received an award for her work with Peace Corps. She blogs at www.atouchoftarragon.blogspot.com.

Terri Tiffany has counseled adults and owned a Christian bookstore; she now resides in Florida with her husband. Her work appears in magazines, Sunday school take-home papers, and anthologies such as *Chicken Soup for the Soul* and *Adam's Media*. Please visit her at www.terri-treasures.blogspot.com.

Tracy Healy graduated from Westmont College in 1999. When she met Brandon, the little guy featured in her story, Tracy was working for ACT (www.autismcenterfortreatment.com), a job that helped prepare her for all of Brandon's special needs. Now she works part-time at Simi Covenant Church in the children's ministry department and is a full-time mommy—the best job of all.

Veta Shepherd is married to her wonderful husband, Lawrence, with four fantastic grown daughters and seven exceptional grandchildren. She is head of the drama ministry at The City of Truth Covenant Church in Oak Lawn, IL.

Yamaris Rosa was born and raised in Philadelphia. She is married to a wonderful man and the proud mother of three children. Yamaris enjoys leading the children's ministry program at her church and singing and dancing with her children, as well as sharing her lemonade story with anyone who will listen.